P9-DUS-252

THE BEDFORD SERIES IN HISTORY AND CULTURE

Black Protest
and the Great Migration
A Brief History with Documents

Eric Arnesen

George Washington University

BEDFORD/ST. MARTIN'S   Boston ♦ New York

For Bedford/St. Martin's

Publisher for History: Patricia A. Rossi
Director of Development for History: Jane Knetzger
Developmental Editor: Sarah Barrash Wilson
Editorial Assistant: Julie Mooza
Associate Editor, Publishing Services: Maria Teresa Burwell
Senior Production Supervisor: Dennis J. Conroy
Production Associate: Christie Gross
Marketing Manager: Jenna Bookin Barry
Project Management: Books By Design, Inc.
Text Design: Claire Seng-Niemoeller
Indexer: Books By Design, Inc.
Cover Design: Billy Boardman
Cover Photo: The Migration Series, Panel No.1: During World War I there was a great migration north by southern African Americans, 1940–41 (casein tempera on hardboard), Lawrence, Jacob (1917–2000)/The Phillips Collection, Washington, D.C., USA/Acquired 1942/The Bridgeman Art Library. © 2014 The Jacob and Gwendolyn Lawrence Foundation, Seattle/Artists Rights Society (ARS), New York.
Composition: Stratford Publishing Services, Inc.
Printing and Binding: Haddon Craftsmen, an RR Donnelley & Sons Company

President: Joan E. Feinberg
Editorial Director: Denise B. Wydra
Director of Marketing: Karen R. Melton
Director of Editing, Design, and Production: Marcia Cohen
Manager, Publishing Services: Emily Berleth

Library of Congress Control Number: 2002104745

Copyright © 2003 by Bedford/St. Martin's

Manufactured in the United States of America.

For information, write: Bedford/St. Martin's, 75 Arlington Street, Boston, MA 02116 (617-399-4000)

ISBN: 0-312-39129-3

Acknowledgments

How the Arkansas Peons Were Freed. Courtesy of the Pittsburgh Courier Archives.
George E. Haynes, *Negro Migration: Its Effect on Family and Community Life in the North.* Courtesy of National Urban League OPPORTUNITY: Journal of Negro Life.
Excerpt from Alain Locke, *The New Negro.* Reprinted with the permission of Scribner Publishing Group from THE NEW NEGRO by Alain Locke. Copyright © 1925 by Albert and Charles Boni, Inc. All rights reserved.

Foreword

The Bedford Series in History and Culture is designed so that readers can study the past as historians do.

The historian's first task is finding the evidence. Documents, letters, memoirs, interviews, pictures, movies, novels, or poems can provide facts and clues. Then the historian questions and compares the sources. There is more to do than in a courtroom, for hearsay evidence is welcome, and the historian is usually looking for answers beyond act and motive. Different views of an event may be as important as a single verdict. How a story is told may yield as much information as what it says.

Along the way the historian seeks help from other historians and perhaps from specialists in other disciplines. Finally, it is time to write, to decide on an interpretation and how to arrange the evidence for readers.

Each book in this series contains an important historical document or group of documents, each document a witness from the past and open to interpretation in different ways. The documents are combined with some element of historical narrative—an introduction or a biographical essay, for example—that provides students with an analysis of the primary source material and important background information about the world in which it was produced.

Each book in the series focuses on a specific topic within a specific historical period. Each provides a basis for lively thought and discussion about several aspects of the topic and the historian's role. Each is short enough (and inexpensive enough) to be a reasonable one-week assignment in a college course. Whether as classroom or personal reading, each book in the series provides firsthand experience of the challenge—and fun—of discovering, recreating, and interpreting the past.

Lynn Hunt
David W. Blight
Bonnie G. Smith
Natalie Zemon Davis
Ernest R. May

Preface

The Great Migration of the World War I era involved the journey of unprecedented numbers of African Americans from southern to northern states. The magnitude of the migration quickly generated a significant public debate over its causes, implications, and significance. To some, particularly white southerners, the migration could be blamed on northern labor agents luring away black workers with false promises of high pay and wonderful conditions. To others, particularly the migrants, it reflected southern blacks' desire to escape racial and economic oppression and to create better lives for themselves and their families. To still others, the migration generated problems in the realm of acculturation and adjustment, race relations, and struggles over resources such as jobs and housing. Whether one opposed, cautiously approved, or enthusiastically endorsed the migration, one thing was clear: the Great Migration represented an undeniable turning point in the history of African Americans and race relations in the United States.

The character and tempo of black politics and protest also changed dramatically during the war and immediate postwar years. An older, cautious, conservative, even accommodating approach to race relations, embodied most clearly in the philosophy of Booker T. Washington, increasingly appeared anachronistic. More vocal and militant challenges had emerged from civil rights activists like W. E. B. Du Bois and organizations such as the National Association for the Advancement of Colored People. Socialists like A. Philip Randolph and nationalists like Marcus Garvey articulated powerful critiques of white America and blacks' subordinate place in it.

But the new mood was by no means restricted to African American leaders. Contemporaries increasingly referred to a "New Negro" who, in the words of the radical *Messenger* magazine, would no longer "turn the other cheek," for the New Negro would fight to make "America safe for himself."[1] Indeed, a new impatience with the racial status quo, and a new willingness to challenge it, was evident in the countless actions of black migrants, black women's clubs and suffrage groups, black unions and labor associations, and local chapters of civil rights groups.

Black Protest and the Great Migration examines two related themes. The first is how contemporaries viewed and explained the reasons behind the migration, on the one hand, and understood the migration's implications and meanings, on the other. This subject consumed the energies of vast numbers of people—white politicians, planters, employers; black and white journalists and editors; educators, religious leaders, black civil rights activists, and migrants. The second theme concerns the character and contours of black protest. The new mood among black Americans could be found not only in established organizations but in the perspectives and initiatives at the grassroots level.

This book's introduction and its documents seek to convey the extent and range of individual and collective protest across the nation. The introduction, "The Great American Protest," explores the book's themes by providing an overview and interpretation of both the origins, consequences, and meanings of the World War I–era migration and the evolution of black politics and protest during and after the war. The document section that follows is divided into six chapters. Chapter 1, "The Great Migration Begins," examines conditions in the prewar South that created the desire among southern blacks to migrate, the often negative response of white southerners to the migration, the lack of enthusiasm that some southern black leaders expressed over the migration, and letters from migrants themselves explaining what they hoped to accomplish. Chapter 2, "The Promised Land?" explores what awaited migrants in the wartime North. Migrants hoping to escape the oppression and poverty of the South looked forward to jobs, housing, political rights, and better education for their children in the North, a region some viewed as a "land of hope." But as critics of the migration pointed out, the reality—harsh housing and employment conditions, employer and union racism, and racial violence—fell short of the promise. African Americans in the North quickly developed critiques of northern racism and engaged in struggles against it. Chapter 3, "The Evolution of Black Politics," traces the multitude of political stances adopted by blacks during and after the war, ranging from expressions of patriotism to nationalism, civil rights militancy, and support for

---

[1]The *Messenger* quoted in Nathan Huggins, *Harlem Renaissance* (New York: Oxford University Press, 1971), 53.

women's suffrage. Chapter 4, "Black Workers and the Wartime Home-front," focuses on the experiences of black men and women in northern and southern workplaces. It shows that black protest was neither restricted solely to the North nor confined to the ranks of the black middle class and its organizations; rather, working-class African Americans engaged in widespread individual and collective challenges to racial and economic inequality in their workplaces and in the broader labor market. Chapter 5, "Opportunities and Obstacles in the Postwar Era," focuses on the postwar racial reaction that manifested itself in intense white violence against blacks and concerted efforts to stop black social, economic, and political advances. Chapter 6, "Postwar Migration," carries the story into the 1920s to explore continued migration to the North, the ways in which contemporaries interpreted that migration, and the cultural, political, and organizational development of northern black communities.

A NOTE ABOUT THE TEXT

The documents in this volume have been chosen from newspapers, periodicals, journals, and trade publications from the North and the South, big cities and small towns, and black and white publications to highlight a variety of perspectives on the issues of black protest and the Great Migration of the World War I era. Many of the selections reprinted in this volume are excerpts from longer articles; ellipses in the text indicate omissions. Original spelling and punctuation have been preserved in most cases to retain particularities of the publication and time period. Headnotes preceding the documents call attention to sources, authors, and context, providing information that is pertinent for students' critical reading of the documents. Concluding the volume are a chronology of important events, questions for consideration, and a bibliography to help students to further focus on — and think critically about — black protest and the Great Migration.

ACKNOWLEDGMENTS

When completing any substantial project, one takes considerable pleasure in finally expressing one's appreciation to those whose efforts made the project possible. Kevin Gaines, University of Michigan; Tera Hunter, Carnegie Mellon University; Daniel Letwin, Penn State University; Nelson Lichtenstein, University of California, Santa Barbara;

Joseph McCartin, Georgetown University; Steven Reich, James Madison University; and an anonymous reviewer subjected the introduction and the documents to close scrutiny, suggesting new avenues to explore, saving me from occasional embarrassments, and providing me with more useful suggestions than I could ultimately pursue. Steven Reich, Joseph McCartin, Jason Digman, Gareth Canaan, and Carla Burnett also shared with me a variety of documents they had located from their own research and writing on the era of World War I. David Blight, the series' advisory editor, provided encouragement and guidance along the way, while my editor at Bedford, Sarah Barrash Wilson, now probably knows the book better than I do; from the start to the finish, she worked tirelessly to craft the manuscript and refine its scope.

My parents, Alice and Jack Arnesen, are not historians, but as critical readers, their comments (always provided in the most timely of manners) made this a far more readable volume. Finally, as usual, Katrin Schultheiss, who *is* an historian, contributed in immeasurable ways to the writing of this book. She entertained our children — Rachel, Samuel, and William — when deadlines loomed, but far more important, she regularly debated the book's arguments with me and provided copious and invaluable criticism of the text. Her support and insights, and our ongoing dialogues about history, continue to sustain me.

                                                    Eric Arnesen

Contents

PART ONE

Introduction: "The Great American Protest"

ORIGINS OF THE GREAT MIGRATION

The First World War inaugurated a dramatic transformation—some called it "revolutionary"—in the lives of many black Americans. Although astute observers had already discerned a small but growing number of southern black migrants to the North, few would have predicted the magnitude of the changes to come by the end of the war. By 1916, the number of migrants was increasing rapidly and by 1917, no one could have missed the obvious: An unprecedented number of southern African Americans were participating in what historians call "the Great Migration."

Most historians agree that roughly 450,000 to 500,000 black southerners relocated to the North between 1915 and 1918,[1] and following a brief but severe economic depression shortly after the end of World War I, at least another 700,000 southern blacks made their way north during the 1920s.[2] As one observer noted in 1918, the Great Migration constituted nothing less than a "veritable mass movement," an "exodus" on an "unprecedented scale."[3] This migration intensified a gradual demographic shift that transformed an overwhelmingly southern, rural people into a northern and urban people by the decades following World War II.

1

In an effort to comprehend, convey the scope, and assess the character of this population movement, black activists, journalists, government officials, and other contemporaries resorted to a wide range of metaphors. By 1917, the term "exodus" was widely used to describe the migration, replete with its biblical imagery of the enslaved Israelites' triumphal flight from slavery and persecution in Egypt to eventual refuge in the promised land of Canaan. The imagery of flowing water was also prevalent in the analyses of the migration process. The African American weekly, the *Birmingham Reporter,* described the migrants as an "increasing tide of humanity" who simply moved "off from the southland in search of a better location."[4] Decades later, historians too adopted similar language. What had been a "trickle" of migration, historian Neil McMillan observes, had become a "torrent" by the war years.[5]

Black southerners had ample reason for wanting to leave the region of their birth and upbringing. After the failure of Reconstruction, most southern blacks remained rural agricultural workers. In the system of sharecropping that followed on the heels of slavery in many parts of the South by the 1870s, white southerners retained control of the land, sources of credit, supplies, and the final crop raised on their property. Black men and women provided the necessary labor to grow cotton, living off the supplies provided by landowners until the crop was harvested. At the end of the harvest, relatively few sharecroppers came out ahead. At best, they broke even, or at worst, found themselves even deeper in debt to the landholder. Those black sharecroppers who chose to question or challenge landholders' fraudulent accounting practices often found themselves evicted from their plots, arrested, or physically harmed. The sharecropping system ensured that most black sharecroppers remained in poverty and exercised little power in the economic arena. More than a half century after emancipation, the *Houston Informer,* a southern black weekly newspaper, summed up the thinking of many, if not all, African Americans: "It appears that quite a number of Southern communities not only do not know that slavery has been abolished in this country, but on the contrary they are maintaining a species of peonage far worse than anything conceived or practiced during the period of human bondage."[6]

The economic changes wrought by the outbreak of the war in Europe in August 1914 only temporarily affected southern blacks' living standards. In 1914–15, the South confronted an agricultural depression, as the region was cut off from one of its lucrative overseas markets for cotton. Widespread flooding in 1916 contributed to economic hard times, as did infestations of the boll weevil, a cotton-destroying insect that struck with particular intensity in 1915–16 and continued to ruin crops well into the early 1920s. The price of cotton soon rose, producing a short-lived economic boom. After the war, however, the price of cotton again dropped dramatically.[7]

Harsh economic conditions were only one part of the equation. By the end of the nineteenth century, African American southerners possessed few political, social, or legal rights and remained subject to the threat of white violence for daring to question their place in the southern order. Although the end of Reconstruction in 1877 deprived most black men of the franchise, some continued to vote through the 1880s and 1890s. The wave of disfranchisement laws and constitutional provisions that swept both the lower and upper South from the late 1880s through 1910 effectively put an end to black voting for roughly half a century. Southern municipalities and states passed "Jim Crow laws" by the century's end, relegating blacks to separate facilities: separate parks, separate train cars, separate water fountains, separate schools, and the like. Although in theory the facilities or services for blacks were supposed to be equal to those provided to whites, in practice they were often inferior. Yet the U.S. Supreme Court ignored that reality when it upheld the legality of a Louisiana state law requiring segregated railroad cars in 1896: The landmark ruling, *Plessy v. Ferguson*, officially justified the fiction of "separate but equal" for the next half century.[8]

Before the law, southern blacks charged with crimes could expect nothing resembling justice. Judges discounted black testimony against whites and often presumed blacks to be guilty; juries excluded blacks from service and were reluctant to convict whites accused of crimes against blacks. Utilized by white officials, landowners, and employers, the law was also an effective weapon against blacks, limiting their mobility and their ability to challenge existing conditions. The convict lease system transformed the growing number of convicted black prisoners into a virtual slave labor force that was used for railroad construction and coal mining. Legal and extralegal violence against African Americans increased in the late nineteenth century as well. Antilynching activist Ida B. Wells-Barnett documented the lynching of 160 blacks in 1892; Bishop Henry McNeal Turner, a black nationalist leader, concluded in the late 1890s that if the bodies of all black victims of lynching were "laid one upon the other," they would "reach a mile high." Justice, for southern blacks, was an elusive ideal at best.[9]

Some white southerners trying to comprehend the migration blamed outside agitators and labor agents or attributed population movement to floods or the boll weevil; others begrudgingly acknowledged that "better treatment" toward their black workforce might be required to stop the migration. But the "spokesmen of the Negro are unanimous," one observer made clear. "The colored people . . . are migrating because the South has stolen their political rights and curtailed their civil rights, because it refuses common justice to the Negro and education to his children, because it segregates him in the cities, condemns him to the Jim Crow car, refuses to respect his property, and holds over him the ultimate terror of mob violence and Judge Lynch."[10]

Indeed, long before the Great Migration of the World War I era, a small minority of black southerners registered their discontent through geographical migration. Despite the sharecropping system and a network of labor-repressive laws designed to keep them poor, indebted, and "in their place," southern blacks were hardly rendered immobile. At the end of a given year in the late nineteenth century, as many as 30 to 40 percent of black sharecropping families moved from one plantation to another in the same area, a process known as "shifting." Indebtedness and the growing need for cash income prompted some family members to abandon full-time agriculture and to engage in seasonal migration. With few economic opportunities open to them, black women found jobs as domestic servants or washerwomen in towns and large urban centers. Turpentine, timber, and railroad construction camps, brickyards, cottonseed presses, docks, and coal mines attracted many black men when their labor on the farm was not in demand, although the work was low paying, difficult, and often dangerous. At other times of the year, many of those temporary wage workers would reverse course and head home. Well into the early twentieth century, Alabama coal operators complained of shortages of black labor during planting and harvesting time, as black miners returned home to help their families. As Peter Gottlieb and other historians have argued, for many southern blacks, northward migration was not just a one-time affair. In many cases, migration developed in stages, starting with regional movements that took people from the farm to various southern industries or urban centers, and sometimes back again.[11]

Pre–World War I migration at times involved organized campaigns by blacks to escape immediate oppression or to find greater opportunities elsewhere in the South or West. (See Figure 1.) For blacks from

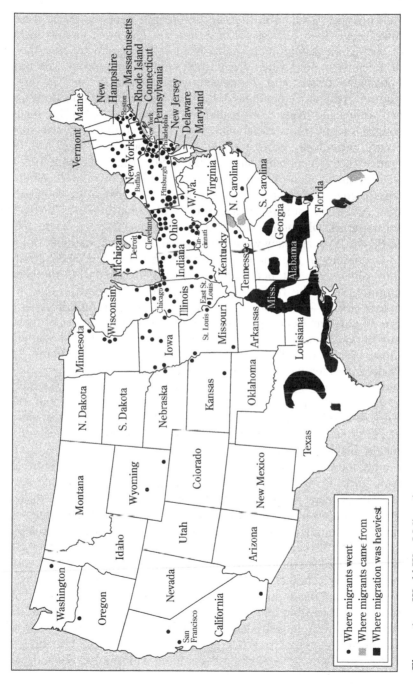

Figure 1. World War I Migration

Legend:
- Where migrants went
- Where migrants came from
- Where migration was heaviest

Georgia and Alabama in the late nineteenth century, the destination might have been Mississippi or Arkansas. The most famous instance of prewar black migration occurred in 1879–80, shortly after the end of Reconstruction, when freed men and women from Mississippi, Louisiana, Texas, and Tennessee participated in an "exodus" to Kansas. Against tremendous odds—including opposition from southern whites and many black leaders—as many as 25,000 "Exodusters" sought escape from racial violence and destitution by leaving the South. Periodically, other, smaller groups would seek their own deliverance through mobility, and by the 1890s, the Oklahoma Territory was the destination of a substantial black migration as well. When the federal government opened the territory to migration by people other than American Indians, an influx of "Oklahoma boomers" arrived to set up farms. Oklahoma's black population rose from 21,609 in 1890 to 55,684 in 1900, as many were attracted to all-black towns like Boley.[12]

Conditions in the South had long been oppressive and harsh, but they alone had not been sufficient to generate large numbers of migrants from the region. The alternative to the South—life in the urban North—was also unappealing for African Americans in the pre–World War I decades. Racial prejudice remained strong in many northern communities, where black migrants and "old settlers"—those blacks who had earlier made the North their home—confronted residential discrimination, de facto segregation, occasional racial violence, and a highly discriminatory job market. A small but growing number of southern blacks journeyed north temporarily to work on the farms of New Jersey, Delaware, or Pennsylvania, and others took seasonal jobs in hotels and resorts as waiters, janitors, and maids. Black women, particularly those along the South Atlantic coast, readily found work as live-in domestic servants in Washington, D.C., New York, Boston, and other northeastern cities.[13] Domestic service was the primary job open to black women, while black men worked in a variety of low-paid positions in domestic and personal service and as unskilled common laborers. The skilled trades and most skilled and semiskilled factory work remained closed to black northerners. This lack of broader employment opportunities constituted a serious barrier to many potential black migrants.[14]

Black Americans in northern urban centers were excluded from most manufacturing and skilled work for a variety of reasons. First, many northern industrialists shared the racial prejudices of their southern counterparts. White employers declined to hire blacks or relegated them to janitorial or common labor jobs. Second, white workers—both unionized and non-unionized—often refused to work with them, threatening to walk off the job (or actually doing so) if their employers contravened traditional racial divisions of labor. Finally, industrial enterprises had other, large sources of labor upon which to draw. Between 1870 and 1910, an average of a half million immigrants a year came to the United States in search of work. The industrial revolution, centered in much of the North and upper Midwest, was fueled largely by unskilled immigrant workers from Europe—first from northern and western Europe and then, by the end of the nineteenth century, from southern and eastern Europe.[15]

WARTIME OPPORTUNITIES IN THE NORTH

The outbreak of World War I in 1914 transformed the economic and demographic landscape. The number of European immigrants coming to the United States fell sharply, from 1.2 million in 1914 to three hundred thousand in 1915 and even fewer in subsequent years. By 1916, employers were beginning to feel the pinch as the demand for labor grew while the supply fell. Contributing to the shrinking labor supply was the conscription and enlistment of millions of American workers into the Army in 1917 and 1918. Facing a growing economy while confronting serious labor shortages, American industrial employers turned to previously untapped supplies of labor, particularly white women,[16] African Americans, and other racial or ethnic minorities. The North drew heavily upon a southern reserve of black labor. Wartime migration thrust a small minority of African Americans into the modern industrial economy. Blacks, especially men, got their first real foothold in industrial jobs in the North, jobs in the dynamic core of the American economy—in the steel mills, in packinghouses, and to a limited degree, in automobile factories. In Detroit, Michigan, the automobile industry increased its number of black employees, with the Ford Motor Company hiring literally thousands of black male migrants. In Pittsburgh, Cleveland, Chicago, and Gary, steel mills hired thousands of southern black men (and some Mexicans), and the packinghouses of Chicago put thousands of black men and women on their payrolls.[17] (See Figure 2.)

Black women in cities dependent on heavy industry, such as Detroit and Pittsburgh, found their options limited to domestic work as laundresses, cleaning women, and maids (but at substantially higher wages than in the South). In cities with more diversified

Figure 2. Black Wartime Workers
The wartime draft and the dramatic dropoff in immigration from Europe that accompanied the war created substantial labor shortages, leading many northern employers to hire black workers for the first time. The prospect of northern employment—with its higher wages and greater opportunities than work in the South—proved attractive to large numbers of black southerners who migrated north in the war years to take up jobs in the manufacturing sector. In this image black workers are making munitions at Oakley Chemical Company. © Corbis.

manufacturing bases, like Chicago, their options were greater, from working on power sewing machines, to working in railroad yards, cigar factories, box factories, and lumber yards. The *Crisis,* the journal of the National Association for the Advancement of Colored People (NAACP),* assessed the changes in November 1918: At the same time as thousands of black men were recruited into the military to fight in Europe, "an army of women is entering mills, factories and all other branches of industry."[18]

Northern jobs offered many advantages over southern ones. Most important, wages in northern industry were often considerably higher than those in southern agriculture. Even if the cost of living in the North was much higher, at the end of the day workers returned home with more money in their pockets. On the eve of the migration, the daily wage of southern black farm laborers was roughly 75¢; for unskilled workers in cotton compresses, lumber mills, and railroad shops, between $1.00 and $1.50; and for skilled workers in construction, between $2.00 and $3.50. Domestic workers earned some of the lowest southern urban wages, with women receiving a weekly wage of between $1.50 and $3.00 (including board) and men $5.00. For comparable work in the North, wages might be double or more.[19]

Many southern whites were unwilling to admit that discriminatory or oppressive conditions played a role in blacks' desire to migrate. Neither would they credit southern blacks with the initiative or intelligence to make an informed decision to leave the South. Instead, southern white politicians, newspaper editors, and planters blamed labor agents for the migration and the resulting "labor famine," and passed laws banning or restricting their activities. To be sure, labor agents, particularly in the early stages of the migration, did constitute an important conduit for information. Hard-hit early in the war by a shortage of European immigrants to lay and repair track or to perform unskilled labor in rail yards, northern- and western-based railroads like the Erie, the Pennsylvania, and the Union Pacific relied on agents to procure replacement labor in the South. In the first half of 1916, by one account, the Pennsylvania Railroad put three to five thousand southern blacks on its payroll as section hands. Labor turnover, however, was heavy, as many of the new workers moved on in search of more attractive employment opportunities that the wartime economy offered.[20] Although most historians agree that labor agents were not

*The NAACP was an interracial organization formed in New York in 1909 following a race riot in Springfield, Illinois. Its agenda called for civil and political rights for African Americans. Its journal, the *Crisis,* became a leading forum for the critique of American race relations and the advancement of civil rights.

the primary factor stimulating migration, white southerners became obsessed with the role they felt the agents played in fomenting discontent and disrupting what they insisted were peaceful labor and race relations. Throughout the South, white legislators took concrete steps to impede agents' efforts. In some cases, agents were required to register, receive official permission, or pay high licensing fees before recruiting labor; in other cases, inducing any laborer to leave his or her community was deemed an illegal offense.[21]

Many southern blacks learned of the new economic and political opportunities awaiting them in the North from friends and family members who had previously migrated, not from labor agents. Before boarding the northbound Illinois Central or other trains, potential migrants directed countless letters to northern brethren and the black press seeking concrete information on living conditions, employment, and housing opportunities in the North. Word of mouth and letters from friends and relatives in the North informed them about where they could find work, at what wages, and under what conditions. Returning friends and relatives too provided what investigator Emmett Scott called a "living example of the prosperity of the North." Every autumn "northern railway stations are black with Negroes waiting for south-bound trains," observed one journalist in 1924. "But hardly any of those Negroes intend to stay south. . . . Almost all . . . are going south to visit friends, show off their fine clothes, describe their fine palaces up North, tell wildly exaggerated tales of 'freedom,' and urge still more Negroes to migrate."[22] This informal but extensive southward flow of information contributed to the chain-like aspect of the migration process, whereby not only family members and friends but often large numbers of people from the same community would relocate in the same northern neighborhoods.

The northern black press constituted an additional—and crucial—source of information and inspiration for southern black migrants. The *Chicago Defender,* the black weekly with the largest circulation in the North and the journal most widely read by southern blacks, railed against the white South, condemning low wages and denouncing the lack of opportunity and freedom. Pullman porters and northern visitors to the South brought multiple copies of the paper with them, which they surreptitiously delivered to eager readers. Distribution of the paper, however, entailed risks. Some blacks were arrested for selling it, and in Georgia, one commentator noted in 1924, "a Negro risks his life every time he buys a *Defender.*"

Opponents of migration had good reason to dislike the *Defender,* for the Chicago paper pulled no punches in its indictment of the white

South. "To die from the bite of frost is far more glorious than [to die] at the hand of the mob," declared a typical article. A relentless prose-lytizer on behalf of migration, the Georgia-born *Defender* editor Robert S. Abbott made clear to prospective migrants that jobs, in abundant numbers and paying high wages, awaited their arrival in the North, as did freedom itself. All a southern black man had to do was "step on a train and ride for a day and a night to freedom," editor Abbott insisted. "You tip your hat to no white man unless you know him and desire to do so. Your wives and daughters walk the streets unafraid. . . . You are a man and are expected to carry yourself as such." Indeed, the *Defender* and other northern black papers repeatedly labeled the North as a "land of promise."[23]

Although some northern black journalists and leaders encouraged migration, many southern black leaders did not. Fearing their own potential loss of supporters or genuinely unimpressed by conditions in the North, many counseled southern blacks to remain in the land of their birth. Some black newspaper editors genuinely feared for the safety of migrants, and filled their columns with news of northern race riots, unemployment, white union hostility, residential overcrowding, and bad weather. It is impossible to determine what, if any, impact such antimigration/antinorthern stances had on southern black read-ers. But if their purpose was to halt or even slow the migration of southern blacks, it was to no avail. "This migration differs from all oth-ers in that it has no visible leader," declared northern minister Dr. Adam Clayton Powell, pastor of the Abyssinian Baptist Church in New York, in 1917. The black church neither started this "cyclone-like movement" nor exerted much influence over it. "The masses have done more to solve the Negro problem in fifty weeks without a leader than they did in fifty years with a certain type of leaders [*sic*]."[24] Only southern whites could halt the migration by addressing blacks' legiti-mate concerns and providing the relief they sought, according to the southern black weekly, the *Birmingham Reporter*. Despite the self-interested pleas of "enlightened" white newspaper editors, few white southerners were willing to provide that substantive relief.

THE PROMISED LAND?

The warnings of prominent whites and even some black leaders notwithstanding, many migrants maintained that the North repre-sented a "promised land" or a "land of hope." Indeed, blacks in the North could participate in the political arena with little fear of personal violence, and black churches, social clubs, and a multitude of fraternal and social welfare organizations proliferated with little white opposition. Between 1900 and 1915, according to historian Allan H. Spear, Chicago's black leaders "built a complex of community organizations, institutions, and enterprises that made the South Side not simply an area of Negro concentration but a city within a city." Chicago's premigration blacks had created a "vision of a 'black metropolis.'" A decade before the Great Migration, one white journalist concluded that the "building up of a more or less independent Negro community" reflected a "growing race consciousness" among northern blacks. Increasing numbers of black-owned businesses established themselves in northern cities; readily available black newspapers provided a steady stream of news relevant to black migrants; and northern schools offered black children a longer and better education than those in the South.[25]

Conditions in the North compared favorably to those in the South, but they fell far short of the region's image as a "promised land." Jobs might be plentiful, at least in some areas, but neither white workers nor trade unions were enthusiastic about the new black arrivals. The American Federation of Labor (AFL), the dominant trade union federation composed largely of skilled white workers, sanctioned the discriminatory practices of many of its constituent unions, most of which rejected blacks as members. White trade unionists often refused to work with black newcomers and resorted to threats and even walkouts to block the introduction of black workers.

When the General Electric Company in Schenectady, New York, hired Wendell King, a young northern black college student, in June 1917, and assigned him to a white crew, approximately 2,500 white machinists and toolmakers (later reports put the number at 6,000) walked off the job in protest. Carrying an American flag, members of the machinists' union insisted on segregating blacks in the workplace—just as blacks were segregated in the armed forces. The company held firm and the eight-day strike failed.[26]

The "interests of Negro Labor is [sic] not given the same consideration as is the interests of white labor, by the Labor Unions," insisted the St. Louis Argus, a black weekly. The AFL has heretofore "been hostile toward the Negro. In fact, the Negro has been barred from union labor; he has been treated as a scab and worse," claimed the African American Southwestern Christian Advocate. The numerous workplace clashes, the long history of trade union discrimination, and in some cases migrants' own lack of familiarity with the labor movement—fewer unions existed in the South than in the North and fewer still existed in agricultural areas—led many African Americans to keep their distance from the AFL. Determined to secure remunerative work in the North, some African American migrants became strikebreakers as a means of securing jobs that would otherwise be closed to them.[27]

The war years witnessed an intensification of racial conflict in the labor market, as migrants encountered sharp and sometimes violent hostility from whites in the workplaces of the North. One of the bloodiest workplace encounters of the war broke out in East St. Louis, Illinois. Unfortunately for the migrants, their arrival coincided with a local employer's anti-union campaign at the Aluminum Ore Works, and white workers directed their frustration toward the newcomers. The estimates of those killed range from forty to two hundred and approximately six thousand blacks were driven from their homes. The riot was nothing less than a "pogrom, engineered by [AFL President Samuel] Gompers and his Trade Unions," in the words of the *Crisis*. City police and members of the Illinois state militia did little to restrain white rioters and in many cases participated in the violence. In response, the NAACP sponsored a silent march of roughly ten thousand people through Harlem. Their signs read: "MR. PRESIDENT, WHY NOT MAKE AMERICA SAFE FOR DEMOCRACY?"[28] (See Figure 3.)

Even when white union leaders recognized the necessity of organizing black workers and took steps to do so, the obstacles to genuine interracial collaboration were numerous. Perhaps the most ambitious northern wartime experiment was undertaken by the Chicago-based Stockyards Labor Council (SLC), which sought to organize the heterogeneous labor force (which included African Americans) in the packinghouse industry. In contrast to many other organizing campaigns, the packinghouse union drive invited black participation, utilized black organizers and speakers, and counseled white members against discriminatory behavior. Many longtime black Chicagoans in the industry supported the union, but those who had only recently arrived from the South did not. Some migrants were unfamiliar with organized labor or were hostile to white unionists based on past experiences in the South. Others felt too economically vulnerable or dependent upon their employers to ally themselves with the SLC and instead sided with packinghouse managers in their conflict with organized labor. Whatever hope the SLC had of bridging the racial gap was shattered in the summer of 1919 with the outbreak of a bloody, five-day race riot in Chicago. Although the core white rioters were not packinghouse workers and the Eastern European immigrant members of the SLC abstained from the violence, the riot exacerbated tensions between

Figure 3. Demonstration Against the East St. Louis Riots
Following the race riot in East St. Louis in July 1917, as many as 10,000 people participated in a silent protest march organized by the NAACP in Harlem, New York. Marchers included black women who were increasingly active in the political arena in the early twentieth century.
© Corbis.

whites and blacks throughout the city, including the packinghouse workers. The SLC's union organizing drive was effectively halted, packers easily defeated a SLC strike, and the labor organization gradually disintegrated.[29]

Appalling housing conditions in the North further belied the region's reputation as a "promised land." In most northern cities, neighborhoods were defined by race, with blacks largely restricted to particular residential areas by custom and, in some cases, legal property deeds. Black migrants, then, were not free to live anywhere they wanted: Their general poverty and racial restrictions forced them to live in geographically circumscribed areas. As their numbers increased, so too did the pressures on the housing stock. Migrants, journalists, and social service workers uniformly agreed that housing conditions were terrible. Rooming houses catering to single black men in wartime Pittsburgh "often beggar description," one investigator concluded. The addition of thousands of migrants meant "the utmost utilization of every place in the Negro sections capable of being transformed into a habitation," with attics, cellars, storerooms, churches, sheds, and warehouses turned into accommodations for the new arrivals. In Newark, New Jersey, another observer found that "old dilapidated buildings" lacking kitchens, toilets, and heat were rented to blacks. Outside of cities or in rural areas, railroads established camps that were little more than bunkhouses or "wooden sheds covered with tar paper," and steel companies utilized "old barns and old houses." Close scrutiny revealed to one white journalist the "frightful congestion behind brownstone fronts in Harlem, worse than Italian overcrowding in Philadelphia, [and] Negroes herding in cellars beneath" barber shops in Detroit. To make matters worse, blacks were forced to pay rents that were "exceedingly high" by white standards.[30]

Neighborhoods joined workplaces as the sites of racial confrontations throughout the North during and after World War I. Northern blacks and new migrants alike confronted highly discriminatory housing markets and de facto residential discrimination. In Chicago, for example, most of the city's blacks were segregated in the South Side Black Belt,* which absorbed tens of thousands of newcomers to Chicago in the first two decades of the century. (See Figure 4.)

---

*The Black Belt extended roughly from 22nd to 39th Streets and from Wentworth to Cottage Grove Avenues on Chicago's South Side.

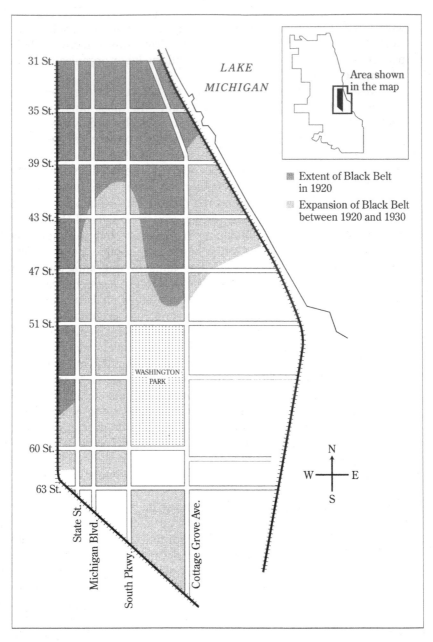

Figure 4. Expansion of the Black Belt

Between 1910 and 1920, the South Side black population almost tripled, from 34,000 to 92,500. Predictably, the housing stock deteriorated and rents were unfairly high (15 to 25 percent higher than for whites). During the war years, little new housing was built despite tremendous need.[31]

The city's black population pushed at its own borders, and some of the old settlers sought better conditions by attempting to move into white neighborhoods. They quickly encountered sharp white resistance, both organized and unorganized. In some cases, "athletic clubs" subjected blacks to "gang lawlessness"; in other cases, organized property owners' associations erected obstacles of their own. When blacks attempted to move south of the Black Belt, they met with fierce opposition from the Hyde Park–Kenwood Property Owners' Association,* which made no secret of its intention to "make Hyde Park white." When persuasion failed, whites resorted to violence: Fifty-eight bombings associated with black residential expansion were recorded between July 1917 and March 1921, targeting new black homeowners and the real estate agents who sold homes to them.[32]

African American migrants encountered not only indifferent or hostile white neighbors and coworkers, but a community of black old settlers who had made the North their home long before the new arrivals burst on the scene. The relationship between newcomers and old settlers was an ambivalent one. Established black professionals staffed social service associations that assisted migrants arriving for the first time in the huge railroad stations of the urban North, directing them to lodging. Officials of Chicago's Wabash Avenue YMCA, as well as of the Urban League and various churches, provided not just recreation but considerable advice about life in the North, as well as job referrals to specific industries or companies.

While trying to help migrants get settled, many social service professionals also maintained close relationships with corporate employers like the Pullman Company† and the various packinghouse firms;

---

*The adjacent Chicago communities of Kenwood and Hyde Park extended from 39th Street to 59th Street and from State Street to Lake Michigan.

†By World War I, the Pullman Company was the single largest employer of African American workers in the nation. Founded by George Pullman in 1867, the company hired a small army of black Pullman porters to serve white passengers on luxurious Pullman sleeping cars; by the end of World War I, roughly twelve thousand blacks labored for Pullman. The company engaged in extensive philanthropy in black communities, particularly in Chicago. Nonetheless, Pullman maintained a strict racial division of labor in its workforce: It neither promoted its porters nor hired blacks for more skilled and higher paying jobs as conductors.

thus they often counseled migrants against joining unions or participating in labor protests. If some old settlers extended a welcoming
hand, others expressed apprehension at rising racial tensions, fearing
that the magnitude of the migration and the migrants' demeanor
undermined their own precarious standing in the urban North. These
longtime black Chicagoans blamed not just racist whites but the
migrants themselves, whom they perceived as unlettered and uncultured and whose behavior ostensibly provoked whites or simply
embarrassed black old settlers. In their eyes, the Great Migration was
not an unqualified boon to be encouraged.[33]

WARTIME BLACK LEADERS, THE NEW NEGRO, AND GRASSROOTS POLITICS

The attitude of black Americans, like public opinion generally, was by
no means united on the question of U.S. intervention into the conflict
in Europe. President Woodrow Wilson had campaigned for re-election
in 1916 on a platform of peace.[34] The American declaration of war in
April 1917 was accompanied by an all-out effort to rally popular opinion and orchestrate patriotic support. Opposition and ambivalence
toward the war never completely vanished, and significant numbers of
white and black men resisted military conscription. But like other
groups of Americans, many northern and southern blacks came to
support the war in concrete ways, including contributing to war bond
drives and the Red Cross, sponsoring enlistment drives in their own
communities, and sending their young men off to war. By the end of
the war in late 1918, roughly 380,000 black men had been drafted or
had enlisted in the nation's armed services.[35]

The very military that welcomed their participation, however, was
not prepared to extend equal treatment or equal justice to its black
troops. The U.S. military was highly segregated and discriminatory.
Black soldiers in the Army worked and fought in all-black units, often
led by white officers; the few black officers were trained in an all-
black facility in Des Moines, Iowa; and black military men were used
heavily in labor gangs to build roads and bridges and to load and
unload ships. No blacks were admitted into the Marine Corps, and the
Navy utilized black men largely to prepare food and stoke ships' boil-
ers. Black soldiers stationed stateside, especially on military bases in
the South, were subject to extensive harassment by white civilians

who objected to the stationing of blacks, especially northern blacks, in their communities.

Racial tensions exploded into violence in Houston, Texas, in August 1917 when a black soldier attempted to stop the beating of a local black woman by police. Tired of regular harassment by white southerners, members of the black Twenty-fourth Infantry Division joined in a battle against white soldiers. In the end, four blacks and perhaps as many as sixteen whites were killed. Military reprisals were swift and decisive: Tried, convicted, and sentenced quickly, thirteen black soldiers were hanged for "murder and mutiny," and sixty-three were given life sentences. "The Negroes of the entire country will regard the thirteen Negro soldiers of the Twenty-fourth Infantry executed as martyrs," declared the Baltimore *Afro-American.*[36]

Although black leaders and newspaper editors pressed for more equitable treatment for black soldiers, they lined up behind the war effort. Not surprisingly, more established and conservative black leaders offered their wholehearted endorsement. Robert Moton, Booker T. Washington's successor at Tuskegee Institute in Alabama, wrote to President Wilson in 1917 that the nation "can count absolutely on the loyalty of the mass of Negroes to our country."[37] The Wilson administration, for its part, took pains to secure black cooperation with the government's efforts, appointing Emmett Scott, who had been Booker T. Washington's secretary and right-hand man for years, to a new position designed to oversee racial matters within the War Department. His goal was simple: to generate black support for the war and to eliminate black dissent. In June 1918, Scott served as co-organizer of a conference of black leaders attended by Moton, *Chicago Defender* editor Robert Abbott, and the editor of the NAACP's journal the *Crisis,* W. E. B. Du Bois. Scott accomplished his goal, for the conference delegates adopted resolutions supportive of the war effort. The Negro is "not disposed to catalogue, in this tremendous crisis, all his complaints and disabilities," they declared. He is "more than willing to do his full share in helping to win the war for democracy."[38]

Whereas it was predictable that conservatives like Moton and Scott would energetically back the government, W. E. B. Du Bois took more than a few people by surprise in July 1918 when he embraced the war with full vigor. Writing in the *Crisis,* whose monthly circulation was nearing eighty thousand, Du Bois published what would quickly become a famous editorial, "Close Ranks," which called on African Americans to prioritize the war over the struggle for racial justice.

Du Bois's uncharacteristic decision was wrapped up with broader personal and political considerations: He believed that blacks' military service would enhance future prospects for civil rights advances and expected to receive a captain's commission in the Army's division of military intelligence. As it turned out, neither came to pass. Du Bois received no captaincy and, less than six months later when the war finally ended, African Americans reaped no benefits—but rather considerable resentment—for their patriotic wartime efforts.[39]

Du Bois's unqualified and enthusiastic endorsement of the Wilson administration's war aims generated much controversy within the small ranks of black radicals. The Boston-based veteran civil rights militant William Monroe Trotter backed the war, but challenged the federal government's policies of segregation. "We have no thought of taking up arms against our country," announced the Boston chapter of the National Equal Rights League, of which he was a member; but the league refused to refrain from protesting discrimination. "As this nation goes forth to fight 'the natural foe of liberty,' let Americans highly resolve that all shall have liberty within her border." As Trotter noted in his newspaper, the *Boston Guardian*, "We believe in democracy, but we hold that this nation should enter the lists* with clean hands."[40]

Such a stance put Trotter—and countless other blacks—at odds with Du Bois. In response to the "Close Ranks" editorial, Trotter charged the NAACP leader with betraying "the cause of the race" and with being "a rank quitter of the fight for our rights."[41] The National Equal Rights League petitioned Congress "as an act of justice, of moral consistency, and to help win the war for world democracy," to pass legislation banning segregation in federal buildings and federal territories; to enforce equal treatment in matters of wages and promotions in federal buildings, to integrate the armed forces, to enforce the Thirteenth, Fourteenth, and Fifteenth Amendments, and, finally, to make "mob murders"—that is, lynching—a federal crime.[42]

The strongest black antiwar voices could be heard in the pages of the *Messenger* magazine, published by two young black socialists, Asa Philip Randolph and Chandler Owen. (See Figures 5 and 6.) In their eyes, the war had no lofty purpose but was rather a struggle between different groups of capitalists. The Great War was not a war for "democracy" but for the "selfish ends" of business. Randolph and Owen got right to the heart of the problem: "Lynching, Jim Crow, seg-

---

* This phrase refers to entering the "playing field" or "arena."

FOLLOWING THE ADVICE OF THE "OLD CROWD" NEGRO

Figure 5. "The Old Crowd Negro"
A. Philip Randolph and Chandler Owen, the militant editors of the *Messenger* magazine, an African American monthly, castigated established black leaders, whom they called "the Old Crowd," for their ostensible conservatism and timidity in the face of racial oppression and racial violence. Pictured in the center is civil rights activist and writer W. E. B. Du Bois, whose 1918 "Close Ranks" editorial is mocked.
The Messenger (September 1919).

regation, discrimination in the armed forces and out, disfranchisement of millions of black souls in the South—all these things," they wrote to President Woodrow Wilson in a public letter in their journal, "make your cry of making the world safe for democracy a sham, a mockery, a rape on decency and a travesty on common justice." Randolph and Owen's position led to one simple conclusion: Black men should not fight in the armed forces of the United States.[43]

THE "NEW CROWD NEGRO" MAKING AMERICA SAFE FOR HIMSELF

Figure 6.   "The New Crowd Negro"
The *Messenger* magazine heralded the emergence of a "New Negro," termed
here the "New Crowd Negro," who repudiated what it saw as the accommodationist, gradualist, and cautious approach pursued by many black leaders. The
"New Negro" neither turned the other cheek nor suspended the struggle for
civil rights during and after the war but instead aggressively challenged white
encroachments on black rights and resisted white attacks on black communities. In this cartoon, the white mobs of the 1919 riots are described as the
"Hun"—a derogatory term for the Germans during World War I—and the
"New Negro" assumes responsibility for the defense of black communities
unprotected by white government officials.
The Messenger (September 1919).

If few African Americans endorsed Randolph and Owen's explicit
antiwar stance, many more shared their anger and impatience with
racial inequality and oppression. During the World War I years, the
social and political horizons of numerous black southerners and

northerners expanded dramatically. Wartime conditions gave rise to "a new consciousness" of the fact that African Americans "have the liberty and the opportunity to move freely from place to place," black government official George Edmund Haynes announced in 1919. Not only did the migration "break down much of their timidity" and give the rank and file "the belief that they could move to another part of the country and succeed in gaining a foothold in its industrial life and activity," it further generated the "united demand of [black] workers for the removal of race discriminations in public courts, public conveyances and for provision in city and country for the same facilities of community improvement for them as for others."[44]

Writer and civil rights activist James Weldon Johnson witnessed the same transformation. "The most vital and far-reaching change" set in motion by the war, he observed in 1919, "is the one that has been wrought within the Negro himself. He has been seized by the spirit that has taken hold of all the submerged classes of the world. He is looking with wider, but wiser eyes at what is happening. . . . [H]e is striving to see that this war will mean for him just what it promises—democracy for all the people of the world."[45]

African Americans seized upon the wartime rhetoric of democracy to express their aspirations and justify their demands. Along with other subordinate groups in American society, such as women and workers, blacks invoked the Wilson administration's stated purpose for American involvement in the European conflict—the lofty aim of making the world safe for democracy—to illustrate the contradiction that the democracy ostensibly being fought for abroad often did not apply to them at home.[46]

Although troublesome to the defenders of the racial status quo, this subtle though often overt change in disposition garnered considerable praise from those critical of the racial order. The militant *Chicago Whip* discerned approvingly in 1920 the "rumbling, roaring, rising, expanding voice of the American Negro . . . beginning to shake gently but perceptibly the foundations of the Southern Overlords, the Magistrates of the Lynch Law and the entire group of those afflicted with nightmares of perpetual White Supremacy." To one white commentator, it was evident that the migration had "stimulated race pride. There is a new self-reliance, a new bearing."[47] Writing in the introduction to his 1925 anthology of black poetry, literature, and criticism, editor Alain Locke of Howard University observed approvingly, "In the last decade something beyond the watch and guard of statistics has happened in the life of the American Negro," namely, the emergence of the "New Negro."[48]

The Great Migration itself was but one manifestation of a willingness to take advantage of new opportunities for individual and collective advancement. On an organizational level, African Americans intensified their push for full citizenship rights and an end to discrimination and exclusion. The name Marcus Garvey is perhaps most associated with the new, more militant, "race-conscious" spirit among African Americans in World War I and in the immediate postwar era. Born in Jamaica in 1887, Garvey emigrated to the United States in 1916, where he founded a branch of his new organization, the Universal Negro Improvement Association (UNIA) in New York. Garvey's vision of black nationalism combined Booker T. Washington's conservative economic and educational philosophy with a strong sense of race pride. The UNIA's goals included the promotion of racial consciousness, the development of a black economic base through the cultivation of black capitalism, the advocacy of black self-determination, and the spread of Christianity in Africa. The UNIA further called for black Americans' eventual return to Africa. No reliable figures exist for UNIA membership, and the organization's claim of 4 to 6 million members is a highly inflated one. Whatever the UNIA's size, however, Garvey clearly appealed to large numbers of black Americans.[49] The carefully choreographed pageantry of UNIA meetings and parades elicited a sense of wonder and pride among participants and spectators alike. Decades later in the 1960s, activist Sylvia Woods remembered how her father, a Garveyite, took her to UNIA meetings in New Orleans. That "was the beginning of my realizing that you have to fight for freedom," she recalled.[50]

The UNIA's glory days were short-lived. By the end of the war, Garvey was engaged in increasingly strident attacks on established black leaders and organizations opposed to him; Du Bois, Randolph, and others ideologically and temperamentally opposed to Garvey's program stepped up their attacks on him. The UNIA's all-black shipping company, the Black Star Steamship Line, supported by the selling of stock to African Americans exclusively, proved to be a commercial failure; Garvey's efforts to establish a beachhead in Liberia collapsed when African leaders spurned his advances. U.S. government officials, fearful of what they saw as Garvey's antiwhite radicalism, kept close watch on Garvey for years. In 1922 Garvey was arrested on charges of mail fraud. Convicted the following year, he began serving his five-year sentence in Atlanta in 1925. The government commuted his sentence in 1926 and deported him. Although he would continue to lead the UNIA from abroad until 1940, membership in the organization declined precipitously and, in the United States, the UNIA remained little more than a shell.

Although less flamboyant than the UNIA, the NAACP grew considerably during and immediately after the war. Founded in New York in 1909, the interracial NAACP attracted middle-class black activists and white philanthropists and reformers who rejected Booker T. Washington's philosophy of accommodation with Jim Crow. In its early years, the civil rights association aggressively advocated an end to legalized segregation and disfranchisement, turning to Congress to lobby for federal antilynching legislation and to the courts to challenge discriminatory laws and practices. Before the war, the NAACP remained a small, elite organization with approximately six thousand members in 1914 and just under nine thousand in 1916. Successful recruitment drives, however, transformed the organization, with ninety thousand men and women enrolled by the war's end. Eighty-five new local NAACP branches representing about thirty-five thousand members formed in 1919. By 1920, sixteen different cities and towns in Georgia boasted NAACP chapters; in Atlanta alone, NAACP membership had quickly grown from seven hundred to three thousand.[51] The affiliation of unprecedented numbers of enthusiastic black workers, sharecroppers, and military veterans broadened the civil rights association's social and geographical composition; by 1919, roughly half of the organization's members were from the South. As their numbers grew, local chapters adopted a more activist stance as they protested lynchings, poor schools, and the lack of social services.[52]

The national black women's club movement, which had first emerged in the 1890s, also intensified its public campaigns during and after the war. When war broke out in Europe in 1914, the National Association of Colored Women's membership exceeded fifty thousand in twenty-eight federations and over a thousand clubs in northern and southern communities.[53] Members and leaders came largely from the ranks of educated and middle-class or elite black women, a group Evelyn Brooks Higginbotham calls the "Female Talented Tenth."* This movement combined elements of Booker T. Washington's self-help and racial uplift philosophy with a more activist civil rights agenda.

---

*Popularized by W. E. B. Du Bois in *The Souls of Black Folk* (1903), the term "Talented Tenth" referred to the stratum of well-educated and skilled African Americans. Historian Evelyn Brooks Higginbotham adapted the term to "Female Talented Truth" to call attention to the leadership role assumed by black women in the late nineteenth and early twentieth centuries.

Promoting Victorian morality and motherhood, clubwomen sought respect for black women but adopted a condescending stance toward those they sought to help—their "poor benighted sisters of the plantation," as Margaret Murray Washington, a club leader, put it.[54] They formed "Mother's Clubs," established day nurseries, kindergartens, and training courses in domestic science, and led attacks on alcohol abuse, saloons, gambling, truancy, and vice. By the 1910s clubwomen in some locations, in Progressive-era fashion, publicized antituberculosis campaigns, ran health education classes, and lobbied government officials for greater educational resources for black children. The crusade against lynching, although always important to black clubwomen, assumed a crucial role in their agenda during the war years, as did the campaign for women's suffrage.[55]

After the ratification of the Nineteenth Amendment granting women the vote in 1920, black women voted and established Republic Clubs across the urban North. In the South, they invariably encountered obstacles to exercising the franchise. Black women in many southern communities formed "colored voters' leagues" to encourage other black women to register to vote, but white election officials quickly and effectively countermobilized to block them. In Savannah, Georgia, whites forcibly turned back close to 1,700 black women from the polls in November 1920; black women were also turned away from voting places in every ward in Atlanta. In subsequent years, local associations, such as the Colored Women's Voters' League of Birmingham and Jefferson County, Alabama, continued to seek the franchise for black women through the payment of poll taxes; these groups had little success, however, until the 1940s and 1950s.[56]

Increased affiliation with national, regional, or local protest and racial pride organizations reflected only one manifestation of the New Negro; countless individual and collective acts undertaken by African American men and women across the country reflected another. To some observers, the Great Migration itself was nothing less than the "great American protest" against the "unbearable living conditions" in the South. "In a way," the Norfolk *Journal and Guide* reflected, "the exodus of Negroes from some sections is a strike on a huge and more or less disorganized scale."[57] But migrants leaving the South were by no means the only African Americans exhibiting a new willingness to question or challenge Jim Crow publicly, to take concrete measures to improve their lives, or to insist upon a greater degree of dignity.

In a quiet, unorganized, but perceptible way, black women in the South and North used wartime labor shortages to move out of domestic service into alternative, less demeaning, and often better paying work in restaurants, factories, and stores, much to the chagrin of the white men and women whose households they had previously cleaned. Those who remained in domestic service often pressed for higher wages and improved conditions. During the 1910s, domestics in New Orleans, Galveston, and Houston formed their own unions, as did black washerwomen in Mobile, Little Rock, Houston, Norfolk, and St. Petersburg, Florida, and female tobacco stemmers in Norfolk, Virginia, and Rocky Mount, North Carolina.[58]

Organizing and taking collective action allowed black women the chance to voice their concerns but also entailed substantial personal risk. In April 1918, the newly formed Laundry Workers Union, representing some 250 African American laundresses in Mobile, Alabama, struck that city's commercial laundries. "We the laundry workers of Mobile . . . have been unable to sustain ourselves on the small wages received for our work," they declared. Particularly objectionable were the long hours and low wages (inside workers labored daily for twelve to sixteen hours and earned $2.50 to $4 a week). Although wartime inflation prompted their walkout, their employers' refusal to consider their demands added another dimension to their protest. "We are protesting against this discourteous treatment," they announced, promising to "stay out until our communications are answered and they agree to deal with our committee." These washerwomen fought a losing battle. Attacks on (presumably black) strikebreakers by strikers and their male sympathizers (one crowd was estimated at several hundred) merely provoked swift police intervention, leading to numerous arrests.[59]

Although unsuccessful, the Mobile women's experience illustrates the extent, often unrecognized, to which African Americans protested workplace conditions and their economic plight during and after the war. Seattle editor Horace Cayton Sr. exaggerated after the armistice when he concluded that in almost every city of the country "the colored man is being brought to realize the meaning of unionism."[60] He nonetheless recognized that levels of labor conflict involving blacks had reached new heights. Rejected or held at arm's length by most of the white labor movement, a small but significant number of African Americans, including those in the South, built their own unions as an expression of their new collective confidence—or daring—in the wartime era.

Not since the 1880s had black men and women organized and struck in such numbers. Among those who organized were phosphate miners in Florida; railroad workers—car cleaners, freight handlers, locomotive firemen, brakemen, Pullman porters, red caps, and dining car waiters—in New York, Chicago, Memphis, St. Louis, Birmingham, Rocky Mount, and Washington, D.C.; building trade laborers in

Norfolk, Charleston, Dallas, Kansas City, and St. Petersburg; and oystermen in Norfolk.[61]

In several significant exceptions to the rule of racial exclusion from the ranks of organized white labor, a number of unions organized along biracial lines, affiliating all-black and all-white union locals under the same organizational banner. Tens of thousands of black and white longshoremen along the Gulf and South Atlantic coasts had enrolled in biracial locals of the AFL's International Longshoremen's Association by the war years, thousands of black and white timber workers joined the Industrial Workers of the World's International Brotherhood of Timber Workers in Louisiana and East Texas, and thousands of black and white coal miners enlisted in the AFL's United Mine Workers of America in the Birmingham district of Alabama and in the coal fields of West Virginia. In Little Rock, Arkansas, black and white women employed in steam laundries successfully organized to raise wages, eliminate racially based wages, and win union recognition. Whether in all-black unions, biracial union federations, or the very rare interracial union, black trade unionists invested hope and energy in workplace associations to improve their members' economic standing, attain their rights, and gain respect on the job.[62]

Few contemporaries applied the term New Negro to black southerners, but the changes in black attitudes and behavior were noticeable in the wartime South. The case of Savannah, Georgia, during and after World War I illustrates sharply the individual and collective initiative taken by that city's black community, the range of issues that propelled blacks into action, and the racial tensions that permeated daily life in wartime. Savannah's black residents, like its white residents, did not hesitate to register their official support for the war effort. One patriotic demonstration in May 1918 brought twelve thousand to twenty thousand African Americans into the streets, with virtually every "society, fraternal organization, trade, school, church and patriotic league" represented in the crowd. A cross-section of the city's black population participated, including barbers, hotel workers, laundry workers, bricklayers, and nurses, the Toussaint L'Ouverture branch of the Red Cross, a local chapter of the Grand Army of the Republic, Baptist and Methodist church groups, and approximately nine hundred waterfront workers, whose banner read "Black men's blood has dyed every battlefield in every war." Although offering moral and material support to the war effort, black Savannah never moved blindly to "close ranks" and suspend activities designed to combat racial or economic oppression.[63]

As racial tensions on the home front escalated as the war progressed, Savannah blacks' dissatisfaction with inequality intensified. Throughout the war and immediate postwar years, the black weekly, the *Savannah Tribune*, relentlessly assailed racial discrimination in employment, law enforcement, and politics. Local African American associations stepped up their activities in response to the heightened racial oppression. Savannah's NAACP chapter, which launched a number of membership drives, lodged complaints with city officials in 1918 denouncing the growing police harassment of blacks. The discriminatory enforcement of a wartime work-card system in particular provoked complaint: "Every Negro man was stopped, questioned and intimidated" by police in the summer of 1918; those who could not provide a "clear-cut reason for not having the card or for not having it punched to date" were required to report to military officials, whereas "No white men were intercepted or quizzed, unless one appeared particularly suspicious."[64] Members of the black plasterers' union, employed on the construction of the new municipal auditorium, threatened to strike over racially based pay in July 1917. Their "demand for more pay," the *Savannah Tribune* concluded, "commensurate with the character and quality of the work they do . . . met with success as it deserved to."[65] Black protests in wartime Savannah at times appeared to grow spontaneously out of the daily humiliations of Jim Crow. Frequent clashes broke out between black and white shipyard workers on the city's streetcars, for example, with the disputes usually centered on the blacks' resistance to segregated seating at the back of the cars.[66]

The growing willingness on the part of black southerners to challenge the racial order did not escape the attention of white southerners, many of whom resented any sign of black initiative or protest, and most of whom never relinquished the most potent weapon in the struggle for racial control—violence. When the war was over, they would move with tremendous speed to suppress black advances and to re-establish the prewar status quo.

RACIAL VIOLENCE AND THE POSTWAR REACTION TO BLACK ACTIVISM

"Now comes the test," declared James Weldon Johnson shortly after the armistice ending World War I was signed in November 1918. Could blacks hold the industrial advantage they had gained? he asked.[67] In subsequent months, Johnson would be displeased by the turn of events and its consequences for African Americans in the postwar world.

The immediate postwar era witnessed the outbreak of a wide range of political, social, economic, and racial conflicts, not just in the United States but in much of the world. The decisive Allied victory over Germany was followed not only by a formal peace but by social and political upheavals on a global scale. The Bolshevik Revolution* in the Soviet Union consolidated its hold, and revolutionaries came to power briefly in Hungary while communists tried, and failed, to take power in Germany. In Great Britain, the Labour Party adopted its program for a socialist postwar order, and in some industrial Italian cities, workers' councils temporarily took over factories. The year 1919 was a year whose events the *Nation* magazine described as part of "a world-wide movement . . . The common man, forgetting the old sanctions, and losing faith in the old leadership, has experienced a new sense of self-confidence, or at least a new recklessness, a readiness to take chances on his own account."[68]

Such observations were not limited to the left-wing press. To the conservative black scholar and leader Kelly Miller, "[r]iot and revolution" were rife and strikes "everywhere abound[ed]." The world was undergoing nothing short of a "process of radical readjustment" in which the "relationship of the rich and the poor, the laborer and the overlord of labor, the strong and the weak, the white and the non-white races of men, must be adjusted in harmony with the progressive spirit of the times."[69]

The United States was not immune to the postwar global upheavals. The Justice Department launched sweeping legal assaults on suspected radicals during the 1919 "red scare," rounding up as many as six thousand suspected revolutionaries, many of whom were immigrants. Conflict also intensified in the nation's workplaces. The year 1919 witnessed the greatest wave of labor militancy in the nation's history, with more than four million workers, approximately 22 percent of the labor force, going out on strike. Black workers, particularly those in the comparatively rare biracial unions in the South, were active participants in many strikes. Black and white phosphate miners in central Florida, longshoremen in New Orleans, Key West, and Savannah, and coal miners in Arkansas, Kentucky, Tennessee, and West Virginia all engaged in dramatic and occasionally violent conflicts with their employers over such issues as union

---

*The Bolshevik Revolution involved the armed overthrow of the Russian czar by Communists in 1917, an event which brought about the founding of the Soviet Union.

recognition, wage increases (at a time of significant inflation), and general relief from harsh conditions.[70]

In many instances, southern white planters, industrialists, and politicians held the federal government responsible for fomenting unrest among black workers. During the war, the government's interest in ensuring sufficient manpower in wartime industries, reducing workplace strife, and ensuring continued production had led to the creation of numerous federal agencies charged with adjudicating labor conflicts. Southern black workers could request the intervention of the National War Labor Board, the U.S. Railroad Administration, the National Adjustment Board, and other governmental bodies in their disputes with employers. Federal officials often investigated their complaints and occasionally supported their claims. The U.S. Labor Department's new Division of Negro Economics, led by black economist George E. Haynes, dispatched 134 black investigators to the South not only to collect information on the labor market but to support the integration of black workers into previously all-white jobs. Governmental labor-related agencies were no panacea for southern black workers, but their unprecedented efforts were appreciated by southern blacks, who petitioned them by the thousands for relief. But where southern blacks saw a potential ally at the national level, southern whites saw a nefarious northern attempt to disrupt the South's racial order by encouraging blacks to form unions or secret antiwhite societies and vowed to resist accordingly.[71]

Southern white employers hostile to both unions and black advancement met the challenge of postwar black labor activism with repression and violence. In November 1919 black trade unionists in the company town of Bogalusa, Louisiana, carried out an organizing drive that won the support of local white unionists, only to be suppressed by gunmen and white vigilantes. The following year, more than ten thousand United Mine Workers union members in Alabama (approximately three-quarters of whom were black) battled coal operators, courts, strikebreakers, and the state national guard over union recognition and brutal conditions, going down to a violent and bitter defeat. The strike of sixteen hundred black and white freight handlers in Galveston, Texas, against Coastwise Steamship Lines also faced a massive state backlash. As the Texas governor declared martial law, Texas Rangers occupied the waterfront for months and the legislature passed an Open Port bill that severely hampered unionism, much to the delight of the anti-union Galveston Open Shop* Association. In

---

*"Open Shop" refers to a workplace that is "union free." Proponents of the open shop after World War I were strongly opposed to unions.

1923, on the docks of New Orleans, a biracial and previously successful Dock and Cotton Council comprising more than ten thousand waterfront workers crumbled in the face of the open shop drive of the New Orleans Steamship Association, a defeat which not only broke the Council but destroyed any further collaboration between black and white dockers.[72] In the postwar years, black trade unionists, like many of their white counterparts, had lost tremendous ground. Few of their associations remained intact; and many of their broader goals remained unrealized.

The year 1919 was a rude awakening for those African Americans who believed that their support of the war would enable them to claim citizenship rights. White Americans generally expressed little gratitude or appreciation for the service of black soldiers, who, upon their return to the United States, found a nation often downright hostile. The summer of 1919, as the eminent historian John Hope Franklin put it, ushered in the "greatest period of interracial strife the nation had ever witnessed." Fearing that blacks' military experience and their widening horizons would threaten the southern racial order, many southern whites sought to reverse wartime black gains and reimpose even harsher lines of racial hierarchy. "What will be the result when tens of thousands of Negroes come home from this war with a record of honorable military service?" asked Georgia senator Thomas Hardwick. "I can conceive that a new agitation may arise as strong and bitter as the agitation for Negro suffrage which swept the North after the Civil War."[73]

Few images "haunted the white supremacist's imagination more than a Black man in uniform," historian Steven Reich has aptly observed.[74] White southerners targeted returning black soldiers and the networks of local civil rights activism that had begun to flourish during the war years. The NAACP came under sharp attack by southern whites. In the Georgia town of Thomasville, a chapter with three hundred members decided to disband after local whites threatened to kill the organization's president. In Texas, the white NAACP executive secretary, John R. Shillady, was brutally beaten by three prominent whites, and state repression forced most of the association's branches in Texas out of business. These were hardly isolated developments. The federal government's Justice Department and military intelligence branch kept black activists around the country under close surveillance, and in many cases, local and state officials in the South joined white employers, planters, and leading citizens in undermining or destroying local civil rights initiatives.[75]

"Our warfare with the German Hun has ceased," one Detroit African American declared in June 1919. "A warfare with the American

Hun is now our task." At the very least, it appeared that many American whites had declared war on African Americans. Southern blacks found themselves confronting a widespread legal and extralegal terror campaign. The number of lynchings nationwide, which had been declining for some years, rose sharply. In 1917, thirty-six blacks were lynched; in 1919, the number was approximately seventy-six, including ten black soldiers still wearing their uniforms.[76] White mobs included members of the new Ku Klux Klan (KKK), which had been re-established in 1915. The KKK's membership grew rapidly from a few thousand during the war to more than one hundred thousand immediately thereafter.[77]

The "racial counterrevolution" reached its climax in the bloody summer of 1919. Race riots erupted in approximately two dozen cities and towns, including Knoxville, Omaha, Charleston, Longview, Texas, Chicago, and Washington, D.C. The riots had different triggering causes: Some involved labor tensions between white and black workers, others focused on rumors of rape, others on competition over scarce resources like housing, and some involved efforts by whites simply to put blacks "in their place." The largest disturbance was the outbreak of racial violence in Chicago in the sweltering heat of July. Tens of thousands of blacks had arrived in Chicago during the war to work in its stockyards, steel mills, and railroads; the city's black population had more than doubled over the decade. Following the armistice, demobilization had dumped literally millions of ex-soldiers into the labor and housing markets, creating intense conflicts over jobs and housing. For five days, whites, initially led by gangs of Irish Americans, attacked Chicago's black community. When the riot finally ended, thirty-eight people were dead and more than five hundred Chicagoans were injured.[78]

A very different kind of violence erupted in rural Arkansas in October 1919, illustrating both the wartime activism of southern African Americans and the newfound determination of southern white planters to restore the prewar racial status quo. Few black share-croppers or tenant farmers had benefited from the high price of cotton during the war in Phillips County, adjacent to the state of Mississippi. Suspecting planter fraud, a number of them organized the Progressive Farmers and Household Union to demand itemized statements of their accounts. Their "sole purpose," James Weldon Johnson later argued, was to obtain "a fair settlement with their landowners for crops and labor." In advancing such a "radical" demand, they anticipated white reprisals and prepared themselves, according to some accounts, by amassing large quantities of weapons and ammunition.

The event that triggered the white counteroffensive was a fight that broke out between whites and blacks at a black church in the town of Elaine that left one white man dead. The accounts are hazy, but it appeared that whites surrounded the church on October 1, fired at it, and that blacks attending the meeting in the church fired back.[79]

Phillips County planters seized upon the incident as proof that the Elaine sharecroppers planned to rise up and massacre the white population. In the words of one white official, the "present trouble with the negroes in Phillips county is not a race riot. It is a deliberately planned insurrection of the negroes" by a group established for the purpose of "the killing of white people." Planters and police struck back against the sharecroppers with a vengeance. At the request of the Arkansas governor, federal troops patrolled Elaine and surrounding areas. By some accounts, more than a thousand black men and women were arrested, held in stockades, and kept away from their lawyers. Those who escaped arrest were literally hunted down by whites known as "headhunters." In the ensuing reign of terror, whites killed at least twenty-five blacks but possibly as many as several hundred.[80]

The trials following the upheaval and violence lasted only five days, and were little more than mock trials. The white court sentenced twelve defendants to death and approximately eighty to jail terms of from one to twenty years. The case was pursued by the NAACP, which appealed to the U.S. Supreme Court. In 1923, the Court issued its decision in the landmark case of *Moore v. Dempsey,* overturning the lower court's ruling on the grounds that those convicted had not received a fair trial. The lives of the defendants had been spared, but their organization had been utterly crushed. Although blacks and whites would pragmatically unite in the Southern Tenant Farmers Union in the 1930s, the landless farmers remained largely powerless in the ensuing decades.[81]

That, of course, was the purpose of the postwar white reaction to black activism: to roll back black advances, dissuade southern blacks from migrating or challenging the racial and economic order, and to restore, as much as possible, prewar conditions. It only partially succeeded. Although repression did not stop northward migration, the efforts of local NAACP chapters and many black labor activists during and immediately after the war were effectively halted by determined white resistance. And although the level and intensity of violence against blacks diminished by the early 1920s, it by no means disappeared. In the spring of 1921, for example, a race riot in Tulsa, Oklahoma, destroyed much of that city's black community. African

Americans needed few reminders that the war to make the world safe for democracy had done little to bring democracy home to them.[82]

CONSEQUENCES OF THE MIGRATION

If the postwar white reaction succeeded in pushing back southern black advances, it did not succeed in re-establishing the prewar racial status quo. The World War I–era "race exodus" from the South heralded a "new era in Negro history in America," and the cessation of hostilities in Europe in November 1918 hardly signaled an end to the vast changes in African American perspectives and opportunities that began during the war. Despite some migrants' loss of jobs to white workers and persistent conflict over housing, black migrants ultimately retained their foothold in the industrial economy and established a firm and permanent presence in the northern and midwestern states, particularly in domestic service, common labor, and unskilled and semiskilled factory production jobs. In some, albeit rare, cases, black male workers in the North experienced modest occupational mobility: By 1930, for example, more than one-third of the semiskilled and skilled positions in Chicago's packinghouses were held by African Americans. "The Negroes who have sought opportunity in Chicago in recent years have found it," one journalist concluded with some exaggeration in 1927. In "scores of industries white and Colored men work amicably side by side . . . Thrifty and steady employment are enabling hosts of Colored workers to acquire homes."[83] However much the North failed to live up to its reputation as the "promised land," it remained an attractive alternative to the persistent oppressiveness of southern life.

The Great Migration of the World War I era was only the beginning of a process with profound demographic, occupational, and political implications for African Americans. A "new southern exodus" began following a sharp but relatively short-lived economic depression after World War I ended, as the demand for labor again intensified. Laws passed by Congress in 1921 and 1924 restricting immigration drastically reduced the number of immigrants from southern and eastern Europe, requiring many employers to continue their dependence on black labor. The 1920s migration soon exceeded the level of the wartime migration of southern blacks to the urban North. The new migrants came for the same reasons as their wartime predecessors. "Almost without exception" the new migrants "describe the exodus as a kind of revenge," one white observer remarked. "They glory in it."[84] White southerners could never again convincingly maintain that African Americans were content with their lot; too many southern blacks had already spoken with their feet.

And they would continue to do so, migrating in even larger numbers in subsequent decades. Although migration slowed during the Great Depression of the 1930s, it increased dramatically from 1940 to 1970, with almost one and a half million southern African Americans relocating to the North in each decade. Changes in southern economic life contributed to the higher numbers. In the 1930s, New Deal agricultural programs paid planters to reduce their crop acreage, which decreased the demand for labor and contributed to a shift from sharecropping to wage labor. Economic development during World War II spurred tremendous population movements, as whites and blacks alike moved to southern and northern cities to fill a new, insatiable demand for labor in shipyards and factories and on military bases. The mechanization of southern agriculture—in particular, the adoption of the mechanical cotton picker—radically reduced white planters' dependence on black labor and doomed the sharecropping system, as did the diversification of southern agriculture. Black southerners increasingly resided in cities and performed nonagricultural work. If the era of the cotton kingdom had ended, and with it the system of sharecropping it rested upon, it remained for southern blacks and their northern allies to carry their crusade against legalized Jim Crow to its successful conclusion in the 1950s and 1960s.[85]

The Great Migration of the World War I era was in many ways removed from the ultimate fall of Jim Crow half a century later, but changes in African American life during that earlier period set the stage for subsequent struggles and ultimate if incomplete victories. In the North, heightened efforts at community building and political mobilization came with the rising population. With greater black patronage, black newspapers thrived, black businesses multiplied, and black churches expanded. The "newcomers who came to Chicago," black sociologist E. Franklin Frazier observed in 1929, "created a voluminous demand for different kinds of services," giving rise to a "large group of professional and business men and women" who constituted "a new leadership" class in the community. Harlem was not just an economic magnet but the cultural capital of black America, providing an institutional base for the flourishing of black arts and letters known as the "Harlem Renaissance." If Harlem had won a "reputation for being the Mecca of the New Negro," Frazier noted, Chicago "has long been known as the political paradise of the Negro." Heavily concentrated in the city's second ward (because of residential segregation), black Chicagoans were able to elect African Americans to the city council and state legislature throughout the 1920s; in 1928, they sent Oscar DePriest to the House of Representatives—the first black man to represent a northern district in Congress. In exchange for black votes, elected Republican officials in Chicago distributed patronage jobs to African American as well as white supporters.[86]

Although the conservative white postwar reaction dampened the sense of optimism about changes in the racial order, the new sensibility of assertiveness and determination among African Americans did not vanish. Expanding black communities in the North quickly proved receptive to the formation of new associations of black protest—the Brotherhood of Sleeping Car Porters in the late 1920s, the National Negro Congress and Don't Buy Where You Can't Work campaigns in the 1930s, and the March on Washington movement in the early 1940s. These organizations and movements pioneered an aggressive and militant style of protest politics that involved grassroots mobilization and confrontation with established authorities. The New Negro, at least in the North, had become a permanent fixture on the urban black scene. Even in the South, that sensibility would manifest itself in countless ways in the decades after World War I, informing the nascent movement for civil rights and black equality that ultimately would destroy Jim Crow and transform America.

NOTES

[1]James R. Grossman, *Land of Hope: Chicago, Black Southerners, and the Great Migration* (Chicago: University of Chicago Press, 1989), 3; Carole Marks, *Farewell—We're Good and Gone: The Great Black Migration* (Bloomington: Indiana University Press, 1989), 1; Lawrence R. Rodgers, *Canaan Bound: The African-American Great Migration Novel* (Urbana: University of Illinois Press, 1997), 11. Some contemporaries and subsequent historians have put the numbers higher: Cooper and Terrill estimate that between 800,000 and 900,000 blacks departed the South, most of whom headed toward northern and midwestern cities. Joe Trotter Jr., suggests a range of 700,000 to a million, with an additional 800,000 to a million moving North and West during the 1920s. William J. Cooper Jr., and Thomas E. Terrill, *The American South: A History*, Vol. II (New York: McGraw-Hill, 1991), 604; Joe William Trotter Jr., *The African American Experience* (Boston: Houghton Mifflin, 2001), 378.

[2]Jay Mandle, *Not Slave, Not Free: The African American Economic Experience since the Civil War* (Durham: Duke University Press, 1992), 69.

[3]"A Negro Exodus," *Contemporary Review*, 114 (September 1918): 229; Gilbert Osofsky, *Harlem: The Making of a Ghetto: Negro New York, 1890–1930* (1963; reprint, New York: Harper & Row, 1968), 18.

[4]"The Exodus and Human Cruelty," *Birmingham Reporter,* 31 Mar. 1923.

[5]Neil R. McMillen, *Dark Journey: Black Mississippians in the Age of Jim Crow* (Urbana: University of Illinois Press, 1989), 267; John Hope Franklin and Alfred A. Moss Jr., *From Slavery to Freedom: A History of African Americans,* 7th ed. (New York: McGraw-Hill, 1994), 340.

[6]"Combating Negro Migration," *Houston Informer,* 12 May 1923; "Migration Justified," *Crisis,* 16, no. 6 (Oct. 1918): 280. On sharecropping and southern agriculture, see: Gerald David Jaynes, *Branches without Roots: Genesis of the Black Working Class in the American South, 1862–1882* (New York: Oxford University Press, 1986); Gavin Wright, *Old South, New South: Revolutions in the Southern Economy since the Civil War* (New York: Basic Books, 1986); Pete Daniel, *The Shadow of Slavery: Peonage in the South 1901–1969* (New York: Oxford University Press, 1973).

[7]Gilbert Fite, *Cotton Fields No More: Southern Agriculture 1965–1980* (Lexington: University Press of Kentucky, 1984), 94, 102, 113, 120; George B. Tindall, *The Emergence of the New South, 1913–1945* (Baton Rouge: Louisiana State University Press, 1967), 33; William H. Harris, *The Harder We Run: Black Workers since the Civil War* (New York: Oxford University Press, 1982), vii.

[8]C. Vann Woodward, *Origins of the New South, 1877–1913* (1951; reprint, Baton Rouge: Louisiana State University Press, 1971); Edward Ayers, *The Promise of the New South: Life after Reconstruction* (New York: Oxford University Press, 1992).

[9]Leon F. Litwack, *Trouble in Mind: Black Southerners in the Age of Jim Crow* (New York: Alfred A. Knopf, 1998), 246–79; McMillen, *Dark Journey,* 197–253; Alex Lichtenstein, *Twice the Work of Free Labor: The Political Economy of Convict Labor in the New South* (New York: Verso, 1996); Jacqueline Jones Royster, ed., *Southern Horrors and Other Writings: The Anti-Lynching Campaign of Ida B. Wells, 1892–1900* (Boston: Bedford Books, 1997), 10; Turner quoted in Philip Dray, *At the Hands of Persons Unknown: The Lynching of Black America* (New York: Random House, 2002), 49; Mary White Ovington, "Reconstruction and the Negro," *Crisis* 17, no. 4 (Feb. 1919): 172.

[10]S.K.R., "An Exodus in America, " *Living Age,* 295 (6 Oct. 1917), 59; "Northward Movement of the Negro," *St. Louis Argus,* 22 Dec. 1916.

[11]Daniel Letwin, *The Challenge of Interracial Unionism: Alabama Coal Miners, 1878–1921* (Chapel Hill: University of North Carolina Press, 1998), 51–52; "Negroes in the Urban Movement," *The Outlook,* 29 June 1912, 457–58; Peter Gottlieb, *Making Their Own Way: Southern Blacks' Migration to Pittsburgh, 1916–30* (Urbana: University of Illinois Press, 1987), 23–26; Marks, *Farewell—We're Good and Gone,* 3; Wright, *Old South, New South,* 205; Henderson H. Donald, "The Negro Migration of 1916–1918," *Journal of Negro History,* 6, no. 4 (Oct. 1921): 393–402.

[12]Nell Irvin Painter, *Exodusters: Black Migration to Kansas after Reconstruction* (1976; reprint, New York: W. W. Norton & Company, 1986); William Cohen, *At Freedom's Edge: Black Mobility and the Southern White Quest for Racial Control 1861–1915* (Baton Rouge: Louisiana State University Press, 1991), 252–56; James Oneal, "The Negro in America," *The Messenger,* 6, no. 11 (Nov. 1924): 337; Joseph A. Hill, "The Recent Northward Migration of the Negro," *Opportunity,* 2, no. 16 (Apr. 1924): 100–105; "The Black Tide," *Atlanta Constitution,* 13 Oct. 1889; "The Exodus," *Huntsville Gazette,* 23 Jan. 1886; "The Colored Exodus from the South," *Christian Recorder,* 11 Feb. 1886; "Another Exodus," *Pensacolian,* 4 Feb. 1888.

[13]R. R. Wright, Jr., "The Migration of Negroes to the North," *Annals of the American Academy of Political Science,* 27, no. 3 (May 1906): 563; Frances A. Kellor, "Assisted Emigration from the South," *Charities and the Commons,* 15, no. 1 (7 Oct. 1905): 12; Cindy Hahamovitch, *Fruits of Their Labor: Atlantic Coast Farmworkers and the Making of Migrant Poverty, 1870–1945* (Chapel Hill: University of North Carolina Press, 1997); Myra B. Young Armstead, *"Lord, Please Don't Take Me in August": African Americans in Newport and Saratoga Springs, 1870–1930* (Urbana: University of Illinois Press, 1999);

Elizabeth Clark-Lewis, *Living In, Living Out: African American Domestics and the Great Migration* (New York: Kodansha International, 1994).

[14]Ray Stannard Baker, *Following the Color Line: American Negro Citizenship in the Progressive Era* (1908; reprint, New York: Harper & Row, 1964), 109–47; Gottlieb, *Making Their Own Way*, 90–91; David M. Katzman, *Before the Ghetto: Black Detroit in the Nineteenth Century* (Urbana: University of Illinois Press, 1973), 107–8; Joe William Trotter Jr., *River Jordan: African American Urban Life in the Ohio Valley* (Lexington: University Press of Kentucky, 1998), 71–92; R. R. Wright, Jr., "The Economic Condition of Negroes in the North. Tendencies Downward. Third Paper: Poverty among Northern Negroes," *Southern Workman*, 40, no. 12 (Dec. 1911): 700–709. Du Bois's early sociological study, *The Philadelphia Negro: A Social Study* (1899; reprint, New York: Shocken Books, 1967), offers a catalog of social ills afflicting black Philadelphians in the late nineteenth century.

[15]Figures cited in Mandle, *Not Slave, Not Free*, 68–69.

[16]Maurine Weiner Greenwald, *Women, War, and Work: The Impact of World War I on Women Workers in the United States* (Westport: Greenwood Press, 1980).

[17]August Meier and Elliott Rudwick, *Black Detroit and the Rise of the UAW* (New York: Oxford University Press, 1979), 5–8; Chicago Commission on Race Relations, *The Negro in Chicago: A Study of Race Relations and a Race Riot* (Chicago: University of Chicago Press, 1922), 357–65.

[18]Kimberley L. Phillips, *AlabamaNorth: African-American Migrants, Community, and Working-Class Activism in Cleveland, 1915–45* (Urbana: University of Illinois Press, 1999), 50, 60–71; Mary E. Jackson, "The Colored Woman in Industry," *Crisis* 17, no. 1 (Nov. 1918): 13; Helen B. Sayre, "Negro Women in Industry," *Opportunity*, 2, no. 20 (Aug. 1924): 242–44; J. Blaine Poindexter, "Blasting Prejudice from the Path of Women Workers," *Chicago Defender*, 13 May 1922.

[19]P. O. Davis, "The Negro Exodus and Southern Agriculture," *American Review of Reviews*, 68 (Oct. 1923): 403, 404; Emmett J. Scott, *Negro Migration during the War*, (1920; reprint, New York: Arno Press, 1969), 16; Trotter, *The African American Experience*, 381; Florette Henri, *Black Migration: Movement North, 1900–1920* (Garden City, NY: Anchor Books, 1976), 54–55.

[20]Eric Arnesen, *Brotherhoods of Color: Black Railroad Workers and the Struggle for Equality* (Cambridge: Harvard University Press, 2001), 43–48.

[21]Scott, *Negro Migration*, 36–37; "Blacks Migrate," *McDowell Times*, 17 Nov. 1916; "Pass Law to Keep Colored Labor," *McDowell Times*, 18 Aug. 1916; "Labor Agent Fine in Alabama," *McDowell Times*, 29 Sept. 1916; "Retaining Our Labor," New Orleans *Times-Picayune*, 26 June 1918.

[22]Scott, *Negro Migration*, 36; Rollin Lynde Hartt, "When the Negro Comes North, I. An Exodus and Its Causes," *World's Work*, 48, no. 1 (May 1924): 86; Jaxon, "Migration of Negroes from South," *Atlanta Independent*, 30 June 1917; Donald, "Negro Migration of 1916–1918," 413–14.

[23]Hartt, "When the Negro Comes North, I, 83; *Defender* quoted in Scott, *Negro Migration*, 31; Chicago Commission on Race Relations, *The Negro in Chicago*, 87–92.

[24]"Hold Big Migration Meeting in New York," *New York Age*, 5 July 1917; Scott, *Negro Migration*, 30; "The Exodus and Human Cruelty," *Birmingham Reporter*, 31 Mar. 1923.

[25]Baker, *Following the Color Line*, 144–45; "Colored Men Seek Political Equality," *Chicago Whip*, 4 Oct. 1919; "Southern Migrants Swell G.O.P. Ranks for Victory," *Chicago Defender*, 25 Oct. 1924; E. Franklin Frazier, "Chicago: A Cross-Section of Negro Life," *Opportunity*, 7, no. 2 (Mar. 1929): 70–73; Allan H. Spear, *Black Chicago: The Making of a Negro Ghetto, 1890–1920* (Chicago: University of Chicago Press, 1967), 91; Abraham Epstein, *The Negro Migrant in Pittsburgh* (1918; reprint, New York: Arno Press, 1969), 30.

[26]"2500 Machinists Draw Line on Negro and Strike; Officials Stand by King," *New York Age*, 21 June 1917; "Strike Settled at Schenectady; 6,000 Men Return to Work; Firm Will Not Remove Negro," *New York Age*, 5 July 1917.

[27]"Draw Line at Munition Plant," *New York Age*, 5 Oct. 1918; "Shall the Negro Join Labor Unions," *St. Louis Argus*, 22 Mar. 1918; "Shall the Negro Unionize," *Southwestern Christian Advocate*, 4 Sept. 1919.

[28]"East St. Louis," *Crisis*, 14, no. 5 (Sept. 1917): 216; "The Massacre of East St. Louis," *Crisis*, 14, no. 5 (Sept. 1917): 219; Lindsey Cooper, "The Congressional Investigation of East St. Louis," *Crisis*, 15, no. 3 (Jan. 1918): 116–21; Congressional committee quoted in Herbert Shapiro, *White Violence and Black Response: From Reconstruction to Montgomery* (Amherst: University of Massachusetts Press, 1988), 117. Banner quoted in David Levering Lewis, *When Harlem Was in Vogue* (New York: Vintage, 1982), 10. The definitive study of the riot remains Elliott Rudwick, *Race Riot at East St. Louis, July 2, 1917* (1964; reprint, Urbana: University of Illinois Press, 1982).

[29]James Barrett, *Work and Community in the Jungle: Chicago's Packinghouse Workers, 1894–1922* (Urbana: University of Chicago Press, 1987), 203, 216; Rick Halpern, "Race, Ethnicity, and Union in the Chicago Stockyards, 1917–1922," *International Review of Social History*, 37 (1992), 25–58; Rick Halpern, *Down on the Killing Floor: Black and White Workers in Chicago's Packinghouses, 1904–54* (Urbana: University of Illinois Press, 1997).

[30]Donald, "The Negro Migration of 1916–1918," 436, 454; Epstein, *The Negro Migrant in Pittsburgh*, 8, 12; Rollin Lynde Hartt, "When the Negro Comes North, II. Where Will the Migration Stop?" *World's Work*, 48, no. 2 (June 1924), 186.

[31]Chicago Commission on Race Relations, *The Negro in Chicago*, 93.

[32]Chicago Commission on Race Relations, *The Negro in Chicago*, 115, 121–23; Hartt, "When the Negro Comes North, II," 184–85; William M. Tuttle Jr., *Race Riot: Chicago in the Red Summer of 1919* (1970; reprint, New York: Atheneum, 1985), 159, 161, 163, 166.

[33]Milton C. Sernett, *Bound for the Promised Land: African American Religion and the Great Migration* (Durham: Duke University Press, 1997), 124–26, 128–30, 137–53; Spear, *Black Chicago*, 167–79; Philips, *AlabamaNorth*, 162–65; Epstein, *Negro Migrant in Pittsburgh*, 68–72; St. Clair Drake and Horace R. Cayton, *Black Metropolis: A Study of Negro Life in a Northern City* (New York: Harcourt, Brace and Company, 1945), 73–76.

[34]Tindall, *Emergence of the New South*, 41.

[35]Jeanette Keith, "The Politics of Southern Draft Resistance, 1917–1918: Class, Race, and Conscription in the Rural South," *Journal of American History*, 87, no. 4 (Mar. 2001): 1335–61; Arthur E. Barbeau and Florette Henri, *The Unknown Soldiers: African-American Troops in World War I* (1974; reprint, New York: Da Capo Press, 1996).

[36]Miller quoted in William Anthony Aery, "Hampton, Virginia Notes: The Negro and the Present Crisis," *Atlanta Independent*, 10 Nov. 1917; Emmett J. Scott, *Scott's Official History of the American Negro in the World War* (1919; reprint, New York: Arno Press, 1969); Martha Gruening, "Houston: An N.A.A.C.P. Investigation," *Crisis*, 15, no. 1 (Nov. 1917): 14–19; Lewis, *When Harlem Was in Vogue*, 10–11.

[37]Baltimore, *Afro-American* quoted in Jervis Anderson, *A. Philip Randolph: A Biographical Portrait* (New York: Harcourt Brace Jovanovich, 1972), 99; Martha Gruening, "Houston," *Crisis*, 15, no. 1 (Nov. 1917): 14–19.

[38]Stephen R. Fox, *The Guardian of Boston: William Monroe Trotter* (New York: Atheneum, 1971), 219–220, Jane Lang Scheiber and Harry N. Scheiber, "The Wilson Administration and the Wartime Mobilization of Black Americans, 1917–1918," in *Black Labor in America*, ed. Milton Cantor (Westport: Negro Universities Press, 1969), 124–29.

[39]W. E. B. Du Bois, "Close Ranks," *Crisis*, 16, no. 3 (July 1918): 111; David Levering Lewis, *W. E. B. Du Bois: Biography of a Race, 1868–1919* (New York: Henry Holt and Company, 1993), 553, 555–60. For two contrasting views of Du Bois's "Close Ranks" editorial, see William Jordan, "'The Damnable Dilemma': African-American Accommoda-

tion and Protest during World War I," and Mark Ellis, "W. E. B. Du Bois and the Formation of Black Opinion in World War I: A Commentary on 'The Damnable Dilemma,'" *Journal of American History* (Mar. 1995): 1562–83, 1584–90.

[40]Quoted in Fox, *The Guardian of Boston: William Monroe Trotter*, 215–16, 217.

[41]Quoted in Lewis, *When Harlem Was in Vogue*, 9, 12.

[42]Quoted in Fox, *The Guardian of Boston*, 220–21.

[43]Anderson, *A. Philip Randolph*, 98; Theodore Kornweibel, *Seeing Red: Federal Campaigns against Black Militancy 1919–1925* (Bloomington: Indiana University Press, 1998), 76–83.

[44]George Edmund Haynes, "Effect of War Conditions on Negro Labor," *Proceedings of the Academy of Political Science* (Feb. 1919): 170–71, 175.

[45]James Weldon Johnson, "The Changing Status of Negro Labor," in *Proceedings of the National Conference of Social Work at the Forty-Sixth Annual Session Held in Atlantic City, New Jersey, June 1–8, 1919* (Chicago: Rogers & Hall Co., 1919), 386.

[46]See, for instance, "Negro Exodus Discussed by Prominent Educators," *McDowell Times*, 31 Aug. 1917; Hartt, "When the Negro Comes North, I," 85; "Savannah Justice," *Savannah Tribune*, 2 Nov. 1918.

[47]"A Cry for Courage," *Chicago Whip*, 17 July 1920; Rollin Lynde Hartt, "When the Negro Comes North, III: Future Results of the Migration," *World's Work*, 48, no. 3 (July 1924): 321; Nathan Huggins, *Harlem Renaissance* (New York: Oxford University Press, 1971), 53.

[48]Alain Locke, ed., *The New Negro* (1925; reprint, New York: Atheneum, 1980), 3.

[49]On Garvey and the UNIA, see Jeffrey B. Perry, *A Hubert Harrison Reader* (Middletown, Conn.: Wesleyan University Press, 2001), 182–200; Judith Stein, *The World of Marcus Garvey: Race and Class in Modern Society* (Baton Rouge: Louisiana State University Press, 1986); Lawrence W. Levine, "Marcus Garvey and the Politics of Revitalization," in *Black Leaders of the Twentieth Century*, ed. John Hope Franklin and August Meier (Urbana: University of Illinois Press, 1982).

[50]Alice and Staughton Lynd, *Rank and File: Personal Histories by Working-Class Organizers* (Boston: Beacon Press, 1973), 114.

[51]August Meier, *Negro Thought in America 1880–1915* (1963; reprint, Ann Arbor: University of Michigan Press, 1966); Tindall, *Emergence of the New South*, 159.

[52]Stein, *World of Marcus Garvey*, 58; Steven A. Reich, "Soldiers of Democracy: Black Texans and the Fight for Citizenship, 1917–1921," *Journal of American History*, 82, no. 4 (Mar. 1996): 1490–98; John Dittmer, *Black Georgia in the Progressive Era 1900–1920* (Urbana: University of Illinois Press, 1977), 206.

[53]Deborah Gray White, *Too Heavy a Load: Black Women in Defense of Themselves 1894–1994* (New York: W. W. Norton & Co., 1999); Anne Firor Scott, "Most Invisible of All: Black Women's Voluntary Associations," *Journal of Southern History*, 56, no. 1 (Feb. 1990): 17.

[54]Evelyn Brooks Higginbotham, *Righteous Discontent: The Women's Movement in the Black Baptist Church 1880–1920* (Cambridge: Harvard University Press, 1993); Washington quoted in Beverly Washington Jones, *Quest for Equality: The Life & Writings of Mary Eliza Church Terrell, 1863–1954* (Brooklyn: Carlson Publishing, 1990), 26; Linda Gordon, "Black and White Visions of Welfare. Women's Welfare Activism, 1890–1945," *Journal of American History* (Sept. 1991), 360–561; Mary Church Terrill, "Club Work among Women," *New York Age*, 4 Jan. 1900.

[55]"The Duty of the National Association of Colored Women to the Race," *AME Church Review* (Jan. 1900); Terrill, "Club Work among Women"; Tera Hunter, *To 'Joy My Freedom: Southern Black Women's Lives and Labors after the Civil War* (Cambridge: Harvard University Press, 1997), 213–16; Jacqueline A. Rouse, "Atlanta's African-American Women's Attack on Segregation, 1900–1920," in *Gender, Class, Race, and Reform in the Progressive Era*, ed. Norallee Frankel and Nancy S. Dye (Lexington: University Press of

Kentucky, 1991), 10–23; Rosalyn Terborg-Penn, *African American Women in the Struggle for the Vote, 1850–1920* (Bloomington: Indiana University Press, 1998), 92–106.

[56]"Votes for Women: A Symposium by Leading Thinkers of Colored America," *Crisis,* 10, no. 4 (Aug. 1915): 178–92; "Race Women Make Good Showing in Suffrage Parade," *Chicago Defender,* 19 May 1914; "Colored Women Attend Suffragette Meeting," *New York Age,* 6 Sept. 1917; "Campaign for Women Nearing Its Close," *New York Age,* 1 Nov. 1917; "Negro Women Seek Permission to Vote," *Savannah Morning News,* 3 Nov. 1920; "The Colored Women's Voters' League," *Birmingham Reporter,* 14 May 1914; Terborg-Penn, *African American Women,* 136–58.

[57]"South Views with Alarm Negro Exodus," Norfolk *Journal and Guide,* 3 Feb. 1917; "The Great American Protest," *Southwestern Christian Advocate,* 12 June 1919; "Negro Exodus Grows Serious," Norfolk *Journal and Guide,* 10 Feb. 1917.

[58]"Servant Problem Closes Many Homes," Norfolk *Journal and Guide,* 24 Feb. 1917; "Waitresses and Cooks Scarce," Augusta, Georgia *Labor Review,* 28 Sept. 1918; "House Servants Are Not Inclined to Domestic Service Again," Richmond *News Leader,* 3 Jan. 1919; "Cooks Almost Obsolete," Memphis *Commercial Appeal,* 12 Mar. 1919; "Colored Women of Houston Organize," *Houston Labor Journal,* 6 May 1916; "Washer Women Form Union for Betterment," *Houston Labor Journal,* 13 Dec. 1919; "Negro Domestics Threaten Strike," *Virginia Pilot and Norfolk Landmark,* 4 Oct. 1917; Hunter, *To 'Joy My Freedom,* 223–7.

[59]"Workers Strike in Laundries to Get Higher Pay," Mobile *Register,* 23 Apr. 1918; "Negro Women Are Under Arrest in Laundry Strike," Mobile *News-Item,* 25 Apr. 1918; "Six Strikers Fined For Interfering with Launderers," Mobile *News-Item,* 27 Apr. 1918.

[60]Seattle *Cayton's Weekly,* 24 May 1919.

[61]On the wartime upsurge in black working-class organizing, see David Montgomery, *The Fall of the House of Labor: The Workplace, the State, and American Labor Activism, 1865–1925* (New York: Cambridge University Press, 1987), 378–82; Eric Arnesen, "Charting an Independent Course: African-American Railroad Workers in the World War I Era," in *Labor Histories: Class, Politics, and the Working Class Experience,* ed. Eric Arnesen, Julie Greene, and Bruce Laurie (Urbana: University of Illinois Press, 1998), 284–308; Earl Lewis, *In Their Own Interests: Race, Class, and Power in Twentieth Century Norfolk, Virginia* (Berkeley: University of California Press, 1991), 48–61.

[62]Joseph A. McCartin, "Abortive Reconstruction: Federal War Labor Policies, Union Organization, and the Politics of Race, 1917–1920," *Journal of Policy History,* 9, no. 2 (1997); 155–83; Eric Arnesen, *Waterfront Workers of New Orleans: Race, Class, and Politics, 1863–1923* (New York: Oxford University Press, 1991); Elizabeth Haiken, "'The Lord Helps Those Who Help Themselves': Black Laundresses in Little Rock, Arkansas, 1917–1921," *Arkansas Historical Quarterly,* 49, no. 1 (Spring 1990): 20–50.

[63]"20,000 Cheering Marchers Turn Out in Biggest Civic Parade Held in this Country by Negroes," *Savannah Tribune,* 1 May 1918; "Negroes Parade in War Demonstration," *Savannah Morning Tribune,* 9 May 1919.

[64]"N.A.A.C.P. Launches Big Membership Drive," *Savannah Tribune,* 20 Apr. 1918; "The Mob in Savannah," *Savannah Tribune,* 15 June 1918; "Work Card System Abused," *Savannah Tribune,* 20 July 1918; "Negro Committee Before Board of Trade," *Savannah Tribune,* 3 Aug. 1918; "Misusing Police Power," *Savannah Tribune,* 24 Aug. 1918.

[65]"Negro Plasterers in 'Near Strike,'" *Savannah Morning News,* 16 July 1917; "The Plasterers' Strike," *Savannah Tribune,* 21 July 1917; "Discrimination at Ship Yard," *Savannah Tribune,* 5 Oct. 1918; "The Negro Before the Law," *Savannah Tribune,* 20 Nov. 1920.

[66]"Street Car Troubles," *Savannah Tribune,* 17 Aug. 1918; "Near Race Riot Here Tuesday," *Savannah Morning News,* 8 June 1918; "Near Strike at Shipyards," *Savannah Tribune,* 8 Aug. 1918.

[67]James Weldon Johnson, "Views and Reviews: Now Comes the Test," *New York Age,* 23 Nov. 1918.

[68]"The Revolt of the Rank and File," *The Nation,* 109 (25 Oct. 1919): 540; Stein, *World of Marcus Garvey,* 54–55.

[69]Kelly Miller, "Radicalism and the Negro," *The Competitor,* 1, no. 2 (Feb. 1920): 39; Nell Irvin Painter, *Standing at Armageddon: The United States, 1877–1919* (New York: W. W. Norton & Co., 1987), 365.

[70]Arnesen, *Waterfront Workers of New Orleans,* 229–336, 244–49; Brian Kelly, *Race, Class, and Power in the Alabama Coalfields, 1908–21* (Urbana: University of Illinois Press, 2001), 165–202.

[71]Joseph A. McCartin, *Labor's Great War: The Struggle for Industrial Democracy and the Origins of Modern American Labor Relations, 1912–1921* (Chapel Hill: University of North Carolina Press, 1997), 114–18; Arnesen, *Brotherhoods of Color,* 52–56.

[72]Stephen H. Norwood, "Bogalusa Burning: The War against Biracial Unionism in the Deep South, 1919," *Journal of Southern History,* 63, no. 3 (Aug. 1997): 591–628; James C. Maroney, "The Galveston Longshoremen's Strike of 1920," *East Texas Historical Journal,* 16, no. 1 (1978): 34–38; William D. Angel, Jr., "Controlling the Workers: The Galveston Dock Workers' Strike of 1920 and Its Impact on Labor Relations in Texas," *East Texas Historical Journal,* 23, no. 2 (1985): 14–27; Arnesen, *Waterfront Workers of New Orleans,* 246–52.

[73]Quoted in Dittmer, *Black Georgia,* 204.

[74]Reich, "Soldiers of Democracy," 1481.

[75]Dittmer, *Black Georgia,* 206–7; "Wants Race Equality, League Secretary is Given Sound Beating," *Tampa Morning Tribune,* 23 Aug. 1919; Reich, "Soldiers of Democracy," 1500–1501; Kornweibel, *Seeing Red.*

[76]C. S. Smith, "Close Ranks!" and "Reign of Terror," *Washington Bee,* 28 June 1919. On lynching during and after World War I, see Dray, *At the Hands of Persons Unknown.*

[77]Nancy MacLean, *Behind the Mask of Chivalry: The Making of the Second Ku Klux Klan* (New York: Oxford University Press, 1994); Cooper and Terrill, *The American South: A History,* vol. 2, 622.

[78]Tuttle, *Race Riot,* 3–10, 32–66.

[79]James Weldon Johnson, "Views and Reviews: The Arkansas Hoax," *New York Age,* 18 Oct. 1919; Richard C. Cortner, *A Mob Intent on Death: The NAACP and the Arkansas Riot Cases* (Middletown, Conn.: Wesleyan University Press, 1988); Nan Elizabeth Woodruff, "African-American Struggles for Citizenship in the Arkansas and Mississippi Deltas in the Age of Jim Crow," *Radical History Review,* no. 55 (Winter 1993): 33–51.

[80]*Tampa Morning Tribune,* 7 Oct. 1919; Newport News *Daily Press,* 7 Oct. 1919; Newport News *Times-Herald,* 3 Oct. 1919; Leah Wise, "The Elaine Massacre," *Southern Exposure,* 1, nos. 3 and 4 (Winter 1976): 9–10; Shapiro, *White Violence and Black Response,* 149; Lewis, *When Harlem Was in Vogue,* 22.

[81]Woodruff, "African-American Struggles for Citizenship," 33–51; Cortner, *A Mob Intent on Death*; Howard Kester, *Revolt Among the Sharecroppers* (1936; reprint, Knoxville: University of Tennessee Press, 1997).

[82]Scott Ellsworth, *Death in a Promised Land: The Tulsa Race Riot of 1921* (Baton Rouge: Louisiana State University Press, 1982).

[83]Halpern, *Down on the Killing Floor,* 78; "The Negro's Advance in Chicago," *Chicago Defender,* 27 Aug. 1927.

[84]Hartt, "When the Negro Comes North, I," 85.

[85]Reynolds Farley and Walter R. Allen, *The Color Line and the Quality of Life in America* (1987; reprint, New York: Oxford University Press, 1989), 112–15; Jack Temple Kirby, "The Southern Exodus, 1910–1960: A Primer for Historians," *Journal of Southern History,* 49, no. 4 (Nov. 1983): 585–600.

[86]E. Franklin Frazier, "Chicago: A Cross-Section of Negro Life," *Opportunity,* 7, no. 2 (Mar. 1929): 70, 73; Drake and Cayton, *Black Metropolis,* 348–49; Nathan Irvin Huggins, *Voices of the Harlem Renaissance* (New York: Oxford University Press, 1976).

PART TWO

The Documents

1

The Great Migration Begins

Since the beginnings of the industrial revolution in the early nineteenth century, the American economy, especially in the North and Midwest, had relied upon wave after wave of European immigrants to provide some of its skilled and much of its unskilled workforce. The outbreak of World War I in Europe in August 1914, however, dramatically reduced the number of immigrants coming to the United States. An expanding American economy propelled industrial employers to seek out new sources of labor. For the first time, many northern industrialists began employing African Americans in positions previously barred to them. In 1916, the number of southern blacks migrating to the North began to increase noticeably. By the end of the war in late 1918, an estimated half a million southern African Americans had made the North their home. Although a much smaller number of blacks had made the journey from South to North in the half century before World War I, the unprecedented scope of the wartime migration inspired an outpouring of analysis from politicians, public commissions, black activists, and black and white journalists and editors who sought to make sense of it. The new migration also generated widespread concern among many southern whites and considerable enthusiasm on the part of many—if not all—southern and northern blacks.

W. E. B. DU BOIS

The Migration of Negroes

June 1917

By the decade of the 1910s, W. E. B. Du Bois (1868–1963) was the nation's preeminent black civil rights activist, scholar, editor, and journalist. After the turn of the century, he had publicly criticized Booker T. Washington, the influential head of Tuskegee Institute and a major broker of resources in the area of black education and political patronage, for his advocacy of vocational education for African American students and his accommodationist approach to black politics. In 1909, Du Bois cofounded the NAACP, an interracial civil rights organization. He founded and served as editor of the Crisis, the NAACP's monthly journal which reached a monthly audience numbering in the tens of thousands in the 1910s.

Much has been written of the recent migration of colored people from the South to the North, but there have been very few attempts to give a definite, coherent picture of the whole movement. Aided by the funds of the National Association for the Advancement of Colored People, the *Crisis* has attempted to put into concrete form such knowledge as we have of this movement.

The data at hand are vague and have been collected from a hundred different sources. While the margin of error is large, the actual information which we have gathered is most valuable.

First, as to the number who have migrated to the North, there is wide difference of opinion. Our own conclusion is that about 250,000 colored workmen have come northward. . . .

As to the reasons of the migration, undoubtedly, the immediate cause was economic, and the movement began because of floods in middle Alabama and Mississippi and because the latest devastation of the boll weevil came in these same districts.

Crisis, 14, no. 2 (June 1917): 63–66.

A second economic cause was the cutting off of immigration from Europe to the North and the consequently wide-spread demand for common labor. . . .

The third reason has been outbreaks of mob violence in northern and southwestern Georgia and in western South Carolina.

These have been the three immediate causes, but back of them is, undoubtedly, the general dissatisfaction with the conditions in the South. . . .

To this we may add certain general statements from colored leaders thoroughly conversant with conditions in their communities and in some cases with large parts of the South.

A colored man of Sumter, S. C., says: "The immediate occasion of the migration is, of course, the opportunity in the North, now at last open to us, for industrial betterment. The real causes are the conditions which we have had to bear because there was no escape."

These conditions he sums up as the destruction of the Negroes' political rights, the curtailment of his civil rights, the lack of protection of life, liberty and property, low wages, the Jim Crow car, residential and labor segregation laws, poor educational facilities.

From Oklahoma we learn that Negroes are migrating because of threatened segregation laws and mob violence.

A colored man from Georgia states: "In my opinion the strongest factor in this migration is a desire to escape harsh and unfair treatment, to secure a larger degree of personal liberty, better advantages for children, and a living wage."

The A. M. E. Ministers' Alliance of Birmingham, Ala., names seven causes for the migration: "Prejudice, disfranchisement, Jim Crow cars, lynching, bad treatment on the farms, the boll weevil, the floods of 1916."

A colored business man of North Carolina believes: "There is a silent influence operating in the hearts of the growing class of intelligent Negroes that the insurmountable barriers of caste unnecessarily fetter the opportunities to which every living soul is entitled, namely, a fair chance to earn an honest living and educate his children and be protected by the laws."

In many sections of Mississippi the boll weevil destroyed the cotton crop; rains and high waters in the spring destroyed other crops.

A well-known investigator reports: "Nothing else seemed left for hundreds of the colored tenants to do but to go into the cities or to the North to earn even their food. Nothing was left on the farms and the landowners could not or would not make any further advances. From the country and even from the cities in these unfortunate sections colored people have in many cases streamed northward."

The centres of this migration have been at Jackson, Hattiesburg, and Meridian, Miss., and many have sacrificed property in order to get away.

A widely-traveled and intelligent colored man writes:

"I recently made a trip through the South as far down as New Orleans, La., and I saw hundreds who were making their way northward. When in New Orleans, I learned that there were about 800 in the city from the inland district waiting to go, and who expected to leave during the next week. I went with a friend down where I could meet some of the leaders and talk with them. I met them, and they informed me that they were willing to go anywhere rather than continue to live like they had been. These were heading toward Chicago. I was shocked at the statement made by some of them as to how they lived on those big inland farms, and how badly they were treated by the whites. Many of these men were in overalls. I told them that they were unprepared for the climate; but they were willing to run any risk to get where they might breathe freer. Who blames them?"

Many of the southern whites, through their newspapers, are confirming this general unrest. A white woman says:

"That which a regard for common justice, fair play, human rights could not accomplish, a fear for our bank account is doing, and we are asking: Why is the Negro dissatisfied? What can we do to keep him in the South? We can't afford to let him go; he means too much for us—financially. He works for little; his upkeep costs us little, for we can house him in any kind of shack, and make him pay us well for that; we do not have to be careful of his living conditions; he is good-natured, long-suffering, and if he should happen to give us trouble we can cope with that and the law will uphold us in anything we do."

The Columbia, S. C., *State* asks: "If you thought you might be lynched by mistake, would you remain in South Carolina? Ask yourself that question if you dare."

The Greenville, S. C., *Piedmont* feels that,

"The truth might as well be faced, and the truth is that the treatment of the Negro in the South must change or the South will lose the Negro."

The Greenville, S. C., *News* says:

"The Abbeville outrage may yet prove more of an economic crime than an offense against the peace and dignity of the state. Where is our labor to come from if not from these people who have lived here beside us for so many generations? Immigration has been a distinct failure in the South; it is expressly declared to be against the policy of South Carolina by our laws."

It is interesting to note that this migration is apparently a mass movement and not a movement of the leaders. The wave of economic distress and social unrest has pushed past the conservative advice of the Negro preacher, teacher and professional man, and the colored laborers and artisans have determined to find a way for themselves. For instance, a colored Mississippi preacher says:

"The leaders of the race are powerless to prevent his going. They had nothing to do with it, and, indeed, all of them, for obvious reasons, are opposed to the exodus. The movement started without any head from the masses, and such movements are always significant."

The character of the people who are going varies, of course, but as the Birmingham, Ala., *Age-Herald* remarks: "It is not the riff-raff of the race, the worthless Negroes, who are leaving in such large numbers. There are, to be sure, many poor Negroes among them who have little more than the clothes on their backs, but others have property and good positions which they are sacrificing in order to get away at the first opportunity."

"Various reasons are assigned for the migration of Negroes from the South to the North. It was believed for a while that they were lured away by the glowing reports of labor agents who promised high wages, easy work, and better living conditions. But there is something more behind their going, something that lies deeper than a temporary discontent and the wish to try a new environment merely for the sake of a free trip on the railroads. . . .

"The entire Negro population of the South seems to be deeply affected. The fact that many Negroes who went North without sufficient funds and without clothing to keep them warm have suffered severely and have died in large numbers, has not checked the tide leaving the South. It was expected that the Negroes would come back, sorry that they ever left, but comparatively few have returned. With the approach of warmer weather the number going North will increase."

How great this migration will eventually prove depends upon a number of things. The entrance of the United States into the war will undoubtedly have some effect. When the war ends it is doubtful if the labor shortage in Europe will allow a very large migration to the United States for a generation or more. This will mean increased demand for colored laborers in the North. A writer in the New York *Evening Globe* predicts that 1917 will see 400,000 of the better class of Negro workers come to the North.

At any rate, we face here a social change among American Negroes of great moment, and one which needs to be watched with intelligent interest.

MARY DeBARDELEBEN

The Negro Exodus: A Southern Woman's View

March 18, 1917

The Southwestern Christian Advocate *was one of dozens of African American newspapers published in the early twentieth century. Although some were affiliated with particular religious denominations, most were secular. Sharing no single viewpoint, black weeklies provided extensive coverage of local, regional, and national news about African Americans, their position in the United States, and the state of race relations. The* Southwestern Christian Advocate *was published in New Orleans and was sponsored by the Methodist Episcopal Church. In this article, one of the South's rare white racial liberals expressed sympathy toward the migrants, calling on churches to address their plight.*

The papers have been full of late of the tragedy of the German expulsion or deportation of the Belgian [*sic*] laborers. Our hearts have been stirred, our indignation aroused as we read of fathers, sons, husbands and brothers torn from their children, their wives and sweethearts, from the old loved surroundings, and borne forcibly to labor in regions strange and new under conditions galling and humiliating.

But there is another deportation, another expulsion going on under our very eyes that concerns us more nearly—some of the causes for which should make us, as citizens of a great, free nation, hang our heads in shame, should send us, as professing Christians, to our knees, crying aloud for forgiveness for our cruel neglect.

Thousands Take Flight

I speak of the great exodus of the Negroes from our Southland. There is much being said about it in the press these days. O, yes, we are beginning to talk and question now, for we are beginning to fear for our pocketbooks. That which a regard for common justice, fair play, human rights could not accomplish, a fear for our bank account is doing, and we are asking: Why is the Negro dissatisfied? What can we do to keep him in the South? We can't afford to let him go; he means too much to us—financially. He works for little: his upkeep costs us little, for we can house him in any kind of shack, and make him pay us well for that; we do not have to be careful of his living conditions; he is good-natured, long-suffering, and if he should happen to give us trouble we can cope with that and the law will uphold us in anything we do. Am I exaggerating? If we do not thus reason audibly, this is at least the attitude we, as a white race and employers of labor, assume or allow assumed.

But the Negro is going, going in scores, in hundreds and in thousands. In some sections of South Georgia there are stretches of country almost destitute of Negro population. Country churches which once had congregations of two and three hundred have now only twenty or thirty members. One Negro Conference of the Colored Methodist Episcopal Church that had a membership in 1915 of 11,000 has now barely 5,000. At a recent session of this Conference men who had been pastors of these people stood on the floor of the Conference and with tears in their eyes and sobs in their throats pleaded to be allowed to go with their congregations. "Not that we want to go for our own sakes," they said, "but for the sake of our people. We know it means suffering and hard living, but we will work with our hands for our support, that we may minister to our people, may keep them together, that they may not drift and be swallowed up in the great cities of the North, with no spiritual or moral guidance to keep them from the downward path."

They are going at night, these refugees; the trains are full of them, and they are going with a mighty fear upon them. A friend of mine was talking to an old man who, with his wife, sons and daughters, was leaving the old home to go out into a great strange world, their poor belongings in clumsy, homely-looking bundles in the seats beside them. The stock was left, they could not sell it, they said: and much of their household stuff, the poor collection of years of labor—but theirs.

Why They Go

"But why do you go?" my friend asked. The old man, with trembling fingers, drew from his pocket a crumpled paper and spread it out before them. At the top of the sheet was crudely drawn a skull and cross-bones; below was written: "You are hereby warned that you and your entire family must be gone from this community within forty-eight hours. Your attention is called to the symbol at top of notice." In the community near which the man lived a woman had been burned at the stake a few months before. Her crime was due to the natural impulse of motherhood. She had dared to protect her child from blows administered by a white man. And so the old man, fearing for his life, was fleeing in the dead of night.

In another town in Georgia four innocent Negroes were foully murdered in the usual way—by an insane mob. The father of the family was lodged in jail for assault on an officer who came to arrest him. The mob therefore seized the family—the mother, two daughters, one of whom was soon to become a mother, and a ten-year-old boy. I cannot go into the revolting circumstances of it all. Suffice it to say that little white boys saw it and hence seeds of brutality, hatred and revenge were planted in their young hearts. Many Negroes are leaving that section. Just what proportion are leaving because of unfair treatment I am unprepared to say, but such outrageous violation of law is certainly playing its part in the exodus.

A Negro woman in Georgia resisted the offensive attention of a white ruffian, with the result that her house, with all her possessions, was burned, and notice served on her to leave the community at once or she would pay the penalty at the rope's end.

It is not simply the poor, irresponsible, thriftless Negro that undergoes such treatment at the hands of a senseless mob, for example, the recent occurrence in South Carolina, where a Negro worth anywhere from $20,000 to $50,000, a law-abiding citizen, was cruelly put to death and his family ordered to leave. His son owned a drug store, where he was doing a good business, all of which had to be sacrificed.

Of course, these outrages are perpetrated by the coarse, brutal mob element. But what are the civil authorities doing about it? With the exception, possibly, of the case cited from South Carolina, where Governor Manning is demanding an investigation, we know of nothing being done to restrain the mob spirit which seems to be rampant. Do we criticise the Germans for barbarities in Belgium and allow with perfect impunity these outrages in our midst? God forgive us for our shamelessness, our self-righteousness, our hypocrisy!

And what is the Church doing about it? Do we know anywhere of any church taking an out-and-out stand against such? We seem to be bound hand and foot. What is it we are afraid of? To bring it closer home; What is our great Methodist Episcopal Church, South, doing about it? Where is her influence? Where is her voice? Who has gagged her? Is she a slave of prejudice? Is she a coward? Or is she asleep? We prefer to believe it is the last, but it is time for her to wake up or a great opportunity will have passed and God will find another instrument through which to voice the wrongs of an oppressed people.

Not only does she seem to be taking no measures to change existing conditions, not only is her pulpit silent with regard to these atrocious wrongs, but she, this great Methodist Episcopal Church, South, wealthy, strong, influential, is actually failing to meet the responsibility of a task already assumed. Paine College is the one avenue through which, as a Church, she has even pretended to minister to the Negro race, by training its leaders, its teachers, its preachers, its parents of the generations to come. So small has been the response to calls for actual sustenance for the school, so meager has been her interest in this, her one institution for the benefit of the Negro race, that, unless there is an immediate and beneficent response, Paine College must close its doors and a great Church acknowledge shamefacedly her failure to measure up to a magnificent, God-given opportunity.

O, Church of the Christ who ministered to the neglected, the outcast and the alien, do you not hear His call today to follow in the footsteps of your Master and minister abundantly to this child race, this oppressed people in our midst? Can you face Him with the blood of this people upon your soul? Will you not "Loose the bonds of wickedness, undo the bonds of the yoke and let the oppressed go free"? Will you not "Deal thy bread to the hungry and bring the poor that are cast out to thy house" of protection, and warmth, and safety? "Then shall thy light," O Church of Christ, "break forth as the morning and thy healing spring forth speedily."

Paine College, Augusta, Ga.

CHARLES S. JOHNSON

How Much Is the Migration a Flight from Persecution?

September 1923

Born in Virginia in 1893, Charles S. Johnson graduated with a bachelor's degree from Virginia Union University, a black religious institution, just as the migration was intensifying in 1916. He pursued his graduate training in sociology at the University of Chicago and served as associate executive director of the Chicago Commission on Race Relations formed after the 1919 race riot. Johnson would quickly emerge as one of the most important African American sociologists in the United States. He founded and was the first editor of Opportunity, *the journal of the National Urban League, an organization founded in 1911 that was devoted to assisting black migrants in finding and retaining employment in the North.*

Desire for more wages and more regular wages, for better social treatment, improved cultural surroundings; the hysteria of a mass movement; simple curiosity and desire for travel and adventure, and free railroad tickets, all have played their part in the divorcement of the southern Negro from the land of his birth.

Reasons are one thing; motives another. The former with all persons are likely to be merely a rationalization of behavior, while the latter usually play first role in inspiring the behavior. All Negroes (no more than all whites) are not uniformly sensitive to their social environment. And altho emphasis upon the pernicious nature of the social environment of southern Negroes should and doubtless will have the effect of improving it, such emphasis is apt to obscure what seem to be even more vital issues and more substantial elements of Negro character. After all, it means more that the Negroes who left the South were motivated more by the desire to improve their economic status than by fear of being manhandled by unfriendly whites. The one is a symptom of wholesome and substantial life purpose; the other, the symptom of a fugitive incourageous opportunism. Persecu-

Opportunity, 1, no. 9 (Sept. 1923): 272–74.

tion plays its part—a considerable one. But when the whole of the migration of southern Negroes is considered, this part seems to be limited. It is indeed more likely that Negroes, like all others with a spark of ambition and self-interest, have been deserting soil which cannot yield returns in proportion to their population increase. The Census of 1920 indicated that the rate of Negro increase declined from 18.0 for the decade 1890–1900, to 11.2 for the next, and to 6.5 for the last. This does not mean that fewer children are being born, for actually more Negro than white babies per family are being born, but that more of them are dying. This desertion of the soil has taken three distinct directions: (a) urbanization—a species of migration; (b) quest for more productive lands; (c) transplantation to industrial communities, practically all of which are in the North. During the past thirty years, 1890–1920, there has been an increase in the rural population of 896,124 Negroes as compared with 2,078,331 for cities. The urban increase has been just about 100 per cent as rapid as the rural. In 1890, 19.8 per cent of the Negro population lived in cities; in 1920, this proportion grew to about 40 per cent. In the Southern States, between 1890–1900, the rural population increased 13.6 per cent, and between 1910 and 1920 it actually decreased 3.3 per cent. The Negro population increase in southern cities, considered as a whole, has been greater than the increase in the North, considered as a whole, despite the half-million added during the last decade. Here, of course, is the economic factor at work, hand in hand, with greater mobility, increased transportation, restlessness and the monotony and uncertainty of agricultural life ever against the allurements of the city.

The greatest inter-state movements of southern Negroes have been further South and West. In 1910, 52.3 per cent of the migration from Southern States was to the area west of the Mississippi; while in 1920, after the tremendous migration to the North, 42.9 per cent were living in the Southwestern States as compared with 42.2 per cent living in the North and West. For 130 years the center of the Negro population moved steadily some 478 miles toward the southwest—from Dinwiddie county, Va., to northern Alabama.

This shifting is further evident in the instability of Negro population in southern counties. Between 1900 and 1910, for example, 33.5 per cent of the counties increased rapidly, 31.1 increased at a rate above the average, while only 3.4 per cent showed an actual decrease, and 9.8 per cent an average increase equivalent to the total increase of the section. In 1879 there was a migration, similar to the one which we now experience, to Kansas. This followed a depression in 1878.

Some 60,000 Negroes left. In 1888–1889, there was a similar movement to Arkansas, which carried 35,000 Negroes. Arkansas, for example, gained, between 1900–1910, 105,516 Negroes, the largest net gain of any state north or south; Oklahoma gained 85,062; and Texas, 19,821; while all the eastern, southern and central states suffered a loss. The counties of most rapid increase in the South between 1910 and 1920 were those south of the region of maximum Negro population density in 1910.

It is further significant here that the white populations have been showing in general outline the same trend of mobility as the Negroes. For example, their rate of mobility was 20 per cent as compared with 16 per cent for the Negroes and they also have left the counties deserted by Negroes, taking the same direction of migration.

Had persecution been the dominant and original stimulus, the direction of Negroes during the sixty years following emancipation would have been north instead of further south.

As a working test, a rough correlation was made between counties of the South in which lynchings had occurred during the thirty year period 1888–1918 and the migration from and to these counties.

Of ten Georgia counties, in which five or more lynchings occurred, the Negro population increased in five. Of the other five, in which the Negro population decreased, there was a corresponding decrease in the white population in three, and an increase in the other two considerably less than the average. To use one example, — in Montgomery County, in which five lynchings occurred, the Negro population decreased from 7,310 to 4,348 and the white population from 12,328 to 4,768. If this were a measure of persecution, the whites are the greater victims.

In Jasper County, Ga., there were nine lynchings, the largest number for any county of the state in thirty years. The Negro population actually increased in this county between 1890 to 1920, while the white population during 1900 and 1910 actually decreased.

Or to take the State of Texas. Of the six counties with five or more lynchings, the Negro population increased in four and decreased in two. Of the two in which there was a Negro decrease, there was a corresponding but more serious decrease in the white population. In Waller County, the Negro population decreased from 6,712 in 1910 to 4,967 in 1920; the white population decreased from 6,375 in 1900 to 5,426 in 1910 and to 4,082 in 1920. In Harrison County, with the largest number of lynchings (16), the Negro population showed a similar increase from 13,544 to 15,639.

In the State of Alabama, Jefferson County, with ten lynchings, increased from 90,617 in 1910 to 130,211 in 1920—the largest recorded increase in any county; Dallas County, with the largest number of lynchings (19), lost only 1,246 Negroes, while Sumter, with no lynchings at all, lost 3,491.

In spite of a considerable progress by Negroes, the great bulk of this population is in an almost hopeless struggle against feudalism. In four of the most congested Southern States: Georgia, Alabama, Mississippi, Louisiana, containing . . . over 36 per cent of all the Negroes in the country, 83.3 per cent of them are landless. The per cent of tenant farmers instead of changing over into owners actually increased in practically every Southern State during the past decade, while the per cent of owners decreased. Altho this was to some extent true of white farmers, the proportion among Negroes was just twice as great. The large plantation owners it seems are gradually taking over the land, thus reducing tenants, white and colored, to a state of unrelieved and helpless peasantry.

Cotton is a peculiar crop. Its nurture requires about seven times as many hands as other crops and only then for certain periods of the year. It does not yield readily to labor saving devices. It can be grown profitably only with cheap labor, and plenty of it, and Negroes have been the South's cheap labor. Immigrants are not welcomed because of their tendency and frequent ability in time to purchase their own plots of ground. As a matter of fact, small white tenants are not as desirable in the plantation scheme as Negroes; and if Negroes persist in leaving, the plantation system itself, an anomaly in this country and notoriously unstable, is doomed.

Knowing just why Negroes left the South and what they were looking for will carry one further toward making their adjustment easier. The thought of flight from persecution excites little sympathy either from the practical employer or the northern white population among whom these Negroes will hereafter live. Every man who runs is not a good worker and from the point of view of the Negroes who have come, they cannot sustain themselves long on sympathy. It is indeed not unthinkable that the high mortality so conspicuous in the abnormally reduced rate of Negro increase will be strikingly affected by the migration. The relief of overpopulation in certain counties of the South will undoubtedly give each Negro child born a better chance for survival, while, on the other hand, the presence of Negroes in cities exposes them to health education and sanitary regulations. The death rate of Negroes in northern cities, in spite of the fact that migrations there are principally of adults to whom death is more imminent, is not as great as in most of the Negro counties of the South.

WHITE SOUTHERNERS RESPOND TO THE MIGRATION

McDOWELL TIMES

1100 Negroes Desert Savannah, Georgia

August 11, 1916

Southern white employers opposed the Great Migration on the grounds that it deprived them of their labor supply. Accordingly, they placed as many obstacles as they could in the way of potential migrants. Attributing the migration of southern blacks to northern labor agents who were stirring up discontent, promising high wages in the North, and advancing migrants the train fare to make the journey, southern white politicians and police officers harassed both those blacks seeking to migrate and labor agents operating in their communities. The McDowell Times, a small, black West Virginia weekly newspaper, regularly published stories and editorials highlighting the experiences of African Americans throughout the South.

Two Special Trains Required to Transport Colored Laborers to Philadelphia

SAVANNAH, GA., AUG. 5—The Savannah union station was a black paradise Monday, when nearly 1,100 colored laborers, ranging in age from 21 to 45 years, started for Philadelphia on two special trains.

They are to work along the lines of the Pennsylvania railroad. A crowd of 2,500 relatives and friends crowded the station and down to the train shed to see them off. Policemen had some difficulty in restraining the crowd which surged up against the gates when they were opened to admit those who were to board the trains.

There was nothing of the sorrow of parting in the crowd, everybody who left being in an excursion mood, and those who stayed behind being sure that they would be well taken care of by the wages sent home.

Two hours before the train left the two agents of the Pennsylvania who had been arrested Saturday and released on bond were rearrested, charged again with having violated the state law of acting as immigrant agents.

Bail of $1,000 was immediately furnished for each of the men, and they were at the station to assist in the work of getting the laborers aboard the train.

NEW ORLEANS TIMES-PICAYUNE

Luring Labor North

August 22, 1916

The Times-Picayune *was one of New Orleans' most widely read and influential daily white newspapers. Reflecting—and shaping—opinion among southern whites, it viewed the migration as a danger to southern employers and placed the blame for the migration not on conditions in the South but on labor agents and the demand for labor in the North. Like much of the white press, the* Times-Picayune *refused to capitalize the word Negro, a small but clear sign of disrespect.*

Vigorous protests are going up from Georgia and Florida, especially from Savannah and Jacksonville, against the work of the labor agents from the North, who are luring negro labor from the South Atlantic states to the great injury of employers in that section. There have been complaints on this score for some time, but the drain has, of late, become so great as to call for action. A steady drift of negroes has started Northward, attracted by reports of the big wages paid there. Just now—and, like everything else, due to the European war—the movement has reached immense proportions. The war has cut down immigration to the minimum and, as a matter of fact, as many people are leaving the country each year as are entering it. It is from the great mass of unskilled labor from Southern and Eastern Europe, that Northern employers, mine owners and others, have obtained the greater part of their labor. With this immigration shut off and the demand for unskilled labor as great as it is now, and growing greater,

Northern employers have turned to the South to supply the deficiency with the negroes; and they have, by their efforts and inducements, persuaded thousands of the latter to move North.

The result is naturally demoralizing labor circles, and many planters and manufacturers will not have enough men to supply their needs or take off their crops. Similar movements have been started at various times, and have always been harmful. The negroes are brought North almost wholly for temporary work, and when no longer needed are fired and told to find their way back home as best they can. So great has the abuse become that a number of states have passed laws on the subject of these agents, requiring them to furnish bonds for the return of the workmen they have thus lured away. Occasionally, there has been forcible interference with the agents, on the ground that they deceived the negroes and tricked and misled them. . . . Experience with numerous similar exodus movements warns us that something should be done in time to check or prevent the injustice and injury that will otherwise inevitably result from the operations of wholly irresponsible labor agents who give no thought to the men they are bringing North after they have delivered them to the mines or other work they are intended for, at so much per head.

Fortunately for this section this demand for cheap unskilled labor has so far been mainly in the East with the result that the Gulf states have suffered little loss of negro labor. It is well for employers here, however, to be warned in time and to be watchful. With the great demand for rough labor in this country, and the disappearance of the source from which it has previously been largely obtained, immigration, we may expect to see similar raids on negro workers in all parts of the South. It will be well, therefore, to throw such safeguards and protection around both employer and laborer as are necessary to make sure that no harm or demoralization results from the excessive and unusually unscrupulous activities of labor agents from the North.

J. A. MARTIN

Negroes Urged to Remain in South

November 25, 1916

Southern African Americans were not unanimous on the desirability of continued migration. Some black writers used the press, black and white, to remind their readers that the South remained African Americans' "natural home," that racial oppression knew no geographical boundaries, and that the North was no "promised land." The Savannah Morning News *was a daily white newspaper that, like the New Orleans* Times-Picayune, *opposed the migration. Its publication of this article on the conference of the Christian Methodist Episcopal (CME) church, a black religious group, likely served to reassure white readers and caution black readers that the migration was a mistake.*

C.M.E. Conference Report as Much
Race Prejudice in North as South

WADLEY, GA., Nov. 24.—The C.M.E. conference had a very lively session today. The committees on education and the state of the country reported and were listened to with great interest.

The conference is much interested in the colored people leaving the state and going North. . . . The committee on the state of the country said, among other things:

"As much as we appreciate the fact of spreading the borders of our church in the northern section of this country, we look upon the exodus of our people from the South with a deal of misgivings when we realize the industrial opportunities on the one hand in the South and the high cost of living and scarcity of the soil and the high prices of real estate in the North as compared with the abundance of cheap tillable soil in the South.

"On the other hand, we have long since learned that the racial prejudices and problems are not local, sectional or even national, but are world-wide, and as such they must be handled with that sanity that is

Savannah Morning News, 25 Nov. 1916.

filled with patience and wisdom. They cannot be solved with that fever-ish sentiment that has so often hurt rather than helped in the solution. "We further feel that the problem is many sided. It takes on its com-plications in proportion to the numbers of each race as located in the different sections or communities, or is aggravated by economic condi-tions. In many cases, they are incidentally race questions and would become problems if the issues were at stake between different cul-tured groups of white races or of black races. For instance, the Euro-pean war would not be more horrible if waged between white and black races. For these reasons as a church we feel called upon to offer such statement that may add something worthy as advice to our people in these days of restlessness among them as evidenced by their mov-ing from the South to the North to make better their conditions. This claim founded upon the ground of better wages, first and second for better treatment, both under the law and general sentiment.

"As to prejudice, we find it the same in the North as in the South. Thus the manly and Christian thing to do is to settle the problem upon the soil where it originated. We believe that the Christianity of the South is sufficient for this if exercised by the good white and black people of this section. Believing this to be true, we urge with all of our might that the white and black ministers do all in their power to put down lynching by preaching special sermons and lecturing upon it and other vital questions which are undermining our civilization in the South. If this is done we feel called upon to urge our people to stay in the South and till the fruitful soil. The white people have a great opportunity to encourage our people to stay by carrying out the policy of good treatment."

PERCY H. STONE

Negro Migration

August 1, 1917

Writing in the pages of the Outlook, *a national white weekly magazine, Percy H. Stone, a young black man and a member of the senior class of Hampton Institute, a conservative vocational and teacher training school for African Americans in Virginia, regarded black migration as a mistake.*

Outlook, 116, no. 14 (1 Aug. 1917): 520–21.

... At the outbreak of the present world war the call of country, father-land, and munition factory stripped the Northern and Central Western industries of their labor units; at the same time came an increased demand for manufactured products. This disastrous condition caused the manufacturer of the North and West to turn, as a last resort, to the only available labor in America.

Since that time general calls for help have been circulated over various sections of the South at different times, and we—some of us—smarting under the pinch of difficult living, crop failure, harsh treatment, and, in some cases, indebtedness, have already responded to the number of five hundred thousand.

In answering this call of an apparently better opportunity we are running a tremendous risk, because it is impossible for us to adapt ourselves to a new climate, new conditions, and new people without a great deal of suffering. The people of the North and West have always been friendly and willing to help us so long as we remained in the South, but now that we are distributing ourselves among them it may lead to a more prejudiced attitude towards us.

Taking advantage of this general movement among us, some would have it, and not without some foundation, that it was primarily to escape race discrimination and mistreatment. True, we resent most bitterly some treatment accorded us, but we have lived in the South since our advent into America. We understand the soil, the climate, and the life in the South; and, being by nature a race of peaceful people, we prefer to remain in the South and solve our problems by industry, thrift, and education.

Yet our plans for economic independence have been thwarted in these abnormal times, and the higher wages, the novelty of new surroundings, and other things are attracting some of us away from the Southland.

Various theories have been advanced as to what will happen at the end of the European war. Some say that the influx of foreigners impoverished by the ravages of war will displace and leave us stranded—a people disappointed and ungrateful in the eyes of the Southern people. But no one can truthfully predict the final outcome. Although a million of my people may cross the Mason and Dixon line in search of an economic outlet, the South will still hold the things most necessary to our racial progress—the opportunity of owning our homes and the chance to develop our best characteristics.

Doubtless some of us who are now leaving the South will return when conditions again become settled, but not all of us will; we know that in this movement some, at least, are making a great mistake and are inviting the criticism of our best friends. Yet there is a possibility of valuable lessons being learned.

Those people in the South who have looked upon our presence as a burden and regarded our labor as an almost worthless commodity in the market will find that, after all, the work of our hands is a vital cog in the South's industrial machinery.

The race problem, thought for so long to be confined to the South, will be spread; and the responsibility for our care and treatment, ours being a backward race, will have more shoulders on which to rest....

...So, if we now allow our outlook to be narrowed down to the immediate present and see in it an opportunity to get away from the disadvantages of the South, thinking to have a less obstructed path of progress in other sections, we leave the soil to which we seem specially adapted and the section that now affords us an opportunity to build up institutions reflecting credit on ourselves; and in our haste to grab the industrial opportunities of other sections we defeat our own purpose, because our economic struggle is not in itself an end, but a means to a more perfect home life and social life.

LETTERS FROM MIGRANTS

Documents: Letters of Negro Migrants
1916–1918

In 1919, the Journal of Negro History, *under the editorship of African American historian Carter G. Woodson, published numerous letters from migrants across the South. In these letters, migrants inquired into employment opportunities in the North and the possibility of financial assistance in migrating, and offered explanations for why African Americans would want to leave the South for a new life in the North. The original spelling has been retained.*

MIAMI, FLA., MAY 4, 1917.

Dear Sir:

Some time ago down this side it was a rumour about the great work going on in the north. But at the present time every thing is quite

Journal of Negro History, 4, no. 3 (July 1919): 290–340.

there, people saying that all we have been hearing was false until I caught hold of the Chicago Defender I see where its more positions are still open. Now I am very anxious to get up there. I follows up cooking. I also was a stevedor. I used to have from 150 to 200 men under my charge. They thought I was capable in doing the work and at the meantime I am willing to do anything. I have a wife and she is a very good cook. She has lots of references from the north and south. Now dear sir if you can send me a ticket so I can come up there and after I get straightened out I will send for my wife. You will oblige me by doing so at as early date as possible.

NEW ORLEANS, LA., 4/24/17.

Dear Sirs:

Being desirous of leaving the South for the beterment of my condition generaly and seeking a Home Somewhcrc in Ill' Chicago or some other prosperous Town I am at sea about the best placc to locate having a family dependent on me for support. I am informed by the Chicago Defender a very valuable paper which has for its purpose the Uplifting of my race, and of which I am a constant reader and real lover, that you were in position to show some light to one in my condition.

Seeking a Northern Home. If this is true Kindly inform me by next mail the next best thing to do Being a poor man with a family to care for, I am not coming to live on flowry Beds of ease for I am a man who works and wish to make the best I can out of life I do not wish to come there hoodwinked not knowing where to go or what to do so I Solicite your help in this matter and thanking you in advance for what advice you may be pleased to Give I am yours for success.

P.S. I am presently imployed in the I C RR. Mail Department at Union Station this city.

NEW ORLEANS, LA., AUGUST 27, 1917.

Dear Sir:

i am wrighting you for help i haird of you by telling my troble i was told to right you. I wont to come there and work i have ben looking for work here for three month and cand find any i once found a place $1 a week for a 15 year old girl and i did not take that. now you may say how can that be but New Orleans is so haird tell some have to work for food and the only help i have is my mother and she have work 2 week now and she have four children young then me and i am 15teen and she have such a hard time tell she is willing for me to go and if you will sin me a pass you will not be sorry i am not no lazy girl i am smart i have got very much learning but i can do any work that come to my hand to do i am set here to day worry i could explane it to you i have ben out three time to day and it only 12 oclock. and if you please sire sine me a pass. it more thin i am able to tell you how i will thank you i have clothes to bring wenter dress to ware. my grand mama dress me but now she is dead and all i have is my mother now please sire sin me a pass and you wont be sorry of it and if you right and speake mean please ancer i will be glad of that but if you would sin a pass i would be so much glader i will work and pay for my pass if you sin it i am so sorry tell i cant talk like i wont to and if you and your famely dont wont to be worry with me I will stay where i work and will come and see you all and do any think i can for you all from little A——— V———. excuse bad righting.

NEW ORLEANS, LA., MAY 7, 1917.

Gentlemen:

I read Defender every week and see so much good youre doing for the southern people & would like to know if you do the same for me as I am thinking of coming to Chicago about the first of June. and wants a position. I have very fine references if needed. I am a widow of 28. No children, not a relative living and I can do first class work as house maid and dining room or care for invalid ladies. I am honest and neat and refined with a fairly good education. I would like a position where I could live on places because its very trying for a good girl to be out in a large city by self among strangers is why I would like a good home with good people. Trusting to hear from you.

MONTGOMERY, ALA., MAY 19, 1917.

Dear sir:

I notice in the Chicago defender that you are working to better the condiction of the colored people of the south. I am a member of the race & want too come north for to better the condiction of my famely I have five children my self and a wife & I want you to seek for me a job please. I will send you the trade I follows while here in the south. I works in the packing houses & also wholesale grocers houses. Either one I can do but I rather the packing the best. you can get a half of dozen womens from here that want work & wants information about jobs such as cooking, nurseing & cleaning up or anything else they can do.

2
The Promised Land?

On the eve of World War I, African Americans in the North enjoyed considerably more political and social rights than did their southern counterparts. With the cut-off of European immigration, the range of jobs now open to blacks increased dramatically as well. For many black southerners, the North appeared as a "promised land" where wages were higher, educational opportunities vastly superior, political rights secure, and where they would suffer fewer, if any, of the daily indignities they suffered in the Jim Crow South. Undoubtedly, life in the North was, for many, a distinct improvement over what they had left behind. But as migrants quickly learned, what some called the "land of hope" by no means welcomed them with open arms. Rising racial tensions in the North reminded migrants and "old settlers" alike that racial equality remained an elusive ideal.

"THE TRUTH ABOUT THE NORTH"

CHICAGO COMMISSION ON RACE RELATIONS

The Arrival in Chicago
1922

Formed by the Illinois governor in the aftermath of a bloody race riot in the summer of 1919, the Chicago Commission on Race Relations conducted a major study exploring the causes and consequences of the Great Migration on the city of Chicago. One of the researchers and writers of the Commission's report was Charles S. Johnson, the University of

The Negro in Chicago: A Study of Race Relations and a Riot (Chicago: University of Chicago Press, 1922), 93–97.

Chicago–trained sociologist who had moved north after graduating from college in 1916. He became the Commission's associate executive director and later went on to work with the National Urban League.

At the time of the migration the great majority of Negroes in Chicago lived in a limited area on the South Side, principally between Twenty-second and Thirty-ninth streets, Wentworth Avenue and State Street, and in scattered groups to Cottage Grove Avenue on the east. State Street was the main thoroughfare. Prior to the influx of southern Negroes, many houses stood vacant in the section west of State Street, from which Negroes had moved when better houses became available east of State Street. Into these old and frequently almost uninhabitable houses the first newcomers moved. Because of its proximity to the old vice area this district had an added undesirability for old Chicagoans. The newcomers, however, were unacquainted with its reputation and had no hesitancy about moving in until better homes could be secured. As the number of arrivals increased, a scarcity of houses followed, creating a problem of acute congestion.

During the summer of 1917 the Chicago Urban League made a canvass of real estate dealers supplying houses for Negroes, and found that in a single day there were 664 Negro applicants for houses, and only fifty houses available. In some instances as many as ten persons were listed for a single house. This condition did not continue long. There were counted thirty-six new neighborhoods, formerly white, opening up to Negroes within three months.

At the same time rents increased from 5 to 30 and sometimes as much as 50 per cent. . . .

Meeting actual conditions of life in Chicago brought its exaltations and disillusionments to the migrants. These were reflected in the schools, public amusement places, industry, and the street cars. The Chicago Urban League, Negro churches, and Negro newspapers assumed the task of making the migrants into "city folk." The increase in church membership indicates prompt efforts to re-engage in community life and establish agreeable and helpful associations. It also reflects the persistence of religious life among the migrants. . . .

Adjustment to new conditions was taken up by the Urban League as its principal work. Co-operating with the Travelers Aid Society, United Charities, and other agencies of the city, it met the migrants at stations and, as far as its facilities permitted, secured living quarters and jobs for them. The churches took them into membership and attempted to make them feel at home. Negro newspapers published instructions on dress and conduct and had great influence in smoothing down improprieties of manner which were likely to provoke criticism and intolerance in the city.

Individual experiences of the migrants in this period of adjustment were often interesting. The Commission made a special effort to note these experiences for the light they throw upon the general process. Much of the adjustment was a double process, including the adjustment of rural southern Negroes to northern urban conditions. It is to be remembered that over 70 percent of the Negro population of the South is rural. This means familiarity with rural methods, simple machinery, and plain habits of living. Farmers and plantation workers coming to Chicago had to learn new tasks. Skilled craftsmen had to relearn their trades when they were thrown amid the highly specialized processes of northern industries. Domestic servants went into industry. Professional men who followed their clientèle had to reestablish themselves in a new community. The small business men could not compete with the Jewish merchants, who practically monopolized the trade of Negroes near their residential areas, or with the "Loop" stores.

Many Negroes sold their homes and brought their furniture with them. Reinvesting in property frequently meant a loss; the furniture brought was often found to be unsuited to the tiny apartments or large, abandoned dwelling-houses they were able to rent or buy.

The change of home carried with it in many cases a change of status. The leader in a small southern community, when he came to Chicago, was immediately absorbed into the struggling mass of unnoticed workers. School teachers, male and female, whose positions in the South carried considerable prestige, had to go to work in factories and plants because the disparity in educational standards would not permit continuance of their profession in Chicago....

The following experiences of one or two families from the many histories gathered, while not entirely typical of all the migrants, contain features common to all:

The Thomas family. — Mr. Thomas, his wife and two children, a girl nineteen and a boy seventeen, came to Chicago from Seals, Alabama, in the spring of 1917. After a futile search, the family rented rooms for the first week. This was expensive and inconvenient, and between working hours all sought a house into which they could take their furniture. They finally found a five-room flat on Federal Street. The building had been considered uninhabitable and dangerous. Three of the five rooms were almost totally dark. The plumbing was out of order. There was no bath, and the toilet was outside of the house. There was neither electricity nor gas, and the family used oil lamps. The rent was $15 per month. Although the combined income of the family could easily have made possible a better house, they could find none.

Mr. and Mrs. Thomas were farmers in the South. On the farm Mrs. Thomas did the work of a man along with her husband. Both are illiterate. The daughter had reached the fourth grade and the boy the fifth grade in school. At home they belonged to a church and various fraternal orders and took part in rural community life.

On their arrival in Chicago they were short of funds. Father and son went to work at the Stock Yards. Although they had good jobs they found their income insufficient; the girl went to work in a laundry, and the mother worked as a laundress through the first winter for $1 a day. She later discovered that she was working for half the regular rate for laundry work. Soon she went back to housekeeping to reduce the food bill.

All the family were timid and self-conscious and for a long time avoided contacts, thus depriving themselves of helpful suggestions. The children became ashamed of the manners of their parents and worked diligently to correct their manner of speech. The children attended Wendell Phillips night school in the hope of improving their community status.

The freedom and independence of Negroes in the North have been a constant novelty to them and many times they have been surprised that they were "not noticed enough to be mistreated." They have tried out various amusement places, parks, ice-cream parlors, and theaters near their home on the South Side and have enjoyed them because they were denied these opportunities in their former home.

The combined income of this family is $65 a week, and their rent is now low. Many of their old habits have been preserved because of the isolation in which they have lived and because they have not been able to move into better housing.

The Jones family. — Mr. Jones, his wife, a six-year-old son, and a nephew aged twenty-one, came from Texas early in 1919. Although they arrived after the heaviest migration, they experienced the same difficulties as earlier comers.

They searched for weeks for a suitable house. At first they secured one room on the South Side in a rooming-house, where they were obliged to provide gas, coal, linen, bedding, and part of the furniture.

After a few weeks they got two rooms for light housekeeping, for $10 a month. The associations as well as the physical condition of the house were intolerable. They then rented a flat on Carroll Avenue in another section. The building was old and run down. The agent for the property, to induce tenants to occupy it, had promised to clean and decorate it, but failed to keep his word. When the Jones family asked the owner to make repairs, he refused flatly and was exceedingly abusive.

Finally Jones located a house on the West Side that was much too large for his family, and the rent too high. They were forced to take lodgers to aid in paying the rent. This was against the desire of Mrs. Jones, who did not like to have strangers in her house. The house has six rooms and bath and is in a state of dilapidation. Mr. Jones has been forced to cover the holes in the floor with tin to keep out the rats. The plumbing is bad. During the winter there is no running water, and the agent for the building refuses to clean more than three rooms or to furnish screens or storm doors or to pay for any plumbing. In the back yard under the house is an accumulation of ashes, tin cans, and garbage left by a long series of previous tenants. There is no alley back of the house, and all of the garbage from the back yard must be carried out through the front. Jones made a complaint about insanitary [sic] conditions to the Health Department, and the house was inspected, but so far nothing has been done. It was difficult to induce the agent to supply garbage cans.

Jones had reached the eighth grade, and Mrs. Jones had completed the first year of high school. The nephew had finished public-school grades provided in his home town and had been taught the boiler trade. He is now pursuing this trade in hope of securing sufficient funds to complete his course in Conroe College, where he has already finished the first year. The boy of six was placed in a West Side school. He was removed from this school, however, and sent back south to live with Mrs. Jones's mother and attend school there. Mrs. Jones thought that the influence of the school children of Chicago was not good for him. He had been almost blinded by a blow from a baseball bat in the hands of one of several older boys who continually annoyed him. The child had also learned vulgar language from his school associates.

The Jones family were leading citizens in their southern home. They were members of a Baptist church, local clubs, and a missionary society, while Jones was a member and officer in the Knights of Tabor, Masons, and Odd Fellows. They owned their home and two other pieces of property in the same town, one of which brought in $20 a month. As a boiler-maker, he earned about $50 a week, which is about the same as his present income. Their motive in coming to Chicago was to escape from the undesirable practices and customs of the South.

They had been told that no discrimination was practiced against Negroes in Chicago; that they could go where they pleased without the embarrassment or hindrance because of their color. Accordingly, when they first came to Chicago, they went into drug-stores and restaurants. They were refused service in numbers of restaurants and at the refreshment counters in some drug-stores. The family has begun the re-establishment of its community life, having joined a West Side Baptist church and taking an active interest in local organizations, particularly the Wendell Phillips Social Settlement. The greatest satisfaction of the Joneses comes from the "escape from Jim Crow conditions and segregation" and the securing of improved conditions of work, although there is no difference in the wages.

SOUTHWESTERN CHRISTIAN ADVOCATE

Read This Before You Move North

April 5, 1917

What southern migrants believed life in the North might be like, and what it was actually like, were often two different things. Journalists and editorialists — black and white, from the South and the North — claimed that migrants often held misconceptions about race relations, available opportunities, and the status of African Americans in the urban North. Whether they sought to warn potential migrants about the difficulties of life in the North in order to dissuade them from leaving the South or simply to describe existing conditions more precisely, they painted a picture that was unflattering. Less-than-ideal conditions in the North — inadequate housing and racial discrimination, for example — provided ample grist for the journalistic mill in the South. This editorial, in a black religious weekly published in New Orleans, acknowledges the advantages of the North but cautions potential migrants about its disadvantages as well.

The migration of the Negro Northward continues to be a serious problem. Three hundred left on one boat from New Orleans for New York a few days ago and a train practically loaded at the same time left for Chicago. The situation around Norfolk is more serious, where the Negroes have plenty of work with good pay. One company where Negro labor has been employed for fifty years expended last year for labor more than $1,500,000 in the city of Norfolk, over $500,000 of this amount in wages for longshoremen and other laborers. Most of this amount went to our people.

The great mistake that some of our people are making in their moving to the North is their going without any definite place to go and with no definite employment in sight. There is enough risk when there is a bona fide offer of good positions in the North of the work that is congenial and work which our people can do, but it is a little less than foolhardy because some of our people are moving North for others to go in a harem scarem way. Those who go without definite employment are making trouble. Going into the cities of the North they have been forced to go into temporary camps, there having been no provision made for them, housing facilities being inadequate and no immediate employment to be had.

These facts lead us to say: In no case should our people attempt to go North until they know where they are going, to what they are going and whether the firms that offer employment are reliable. They must not forget that there are labor agents who get so much per head for men who go North but these labor agents cannot guarantee employment for the shiftless, worthless laborer whether he is in the South or in the North.

There is another thing to which attention should be called, in perfect frankness. Our people who move North should not expect to find everything rosy. There will be considerable disappointment if they think they will not encounter prejudice in the North. There is less prejudice there of a kind. There are better opportunities for education, and there is better protection, but there is the more intense prejudice on the part of the Labor Unions against skilled workmen who are Negroes. We give a warning note to our people against this foolhardy pulling up and moving into the complications of city life without knowing definitely what awaits them.

Moreover, the city with its allurements is no place for our people who are not accustomed to city life. Many Negro boys and girls who have otherwise been innocent in the South will be victims of all sorts of schemes and pitfalls and influences for degradation in the cities. It is well, therefore, when our people contemplate moving North, before they start, that they get in touch with some of the pastors of the churches of whatever denominations in the city where they expect to go. . . .

DWIGHT THOMPSON FARNHAM

Negroes a Source of Industrial Labor

August 1918

For southern migrants, one of the prime attractions of the wartime North was the availability of jobs that had previously been closed to African Americans. Many northern employers hired blacks during World War I not because they wanted to but because they desperately needed labor. Employers, like many other white Americans, often maintained that blacks were culturally and biologically inferior to whites. In the pages of the white business journal Industrial Management, *Dwight Thompson Farnham argued that managers required distinctive strategies for the "handling" of black labor that took into account African Americans' ostensible laziness, ignorance, and childishness. Migrants most likely never read the reflections of northern employers like these. But if they had, they would have encountered familiar and disquieting racial stereotypes and managerial practices virtually guaranteeing that they would be treated as second-class workers.*

The United States Has a Negro Population of 10,000,000 to Help Meet Our Labor Shortage

American industry has given generously of her second million of workers. Every day further calls are made as the training camps are emptied into our transports. . . .

Last year some of our more progressive corporations awoke to the fact that there was a vast reservoir of labor—amounting to over 10,000,000 souls—nearly 11 per cent of the country's population—as

Industrial Management, 56, no. 2 (Aug. 1918): 123–28.

yet practically untapped for manufacturing purposes. With true American initiative these corporations sent agents into the South. Negro settlements were placarded with notices setting forth the high wages and the ideal living conditions prevailing in the North. Trainloads of negro mammies, pickaninnies and all that miscellaneous and pathetic paraphernalia of mysterious bundles and protesting household pets which accompanies our colored citizen on his pilgrimages moved into St. Louis, Kansas City and Chicago, and from there were distributed to the industrial centers of the country.

The South awoke and chased the corporation agents out of town. Southern newspapers began to tell the negro how well off he was at home and who his best friends were. The North began to discuss segregation ordinances. Some communities took the law into their own hands with results which will be a shame and a disgrace upon their names so long as they exist. Corporations shipped carloads of negro workmen into mining and manufacturing villages, tried them out and shipped them out as utterly useless. Last Fall every train south was filled with darkies whose motto, as one expressed it to me, was, "Back to Alabam' or bust." What was the remedy? . . .

The really serious problem which confronts the would-be user of negro labor is that of handling his negroes in such a way as to avoid disastrous loss of operating efficiency. In the South you will hear two contradictory descriptions, "lazy as a nigger" and "slave like a nigger." Both are right and may apply to the same man. The difference is all in the management. I have had foremen who had been accustomed to the supervision of Americans, Slavs and Italians for years come to me in despair—"I can't do anything with the brutes; if I'm good to 'em they shoot craps and sleep, and if I cuss 'em out they shrug their shoulders and say, 'If you doan' like de way a' wukhs, boss, you can jes' give me mah time!'" The mistake most foremen make is that they use the same method with the negro that they use with white labor. . . .

We accuse the negro of laziness. His ancestors picked their food from a bush, fished it out of a stream, or speared it in the next block. Why should he inherit a feverish desire to work? We accuse him of leading a hand to mouth existence. Why should he be obsessed with a desire to emulate the squirrel, when any fruit his ancestors stores would have spoiled and any alligator hams cured would have been carried off by the driver ants? Why should he build him a house for tornadoes and floods to destroy or raise cattle for the tsetse fly to put to sleep? Besides, he didn't feel like it, being wearied by heat and parching winds—and he probably had malaria with like enough a touch of sleeping sickness. Under such conditions you could hardly expect him to be fussy about his clothes or to do much reading evenings. In fact, it is not surprising that he was a bit uncultured at times, given to dining on his enemies and indulging in super-Wagnerian music and voodooism.

The Negro Is Different

Once the plant executives, the foremen who come in contact with the workmen, realize that the negro is different physically, temperamentally and psychologically from any of the white races, the battle is half won. At first the tendency is to regard him either with intense hatred or else as a joke—a remnant of some minstrel show, organized especially to furnish innocent merriment. The man who hates the negro very seldom ever gets on with him. The darky is as quick to feel dislike as a child and resents it accordingly. The man who regards his antics at first with amused toleration is much more likely to eventually control him, although there will be a great many periods of discouragement when the amateur overseer will feel very much as did A. B. Frost's dominie who rescued the bull calf and undertook to lead him to safety with the halter tied about his waist. Sympathy and understanding are necessary but sentimentality is fatal, as experience demonstrates.

Misunderstandings Are Easy

The negro's responsiveness very often leads to serious misunderstandings. He will generally listen respectfully and appreciatively to what you say and seem to understand exactly, when, as a matter of fact, he has not the faintest idea what you are driving at. If you have been used to driving your meaning home to some foreign-born citizen with exhausting gestures and extravagant facial gyrations your first feeling is one of relief at having an honest-to-goodness American to deal with. But when your colored auditor goes and does exactly what you told him not to do, or quits on pay day after accusing you of gross misrepresentation and unfairness, you begin to long for your erstwhile audience of Southern Europeans who had to have the word hammered into them with a club but who understood it once the operation was completed. The remedy is, of course, extreme care and conscientiousness in explaining to the negro exactly what you want him to do and also exactly what you do not want him to do. Then make him tell you in his own words what you said to him and stay and see that he does it that way. . . .

Firmness Needed with the Negro

As in dealing with the child, firmness is absolutely necessary. If you tell a negro to do anything, see that he does it—or that he departs elsewhere immediately. But be sure he understands you before you lose your temper at what seems to be sulkiness or disobedience. When I was in the third grade at school a youngster I knew was punished repeatedly for disobedience and for impudence. It later developed that he was nearly deaf. It is necessary to remember in handling the negro that his responsiveness when addressed and his apparent willingness to please may be assumed to cover a slow understanding which it is not fair to blame him for. He is not above trying you out, however, just as the class of youngsters tries out a new teacher, nor is he any more scrupulous of taking advantage of you, if you prove to be "easy," than is the average young devil who attends our schools. . . .

Someone Must Think for the Negro

From an economic standpoint the man who can think for the greatest number of other men is the most valuable. He grades all the way down from a Lincoln or a Wilson, capable of thinking for a nation, to the working leader of a two man crew. The less thinking a man can do for himself the larger proportion of what he earns has to go to someone else for supervision. The rank and file of negroes require more supervision than the rank and file of whites. By this I do not mean more "driving" nor more "watching," I mean constructive supervision in the sense of thinking for and looking ahead for. We must provide the negro with the foresight of which his ancestor's environment has largely deprived him. . . .

Some Segregation Necessary

A certain amount of segregation is necessary at times to preserve the peace. This is especially true when negroes are first introduced into a plant. It is a question if it is not always best to have separate wash rooms and the like. In places where different races necessarily come into close contact and in places where inherited characteristics

are especially accentuated, it is better to keep their respective folk-
ways from clashing wherever possible. Separate work rooms or even
division into crews on strict racial lines are not at all necessary, if
both races are given to understand that each will be fairly treated,
but that swift justice will be meted out to the man who starts something. . . .

The East St. Louis Riot

NEW ORLEANS TIMES-PICAYUNE

The Negro in the North

June 4, 1917

*Despite growing labor shortages, white workers often perceived black
migrants as threats to their employment security. Several months after the
United States formally entered the war, violent attacks by whites against
blacks in East St. Louis, Illinois, growing out of a tense labor situation,
demonstrated that the integration of African Americans into industrial
workplaces would not be an easy or uncontested process. For the white
New Orleans daily, the* Times-Picayune, *the riot illustrated that the
North was an inhospitable place for southern African Americans.*

The anti-negro riots in East St. Louis, Ill., have about ended, after
accomplishing the results that could with certainty have been predicted of them, and with very little difference on the questions at
issue. Comparatively few persons were killed or seriously wounded,
but the demonstration was sufficiently emphatic to convince the
negroes, as the mayor of the town declared, that the climate of that
portion of Illinois is not good for them. What he meant was that the
white population of the town is opposed to any more negroes, and
were prepared to resort to any lawless methods to keep out the
negroes coming there and to run out all those already settled in the
town. The unanimous sentiment on this subject satisfied the negroes.
The authorities wanted to see them leave, and so advised, and even
went to the length of calling upon the governors of the Southern
states from which the immigrants came to check this movement and
begged the railroads traversing the district to discourage negro travel,
and appealed to the employers of labor to stop employing negroes.

The entire white population was in line on this point, and even the militia seemed lukewarm. The negroes could not, therefore, entertain a scintilla of doubt that their white neighbors in and around this Illinois city did not want them.

They had been deceived by the fact that Illinois is the state of Lincoln, the great emancipator, and it was thought that if the negro was welcomed and safe anywhere from interference and mob violence it was in that commonwealth. Moreover, a portion of the Chicago press has been telling of the unequal treatment the negroes received in the South with such force that it was natural that many of them should look upon Illinois as "the promised land." In St. Clair county the situation was intensified by the fact that the population had absorbed as many negroes as it can well stand without friction. The negroes were first brought there in large numbers some years ago to take the place of white miners then on a strike. As there is a strike under way just now, the whites believed—and they were probably right in their conclusion—that the negroes were being brought in by the thousands to take the places of the whites. Here was ample fuel for a big conflagration. Some minor incident, rumors of an insult by a negro to a white woman, precipitated the riot, and the mob fury was let loose. As we have said, the casualties were comparatively few because there was no opposition to the mob. The negroes fled out of town or were hustled to the jail as a protection from violence. The mob started to storm the jail, but, fortunately, was dissuaded from it. Had the attempt been made, a wholesale slaughter as at Springfield and other Illinois towns would probably have fiollowed. Instead, the mob amused itself marching through the black districts burning the negro homes. The firemen were kept busy two days in checking the flames and a big conflagration was thus prevented, but a number of houses were destroyed.

It is conceded that the mob accomplished its purpose, which was to convince the negroes—both those from the South and those from the North—that they were not desired in East St. Louis. There has been a steady movement of negroes from the town ever since over to the Missouri side of the river, and it is noted that the refugees include a number of old-time negro residents who had reached the conclusion that East St. Louis is a bad place for people of color. The mob demonstration was mainly against the new negro arrivals, the negroes from the South, but it was difficult to distinguish between them and the old residents. All negroes with arms were punished severely, with fines of $200 and imprisonment, and the St. Louis police turned over to the Illinois authorities a number of armed negroes who had fled across the river, and these were similarly fined and imprisoned.

It is universally agreed that the negro exodus from the South to
East St. Louis, St. Clair county and other places in Eastern Illinois is
ended for many years to come. No more negroes will go there or be
admitted. Whether the exodus continues to other sections until similar
demonstrations occur time alone can tell.

. . . The negro is allowed to work in the South, and there is ample
work for all of them, but they are not liked [in the] North, and are
crowded out of nearly every industry, and if they get too numerous
the mobs are turned loose to drive them out. "Stay South, negro, or go
back there," is the advice of the New York World, probably the best
friend the negro has in the North. "Black man stay South," is the
warning of the paper that inherited the traditions and ideas of Lincoln,
and the same advice comes from every portion of the North. The East
St. Louis incident shows a greater unanimity of sentiment on the
negro question than we have ever before seen in this country. It cannot but help to straighten out some of the recent kinks in it.

CRISIS

The Massacre of East St. Louis

September 1917

*NAACP leader W. E. B. Du Bois and Martha Gruening, a white social
worker, NAACP field agent, and* Crisis *staff member, traveled to East
St. Louis following the riot, where they assembled a team of investigators
to examine the causes and impact of the violence. The result of their
investigation was quickly published in the* Crisis, *whose monthly circulation had risen to nearly fifty thousand by September 1917.*

On the 2nd of July, 1917, the city of East St. Louis in Illinois added a
foul and revolting page to the history of all the massacres of the
world. On that day a mob of white men, women and children burned
and destroyed at least $400,000 worth of property belonging to both
whites and Negroes; drove 6,000 Negroes out of their homes; and

Crisis, 14, no. 5 (Sept. 1917): 219–38.

deliberately murdered, by shooting, burning and hanging, between one and two hundred human beings who were black.

Such an outbreak could not have been instantaneous. There must have been something further reaching even than an immediate cause to provoke such a disaster. The immediate cause usually given is as follows: On the evening of July 1, white "joy riders" rode down a block in Market Street, which was inhabited by Negroes, and began to fire into the houses. The Negroes aroused by this armed themselves against further trouble. Presently a police automobile drove up containing detectives and stopped. The Negroes thinking that these were the "joy riders" returning opened up fire before this misunderstanding was removed, and two of the detectives were killed. Some of the policemen were in plain clothes.

One naturally wonders why should the white "joy riders" fire in the first place. What was their quarrel with the Negroes? In answering that question we get down to the real story. It is here we meet with the facts that lay directly back of the massacre, a combination of the jealousy of white labor unions and prejudice.

East St. Louis is a great industrial center, possessing huge packing and manufacturing houses, and is, therefore, one of the biggest markets in the country for common unskilled labor. The war, by the deportation of white foreign workers, caused a scarcity of labor and this brought about the beginning of a noticeable influx of Negroes from the South. Last summer 4,500 white men went on strike in the packing plants of Armour & Co., Morris & Co., and Swift & Co., and Negroes from the South were called into the plants as strike-breakers. When the strike ended the Negroes were still employed and that many white men failed to regain their positions. The leaders of various labor unions realized that the supply of Negroes was practically inexhaustible and that they were receiving the same wages as their white predecessors and so evidently doing the same grade of work. Since it was increasingly possible then to call in as many black strike-breakers as necessary, the effectiveness of any strike was accordingly decreased. It was this realization that caused the small but indicative May riots. Evidently, the leaders of the labor unions thought something must be done, some measure sufficiently drastic must be taken to drive these interlopers away and to restore to these white Americans their privileges. The fact that the Negroes were also Americans meant nothing at such a time as this.

The leader of a labor union must be an opportunist. The psychology of any unskilled laborer is comparatively simple. To the knowledge then that his job is being held by an outsider add his natural and fostered prejudice against an outsider who is black and you have something of the mental attitude of the rioters of East St. Louis. Doubtless it was with some such prophetic vision as this that Edward F. Mason, secretary of the Central Trades and Labor Union, issued a letter. . . .

One point in particular is emphasized, that of color: "The Southern Negro," writes Mr. Mason, "has come into our community. No less than ten thousand of undesirable Negroes," he continues, "have poured in and are being used to the detriment of our white citizens." There is the appeal direct to prejudice. It is not that foreigners— Czechs, Slovaks, Lithuanians—or whatever ethnic division is least indigenous to East St. Louis—it is not that *they* are ousting Americans of any color or hue, but the "Southern Negro," the most American product there is, is being used "to the detriment of our white citizens."

Mr. Mason has no hesitancy in suggesting "that some action should be taken to retard this growing menace" and "to get rid of a certain portion of those who are already here." . . .

Mr. Mason wants to be fair. "This is not a protest against the Negro who has been a long resident"—so runs his superb English—"of East St. Louis, and is a law-abiding citizen of the state." In East St. Louis labor leaders are the arbiters of legal conduct and therefore 10,000 Negroes become undesirable citizens because they are strikebreakers and black.

That the July riot grew out of the meeting called by Mr. Mason . . . , we are not prepared to say; but that it grew out of this attitude is only too apparent. By all accounts of eye-witnesses, both white and black, the East St. Louis outrage was deliberately planned and executed.

Says Richard L. Stokes, writing in the *St. Louis Globe-Democrat* for Sunday, July 8:

> On the night of May 28th a delegation of about 600 union men marched to the City Hall to appeal to the authorities to prevent the importation of any more Negroes. Among them were many of the Aluminum Ore Company strikers. They took possession of an auditorium, and some of the leaders made speeches advising that in case the authorities took no action, they should resort to mob law.

When genuine mob law did finally reign on July 2, the scenes were indescribable. Germany has nothing on East St. Louis when it comes to "frightfulness." Indeed in one respect Germany does not even approximate her ill-famed sister. In all the accounts given of German

atrocities, no one, we believe, has accused the Germans of taking pleasure in the sufferings of their victims. But these rioters combined
business and pleasure. These Negroes were "butchered to make" an
East St. Louis "holiday."

Carlos F. Hurd, an eye-witness, realizes this fact and speaks of it in
the article which he publishes July 3 in the *St. Louis Post-Dispatch,* of
which he is a staff-reporter. Mr. Hurd writes:

> A mob is passionate, a mob follows one man or a few men blindly; a
> mob sometimes takes chances. The East St. Louis affair, as I saw it,
> was a man hunt, conducted on a sporting basis, though with any-
> thing but the fair play which is the principle of sport. The East St.
> Louis men took no chances, except the chance from stray shots,
> which every spectator of their acts took. They went in small groups,
> there was little leadership, and there was a horribly cool deliberate-
> ness and a spirit of fun about it.
>
> "Get a nigger," was the slogan, and it was varied by the recurrent
> cry, "Get another!" It was like nothing so much as the holiday crowd,
> with thumbs turned down, in the Roman Coliseum, except that here
> the shouters were their own gladiators, and their own wild beasts.

He goes on with another horrible account of which he was also an
eye-witness:

> A Negro, his head laid open by a great stone-cut, had been dragged to
> the mouth of the alley on Fourth Street and a small rope was being
> put about his neck. There was joking comment on the weakness of
> the rope, and everyone was prepared for what happened when it was
> pulled over a projecting cable box, a short distance up the pole. It
> broke, letting the Negro tumble back to his knees, and causing one of
> the men who was pulling on it to sprawl on the pavement.
>
> An old man, with a cap like those worn by street car conductors,
> but showing no badge of car service, came out of his house to
> protest. "Don't you hang that man on this street," he shouted. "I
> dare you to." He was pushed angrily away, and a rope, obviously
> strong enough for its purpose, was brought.
>
> Right here I saw the most sickening incident of the evening. To
> put the rope around the Negro's neck, one of the lynchers stuck his
> fingers inside the gaping scalp and lifted the Negro's head by it, lit-
> erally bathing his hand in the man's blood.
>
> "Get hold, and pull for East St. Louis!" called a man with a black
> coat and a new straw hat, as he seized the other end of the rope.
> The rope was long, but not too long for the number of hands that
> grasped it, and this time the Negro was lifted to a height of about
> seven feet from the ground. The body was left hanging there.

These accounts make gruesome reading, but they are all true. . . .
How does East St. Louis feel? According to all accounts she is unre-
pentant, surly, a little afraid that her shame may hurt her business, but
her head is not bowed.

In this connection Miss Gruening supplies the statement of East St.
Louis Postman No. 23, who said: "The only trouble with the mob was
it didn't get niggers enough. You wait and see what we do to the rest
when the soldiers go. We'll get every last one of them."

And here follows a sort of composite statement of the best citizens, editors, and liberty-bond buyers of East St. Louis and its surroundings:

"Well, you see too many niggers have been coming in here. When
niggers come up North they get insolent. You see they vote here and
one doesn't like that. And one doesn't like their riding in the cars next
to white women—and, well what are you going to do when a buck
nigger pushes you off the sidewalk?"

This last pathetic question was put to Miss Gruening by three different editors on as many separate occasions.

The *St. Louis Post-Dispatch* gives the views of District Attorney
Karch on the attitude of the rioters. He says:

> Those men have not left the city, and they have not repented of their
> excesses. They are just as bitter as they were, and the action of the
> Chamber of Commerce in forcing these Negroes down their throats
> is only inflaming the men who participated in the riot.

The District Attorney told of seeing a man on a street car exhibit a
revolver openly Thursday night, and remark that "it had killed niggers, and would kill some more as soon as the damned militia leaves."
Other men near by expressed similar sentiments, he added. They
were laboring men, apparently going home from work.

Karch emphatically confirmed the statements made to the *Post-
Dispatch* Tuesday by City Clerk Whalen, who is president of the Central Trades and Labor Union of East St. Louis, to the effect that large
employers of labor had given marked and continuous preference to
Negroes.

"Their attitude for some time has been that they would give jobs to
white men when they couldn't get any more Negroes," Karch declared.
"This, as Mr. Whalen said, is because the Negroes will not unionize.
Before the tenseness of this situation is relieved, these employers must
convince the laboring whites that they will be given preference over

imported blacks in applying for work. Instead of doing that, they are declaring they will put all the Negroes back to work, and protect them, if they have to keep troops here indefinitely. That kind of flamboyant talk only angers the men who should be quieted.

"As long as the heads of these big plants break up strikes by importing Negro strike-breakers, so long can they expect to have race riots. This is no defense for the rioters; there is no defense for them. It is just a fact that when a man's family is hungry his sense of justice doesn't operate very accurately."

Prejudice is a bad thing. But prejudice in the hands of Organized Labor in America! The Central Trades and Labor Union of East St. Louis has perpetrated a grim jest. Its motto . . . is "Labor omnia vincit." Latin is apt to be a bit obscure, so we translate: "Labor conquers everything." It does. In East St. Louis it has conquered Liberty, Justice, Mercy, Law and the Democracy which is a nation's vaunt. . . .

CHICAGO DEFENDER

Thousands March in Silent Protest

August 4, 1917

The Chicago Defender *was the black weekly with the largest circulation in the nation and an avid proponent of migration. From 1916 through the end of the war, the* Defender's *editor, Robert Abbott, tirelessly denounced the white South and advertised the advantages of northern life for blacks. For this stance, the* Defender *was appreciated by southern African Americans and disliked by southern whites. In this article, the* Defender *covers black protests against the racial violence in East St. Louis.*

NEW YORK, AUG. 3—Aristocratic Fifth Avenue, in Manhattan, Saturday afternoon witnessed a unique parade when some 10,000 people of the Race paraded in silent protest against the race riots in East St. Louis and other places.

No bands blared out martial music and no uniforms relieved the monotony of the trudging thousands. Even the apathetic crowds who sprinkled the line of march seemed to have caught the spirit of silence, and there was no cheering or hand clapping. Only the throb of muffled drums and the shuffling of countless feet, unused to the strain of steady walking, marked the passing of the procession.

Every Class Represented

Every class of occupation in which the Race is engaged, from lawyers, ministers and professional men to ditch digger, were in line. Men, women and children all trudged from Fifty-ninth to Twenty-fourth street in one dumb panorama of voiceless protest against conditions which are deemed unbearable. Big signs bearing printed paragraphs were carried by scores of marchers.

In the belief that the character of the parade might cause some disturbance, the police department had taken elaborate precautions. Policemen lined the avenue on both sides, while a cordon of mounted men headed the parade and one brought up in the rear. But there was not the slightest need for them.

The first marchers to arrive at Madison Square disbanded and then filled the sidewalks and applauded as the rest of the parade came down and were absorbed in the crowd.

Clergymen Head Procession

Headed by the Rev. Hutchins C. Bishop and the Rev. Charles D. Martin, the moving spirits of the scheme, and a dozen other ministers, the parade started. In the first section were some hundreds of small children under the guidance of teachers. A drum corps composed of four boys, their drums draped with black bordered handkerchiefs, furnished the music. Following the youngsters came the women, all dressed in white. Many of them, judging from their looks, dated back to civil war days. The men formed the last section.

While there were some few banners scattered through the other parts of the parade, the main number were among the men. Some of the more striking ones were: "No Negro has ever betrayed the flag, attempted to assassinate the President or any official of the government," "Your hands are full of blood," "The first blood for American independence was shed by a Negro," "Maligned as lazy, murdered when we work," "Race prejudice is the offspring of ignorance and the mother of lynching," "If you hate me on account of my color, blame yourselves and God," "Give every man his equal rights, . . ." "We have fought in six wars, our reward was East St. Louis," "We are willing but unarmed.". . .

3

The Evolution of Black Politics

The era of the Great Migration witnessed an intensification of the struggles waged by black Americans for economic, political, and civil rights. Growing numbers of observers captured a change of mood in black communities that manifested itself in a newly visible "race pride" and the willingness to challenge racial inequities more aggressively. The protests of the New Negro were at times collective, undertaken by such organizations as the NAACP and Marcus Garvey's Universal Negro Improvement Association, which offered a wide range of often conflicting programs for black advancement. But the spirit of the New Negro was hardly confined to the urban North or to established national organizations. Increasingly, individual black men and women, or the local associations they formed, protested the violence directed against them, the discourteous treatment they received, and the racial injustices they endured. If this new assertiveness won the approval of black activists, it alarmed southern white elites who feared its consequences for the racial and economic order in the South.

THE REVEREND J. EDWARD PRYOR

The Patriotism of the Negro

May 4, 1917

African Americans had served in every war fought by the United States since the American Revolution in the late eighteenth century. World War I was no exception. As one black minister reminded his readers in the black West Virginia weekly, the McDowell Times, *there was no cause for whites to question black loyalty during the Great War.*

There seems to be much discussion these days, throughout the country, concerning the Patriotism of the Negro; and what can reasonably be expected of him, during this crucial period of the country's history. Why there should be any question or doubt as to his loyalty, or patriotism, my readers must answer for themselves, as it is not the purpose of these articles to discuss such things at this time, but rather to enlighten those who have no proper conception of the Negro's patriotism and loyalty to his country.

The silence of many of our prominent leaders, and the silence of our people in general, has been in some instances magnified to mean, that we are listless and unconcerned about the country's welfare, and that we harbor resentment because of past conditions, and see in the present condition of things an opportunity to register our protest by being disloyal to our country's best interests. Now they who would place us in any such light, or harbor any such view of our people, must be intensely cruel and utterly devoid of all knowledge of our people and their history. I am sure there can be no question about our patriotism, unless it be found among those who, by their own assumption of exclusiveness, have studiously and purposely blinded their eyes to every evidence of our progress and all the glorious record of loyalty and faithful devotion to the country's best interests under the most trying circumstances that have confronted any people in the world's history. To question the Negro's patriotism is the worst slan-

McDowell Times, 4 May 1917.

der that can be brought against the race, and for this cause alone we cherish the opportunity to use our limited powers in giving the public a clearer view of his patriotism. . . .

W. E. B. DU BOIS

Close Ranks

July 1918

W. E. B. Du Bois's advice to African Americans to "forget our special grievances" for the duration of the war was uncharacteristic of the civil rights leader and proved highly controversial in many black communities. In practice, regardless of what Du Bois advised, many black Americans supported the war effort and simultaneously pressed ahead with their struggle for equal rights.

This is the crisis of the world. For all the long years to come men will point to the year 1918 as the great Day of Decision, the day when the world decided whether it would submit to military despotism and an endless armed peace—if peace it could be called—or whether they would put down the menace of German militarism and inaugurate the United States of the World.

We of the colored race have no ordinary interest in the outcome. That which the German power represents today spells death to the aspirations of Negroes and all darker races for equality, freedom and democracy. Let us not hesitate. Let us, while this war lasts, forget our special grievances and close our ranks shoulder to shoulder with our own white fellow citizens and the allied nations that are fighting for democracy. We make no ordinary sacrifice, but we make it gladly and willingly with our eyes lifted to the hills.

Crisis, 16, no. 3 (July 1918): 111.

THE NEW REPUBLIC

Negro Conscription

October 20, 1917

The participation of African Americans in the nation's armed forces—whether voluntary or by conscription—proved worrisome to many southern whites, who feared that military experience would foster a new spirit of independence and a willingness to challenge the existing racial order. The New Republic, a liberal white journal, posed the issue starkly, calling on the white South to improve relations between the races.

The South is not altogether easy over the conscription of the Negro. The withdrawal of a considerable fraction of the supply of farm labor is embarrassing just now when the pull of the North upon Negro labor is intensified by the drying up of the flow of immigration from Europe. The assembling at mobilization points of large numbers of lusty young blacks accustomed to no other discipline than that of the plantation quite naturally gives occasion for concern. But what chiefly disturbs the South is the probable effect upon the Negro population of the return of the men who have served their campaigns. Will the Negro be the same kind of man when he is mustered out as he was when he was mustered in? Will he accept the facts of white supremacy with the same spirit as formerly? Or will he have acquired a new sense of independence that will make of him a fomenter of unrest among his people?

There are some indeed who dismiss southern anxiety as quite groundless. The Negro problem, they assert, will present the same aspect after the war as before it, whether Negro soldiers serve in France or not. But this is to ignore all the teaching of experience. The South is quite justified in its belief that war will affect the habit of mind and the behavior of the men who engage in it. The Russian peasant who has fought in Galicia is a quite different being from the timid, abject creature who tilled the black lands before the war. He makes a very restive mount for the lords of the earth, as his record in the revolution demonstrates. The German peasant too appears to be changing under the influence of his military experience. The German aristocracy is not so certain as once it was that "Hans bleibt immer Hans."* Unrest among the masses of the working population of England and France is no remote contingency. At all events there are defenders of the existing order in both countries who express grave concern over what will happen when the soldiers return to civil life. In so far as institutions, political or social, are based upon fear they are likely to be challenged by the returned soldier. After facing death in its most hideous forms on the field of battle, will a man cower before a black look, shrink from a threatened blow?

If England and France and America are in no serious danger of political or social disturbances when the soldiers return, this is because the fundamental institutions of those countries are not founded upon the exploitation of fear. Obedience to the law, except in sporadic instances, rests upon a general recognition of social utility, not upon fear of the police. We leave their possessions to the privileged, not because they hold the keys to the jail, but because the system that produces them serves the social purpose better than any other system we have been able to devise. We may expect that the system will be subjected to severer popular scrutiny after the war. We may expect it will have to undergo many modifications. The government and the employers may be required to show cause why they should permit crises of unemployment to arise. Hours of labor, scales of wages, sanitary and safety arrangements, provisions for disability and superannuation, may be overhauled. All this may give rise to some embarrassment to the lords of the earth, and to much murmuring. But in the long run they will find the new order as satisfactory as the old. They claim title by virtue of service; they cannot object seriously to a more precise definition of their obligation to serve.

Do the relations between blacks and whites in the South rest upon mutual service, or does the social system of the South rest upon fear? Southerners themselves are far from unanimous on this point. There is a type of southerner who swears that the proper function of the white man is to keep the fear of God or Devil in the breast of the black. There is another type of southerner who conceives the function of the white man as that of guide and protector of the black man. The latter, to judge rather by general effects than by expressed opinions, is the prevailing type. Relations between the races are generally far more cordial than could possibly be the case if the southern social system were based wholly, or even chiefly, upon fear.

*"Hans will always be Hans."

The southern white profits by the labor of the black and he gives service in return. The Negroes of the South, we may well believe, are better off than they would be in a black republic. It does not follow that they are so well off as they ought to be. It does not follow that the whites are performing to the full the obligation they owe. Grant that the South has done much for the Negro; it has not done enough. The northern white will have to give more service in return for his privileges, just as the Prussian aristocrat, the French and British and American factory owners will have to give more. This is a necessary consequence of a war that stirs democracy to its greatest depths.

There is much that the South ought to have done for the Negro that it has not done. It ought to have put down the temperamental Negro baiter, the man who goes out of his way "to put the nigger in his place," acting on a psychology more crude and stupid and brutal than the worst Prussia can exhibit. The South ought to have assumed greater responsibility for the Negro's civil and economic welfare. The best men of the South know that there are cormorants of sharp business preying upon the Negroes. They know that the Negro is handicapped when he buys land and when he sells it; that he is handicapped in every legal transaction; that if he is ambitious, his road to advancement is inhumanly steep and slippery unless he chances to have the personal protection of a white man of the best type. But the men of the best type have not organized for the defense of the legitimate interests of the Negro. They intervene in specific cases of injustice, but they leave untouched institutions that make for injustice.

Conscription of the Negro brings the South face to face with the necessity of overhauling its scheme of racial relationships. It is a necessity that many would avoid. They would be willing to send more of their own sons to battle if their local institutions might remain unchallenged by new problems. But local institutions cannot go forever unchallenged. Is the South willing to admit that white supremacy cannot rest on any sounder foundation than fear? If it can rest on service, the problems arising out of Negro conscription cannot be insoluble.

LEON A. SMITH

Protest to Boston Herald

April 20, 1918

During the era of the Great Migration, black Americans wrote numerous letters to the editors of white and black newspapers and periodicals. The Boston Guardian, *a black weekly edited by civil rights activist William Monroe Trotter, printed a letter directed to the* Boston Herald, *a white daily, by a black reader protesting the* Herald's *use of racist language.*

BOSTON, MASS.
APRIL 13, 1918.

Dear Sirs:

As has been my custom for a number of years and is still my custom at the present time, I take your paper daily. In looking through the columns on this morning (Saturday morning, April 13, 1918) on Page 14, it gave me great discomfort and displeasure to see the Colored draftees at Camp Deven, Ayer, Mass., that arrived from Florida termed as "Southern Darkies."

This is a war of democracy. Our boys are in France fighting to uphold America and the good old Stars and Stripes as are the men of the other race. Our boys are in camps training to go to France to do their equal share and bit as are the white boys. If relying on Lincoln's Statement that "All Men Are Created Equal," then why should degrading and insulting statements be cast at us on account of color. We are American citizens as well as the white man and are proud of it. Whether we be from the South or the North or the East or the West we are still American citizens and our boys in uniform are American soldiers.

An early reply from you on this matter will be very appreciative.

Yours truly
LEON A. SMITH.

Boston Guardian (20 April 1918).

MARTHA GRUENING

Houston: An NAACP Investigation

November 1917

Those African Americans who believed that service to their country would bring them respect and justice found their hopes quickly dashed. Black soldiers stationed in the South were segregated in all-black units, subjected to the specific Jim Crow laws of southern communities and states, and harassed by military police and local law enforcement officials. In August 1917, black soldiers' anger exploded. The "Houston riot," the subsequent arrest and hasty court-martial of the black military rioters, and the execution of thirteen of those convicted were seen by many African Americans as examples of southern oppression and unjust treatment by the U.S. military. White social worker and NAACP activist Martha Gruening, who had just completed her investigation with W. E. B. Du Bois into the East St. Louis riot, traveled to Houston and published this account in the pages of the NAACP's monthly journal, the Crisis.

The primary cause of the Houston riot was the habitual brutality of the white police officers of Houston in their treatment of colored people. Contributing causes were (1) the mistake made in not arming members of the colored provost guard or military police, (2) lax discipline at Camp Logan which permitted promiscuous visiting at the camp and made drinking and immorality possible among the soldiers.

Houston is a hustling and progressive southern city having the commission form of government and, as southern cities go, a fairly liberal one. Its population before the Negro exodus, which has doubtless decreased it by many thousands, was estimated at 150,000. Harris County, in which it is situated, has never had a lynching, and there are other indications, such as the comparative restraint and self-control of the white citizens after the riot, that the colored people perhaps enjoy a greater degree of freedom with less danger than in many parts of the South. It is, however, a southern city, and the presence of the Negro troops inevitably stirred its Negrophobe element to protest. There was some feeling against the troops being there at all, but I could not find that it was universal. Most of the white people seem to

Crisis, 15, no. 1 (Nov. 1917): 14–19.

have wanted the financial advantages to be derived from having the camp in the neighborhood. The sentiment I heard expressed most frequently by them was that they were willing to endure the colored soldiers if they could be "controlled." I was frequently told that Negroes in uniform were inevitably "insolent" and that members of the military police in particular were frequently "insolent" to the white police of Houston. It was almost universally conceded, however, that the members of the white police force habitually cursed, struck, and otherwise maltreated colored prisoners. One of the important results of the riot has been an attempt on the part of the Mayor and the Chief of Police of Houston to put a stop to this custom.

In deference to the southern feeling against the arming of Negroes and because of the expected co-operation of the city Police Department, members of the provost guard were not armed, thus creating a situation without precedent in the history of this guard. A few carried clubs, but none of them had guns, and most of them were without weapons of any kind. They were supposed to call on white police officers to make arrests. The feeling is strong among the colored people of Houston that this was the real cause of the riot. "You may have observed," one of them said to me, "that Southerners do not like to fight Negroes on equal terms. This is at the back of all the southern feeling against Negro soldiers. If Corporal Baltimore had been armed, they would never have dared to set upon him and we should not have had a riot." This was the general feeling I found among the colored people of Houston. . . .

On the afternoon of August 23, two policemen, Lee Sparks and Rufe Daniels—the former known to the colored people as a brutal bully—entered the house of a respectable colored woman in an alleged search for a colored fugitive accused of crap-shooting. Failing to find him, they arrested the woman, striking and cursing her and forcing her out into the street only partly clad. While they were waiting for the patrol wagon a crowd gathered about the weeping woman who had become hysterical and was begging to know why she was being arrested. In this crowd was a colored soldier, Private Edwards. Edwards seems to have questioned the police officers or remonstrated with them. Accounts differ on this point, but they all agree that the officers immediately set upon him and beat him to the ground with the butts of their six-shooters, continuing to beat and kick him while he was on the ground, and arrested him. In the words of Sparks himself: "I beat that nigger until his heart got right. He was a good nigger when I got through with him." Later Corporal Baltimore, a member of the military police, approached the officers and inquired for Edwards, as it was his duty to do. Sparks immediately opened fire, and Baltimore, being unarmed, fled with the two policemen in pursuit shooting as they ran. Baltimore entered a house in the neighborhood and hid under a bed. They followed, dragged him out, beat him up and arrested him. It was this outrage which infuriated the men of the 24th Infantry to the point of revolt. . . .

Police brutality and bad discipline among the soldiers led up to the riot, which cost the city of Houston eighteen lives. . . .

. . . The Houston *Post* and the white people generally explained it as another illustration of the well-known fact that "the South is the Negro's best friend"; that race riot and bloodshed are really indigenous to northern soil; and that the relations between black and white in the South are highly cordial. The colored people of Houston, however, are migrating North, and to this more than to any element in the case I attribute the new restraint in the attitude of white Houstonians. While I was in Houston, 130 colored people left in one day. In June, one labor agent exported more than nine hundred Negroes to points along the Pennsylvania Railroad. The Houston Chamber of Commerce became so alarmed over the Negro exodus that it telegraphed to the head of the railroad asking that this exportation be discontinued. The railroad complied with this request, but the colored people continued to leave. Colored men and women in every walk of life are still selling their homes and household goods at a loss and leaving because, as one of them, a physician, put it to me, "Having a home is all right, but not when you never know when you leave it in the morning if you will really be able to get back to it that night.". . .

SAVANNAH TRIBUNE

Racial Clashes

July 26, 1919

After the war, returning black soldiers confronted widespread resentment and resistance from whites who feared that the black veterans would "forget their place" and insist upon their political, social, and economic rights. The weekly African American newspaper the Savannah Tribune *provides a glimpse at white southerners' treatment of returning soldiers and southern blacks' call for justice.*

We have discovered beyond question that now that the war is over, a great many of the whites of the rural districts, and in the cities too, resent the presence of Negroes in uniform. From their treatment of these Negroes, it appears they feel that Negroes, discharged, have no right to walk around, visit about or otherwise enjoy their return home, as other men are doing. Or, it is felt, the resentment is borne of a fear that these Negroes who have been in the camps and across the seas will forget "their places," and hence it will be well to have them get rid of the uniform as early as possible. We have observed and proved this resentment in a score of the trouble, and we have heard many comments which indicate that there are thousands who have this state of mind as regards Negro ex-enlisted men.

While the war continued there was the most cordial welcome to Negro draftees everywhere, because it was not then known to what extremes the demands and exigences of war would go, nor how necessary might be the Negro soldier in helping to save the nation. When the war was over, the breach which has prevented inter-racial cooperation, fellowship, protection to Negroes, and all the benefits of civilization, immediately sprang open again, and wider, apparently, than before, because of this supposed arrogance of Negro soldiers.

We have proved that most of the so-called "uppishness" of Negroes, which appears to grate upon the narrow and fearful white men of the rural districts, is imagined, rather than real, and that the great majority of young Negroes returned from the war are immensely better off in every way than before they went away. They are more mannerly, of better personal appearance and health, better trained, of maturer judgment and more refined.

We have seen, on the other hand, lots of mischief-making among many of the returned young white men, in public places, on public high ways, on cars and trains, and this often at the expense of Negroes. This has been a fruitful source of disorder, quite as much as any other.

There ought to be as much patience, tolerance and help extended to the Negro ex-soldier as to any other. There ought to be provided the same fair opportunity and preferences of work and pay. There ought to be the same consideration of his feeling, his dignity and his pride in the service he has rendered. He has made sacrifices, endured the same privations, made the same free offer of his life to save the honor of the common fatherland.

Racial clashes should never arise from resentment of the Negro in uniform. The uniform should be a reason for ceasing strife. . . .

CLEVELAND GAZETTE

League Asks Full Manhood Rights

May 19, 1917

The National Equal Rights League, an organization founded by Boston activist William Monroe Trotter, was a small, militant civil rights organization. In contrast to Du Bois's view that black Americans should "close ranks" during World War I, League members did not believe that the struggle for equality on the home front should be put aside for the duration of the war. Instead, they pledged loyalty to the government at the same time they insisted that the American republic protect blacks' legal and civil rights. The Cleveland Gazette *was an African American weekly newspaper.*

BOSTON.—The Boston branch of the National Equal Rights league sends out the following memorial to the people of the United States. The league pledges loyalty to the government and asks that colored Americans be protected in their legal and civil rights along with other loyal citizens of the American republic.

The league in its memorial says:

"... As the United States of America enters this awful war the world speculates whether Americans of color will be loyal because of the denial of rights to a majority of them. . . .

"The Boston branch of the National Equal Rights league, meeting when the country is at war, realizing its responsibility as a branch of the only nation wide organization formed by and of and led by colored citizens to oppose race and color discrimination, declares false all charges of disloyalty . . .

"Colored Americans would be less than human if they did not feel bitterly every bar from employment, from public accommodation, because of our race and color. Deep is the resentment against enforced segregation by city, state or the federal government whether in the civil or military service. But we have no thought of taking up arms against this our country. Ours it has been to save the government from rebellion. This work of our fathers we shall not destroy. There is not gold enough in all the treasuries of the nations of the earth to corrupt us, for it is not a question of money, but of equality of rights.

"To the national government which call[s] us all to war, to our fellow Americans of every race variety, we would appeal in the name of fair play, of justice and humanity. We are all citizens of a common country.

"There is need no longer of subjection of Americans to the race prejudices of fellow Americans. In the presence of a common danger and a common obligation, with a war devastating Europe caused by racial clannishness and racial hatred, under Almighty God let the United States of America and the people thereof give up race proscription and persecution at home. Let the door of the workshop, the school, the college, the civil service, the army, the navy, the military school, the naval school now and henceforth open alike to every citizen of the republic without regard to race and without distinction of color. Let the right to travel, to vote, to have court protection be free, without barrier or denial.

"Give, Mr. President and all our governors, the same encouragement for volunteering or enlisting to white, to brown, to yellow, to black, Americans all, by vouchsafing the same free chance to enlist, to rise on merit, and on return home the same right to civil service and to civil rights without bar or segregation.

"Now is the time for all in authority to declare for the abolition of all racial discriminations and proscriptions and for all to join in our unhyphenated Americanism for victory under the favor of the God of all mankind.". . .

CRISIS

The Heart of the South

May 1917

The NAACP's membership grew dramatically during the World War I years, and its geographical reach and social base expanded accordingly. The association sponsored aggressive membership drives in the South, attracting significant new membership from that region for the first time.

Crisis, 14, no. 1 (May 1917): 18–19.

Although local chapters were guided by the national office's programs, they also organized around issues of concern to their particular communities.

The organization of a dozen, lusty, young branches as a new Dixie District in the heart of the South marks the beginning of a new era in the history of the N.A.A.C.P. We are not unmindful of the good work done there by the branches at New Orleans, El Paso, and Key West. Nevertheless, we have heretofore been essentially a northern organization calling the attention of the nation to the worst of the evils oppressing colored folk, reporting the shrieks and moans that came to our ears from across the Line when some particularly brutal barbarity cried to heaven, a voice trying to speak for inarticulate millions. With the entry of Atlanta into the fight, flanked by Richmond, Norfolk, Durham, Greensboro, Raleigh, Augusta, Athens, Savannah, Charleston, Columbia, Jacksonville, and Tampa, we feel that the hosts of the cotton kingdom have suddenly become articulate and the National Association a real first line defense facing the enemy at proper range.

That the younger sons will come to grips with their local problems in short order we have no doubt, but to Atlanta belongs the honor of launching a fight of first importance without waiting for the ink to dry on their application for a charter.

Each of these new southern branches has local problems facing them as important as the one with which Atlanta has come to grips. Richmond is taking steps to see that colored principals are placed at the head of the colored public schools in the city, and Charleston has a similar problem to attack.

The Savannah Branch is taking steps to defeat for appointment to a Federal judgeship a man who had openly expressed sentiments hostile to the race, and who refused to receive a delegation of colored postal employees, although he was at the time a member of Congress from Savannah. Columbia has a fight on its hands against a residential segregation ordinance which passed its first reading in the City Council during the last days of March. R. G. Finlay, rector of Trinity Church, and three professors on the faculty of the University of South Carolina, the white members on the colored auxiliary to the Associated Charities of Columbia, have written us that they are preparing to oppose the ordinance; and the new branch should lose no time in joining forces with them. Jacksonville has taken steps to secure justice in the courts for a colored man who killed a wealthy white man whom he found in his home. Efforts have been made by the police to hold this colored man on some trumped up charge of robbery and of not being married to the woman in the case. The Jacksonville Branch has engaged a special attorney to look after his interests. Mr. Wilson Jefferson, President of the Augusta Branch, writes that "On March 5 we got out perhaps the largest crowd ever assembled for a meeting of the character of ours in this old town, to hear James W. Johnson. . . . I am not going to be satisfied until my people know the truth about some things very close to their future well-being and happiness." So all through the South the new branches are bravely taking up the fight.

The roll of paid-up members as we go to press, made up at a later date than the membership statistics below, is eloquent of the good work accomplished by the Field Secretary on his first organizing effort:

ATLANTA, GA	139
TAMPA, FLA.	107
RICHMOND, VA.	63
SAVANNAH, GA	60
COLUMBIA, S. C.	46
JACKSONVILLE, FLA	31
ATHENS, GA	29
RALEIGH, N. C.	29
CHARLESTON, S. C.	29
AUGUSTA, GA.	28
GREENSBORO, N.C.	27
NORFOLK, VA.	26
DURHAM, N.C.	<u>25</u>
	639

"There is no doubt that a new spirit is awakening in the South," Mr. Johnson says, "and that the National Association for the Advancement of Colored People offers the precise medium for the exercise of that spirit. When the Association has spread over the entire South, as it is certain to do, and the thinking men and women of the race feel and know that they are leagued together with thinking men and women of both races all over the country for one and the same purpose, when each group feels and knows that it has the co-operation and support of all the other groups, many are changes that are going to be brought about.

"I am not only gratified by the campaign in the South, but I have been encouraged and inspired by it. And I ought to add that I had a most enjoyable time; the six thousand people whom I met not only listened to what I had to say and responded to my efforts, but, without exception, treated me in full accordance with the fine old traditions of Southern hospitality."

How ready the South is to join forces with and subscribe to the uncompromising demands of the N.A.A.C.P. is further testified to by a letter received from Tampa just as we go to press, asking for a charter as a branch:

"We are enclosing check for one hundred and nineteen dollars ($119.00) as per list enclosed. The report would have been sent several days ago but for the ambition of the membership to send not less than one hundred members. We are sending one hundred and seven and our motto is to increase the membership to five hundred within the net [*sic*] few days."

Under date of March 31, a circular letter is being sent out to the entire Association membership with a blank enclosed urging each member to send in at least one new member from among his or her friends. It is not only because in numbers lies our strength that we make this earnest plea. It is not only because the N.A.A.C.P. is fighting for the rights of all colored people that it should be supported by every one, white or black, who has the future of democracy in America at heart. We are in the war and always in times of international stress the support of many large contributors who support organizations dealing with internal problems is withdrawn. The first year of the European war was so lean that the Association had to curtail its activities all along the line for lack of funds; yet it is a moment when we must be particularly alert if we would take advantage of war-created opportunities to advance the status of colored people, as the disfranchised women of England and the oppressed masses of Russia have advanced theirs.

All new memberships received from this appeal will of course be entered to the credit of the local branch of the city from which they come, and we count upon the active cooperation of all branch officers in shoving the Association membership well across the 10,000 mark within the next month.

MARY WHITE OVINGTON

Reconstruction and the Negro

February 1919

The term Reconstruction—*first applied to the period following the Civil War in the South—came into vogue again following World War I. The term now reflected the notion, and for many the hope, that American society would be "reconstructed" along more democratic lines after the war. For some elite southern whites, the term conjured up frightening images of the first Reconstruction, when blacks gained some rights and whites' control weakened. In this essay for the* Crisis, *white NAACP leader Mary White Ovington posed the question of what a new Reconstruction might mean for African Americans.*

Six months ago the word on everyone's lips was War: the need of continuing the struggle against the Central Powers. Today, the first thought of those who think at all is Reconstruction; what will be done for the people, in the land of the victor and the land of the vanquished? Out of this terrible slaughter, this immeasurable loss of property and life, what advance will be made toward justice and humanity?

Every oppressed group, workingmen, carving out others' fortunes while they themselves remain in poverty; women, deprived of their rights as citizens; small nationalities, disrupted by the ambitions of aggressive empires; so-called "inferior races," persecuted by the race at the moment in power; each and everyone of these groups is engaged in a separate struggle to secure something of value for itself in the chaos that comes at the close of a great war. Now, they realize, while systems are fluid, before the structure of society becomes rigid again, is the opportunity to win the reality of democracy.

Probably among all the peoples clamoring for liberty and the right to fuller self-expression in this year of 1919 none has a more uphill road than the American Negro.

What is the Reconstruction that the Negro demands?

Mr. J. R. Hawkins, of Washington, D. C., in an able speech made before the District of Columbia Branch of the N. A. A. C. P., which has been commented upon by a portion of the press, makes an analogy

Crisis, 17, no. 4 (Feb. 1919): 169–73.

between President Wilson's fourteen peace points and the fourteen points desired by the Negro. Mr. Hawkins' fourteen points are:

1. Universal suffrage.
2. Better educational facilities in the South.
3. Abolition of the so-called "Jim-Crow" system.
4. Discontinuance of unjust discriminatory regulations and segregation in the various departments of the government.
5. The same military training for colored youth as for white.
6. The removal of an imaginary dead line in the recognition of fitness for promotion in military and naval service.
7. The removal of the peonage system in the South.
8. An economic wage to be applied to white and colored alike.
9. Better housing conditions for colored employees in industrial plants.
10. Better sanitary conditions in certain sections of our cities and towns.
11. Reform in the penal institutions of the South.
12. A fair and impartial trial by jury instead of lynching.
13. Recognition of the Negro's right and fitness to sit on juries.
14. Fair play. "As the Negro has been among the first to give his best, his all, to his country in every struggle for the defence of its flag, so he wants and expects equal opportunity to serve in the development of his country and the full enjoyment of the fruits thereof."

How, then, can the Negro battle to secure these great things which Mr. Hawkins enumerates—the abolition of segregation in government, in the army, in the daily life of the colored man as he moves from place to place or settles in his permanent abode?

Reconstruction comes at the close of the war—a war fought for democracy—and it comes to aid in better living especially those who have served their country and their country's government. Yet the last place to which the returning colored soldier can look for justice is Washington, the very fountain-head of the government he has so faithfully served. Our government is today in the hands of men inimical to his claims for citizenship, men who degrade the uniform while they degrade him. The railroads are operated by the United States, but colored soldiers are Jim-Crowed as they return to their homes, are denied the right to sleep in Pullmans, are refused food at railroad restaurants. Since 1912 the Negro federal employee has been subjected to many petty acts of discrimination that have aroused race antagonism and created antipathies that never existed before.

But, fortunately, in a republic legislatures change with considerable swiftness and in the coming two years the Negro will find many good friends to press his claims in the new Congress. He cannot, however, expect his friends to do much until he himself presents an immense driving force to stand behind whoever espouses his cause. The power of numbers, but *organized* numbers, is the power that wins the battle. Every reader of *The Crisis,* white and colored, should be a member of the organization for which *The Crisis* stands, of which it is a part. Progress is won when people band themselves together, conviction of the righteousness of their cause in their hearts. In a year the N. A. A. C. P. has linked together forty-three thousand people where formerly it had less than ten thousand. If it continues in the same proportion, it should have 160,000 by January 1, 1920. This would mean groups of men and women, throughout the whole country, who at a given moment could act unitedly for the benefit of the race. This is the first great force to be used to secure the franchise, fair trial by jury, anti-lynching.

And the practical program for this fighting mass? It is not some- thing to be decided on in its entirety. To stamp out segregation by legal decision, as the Supreme Court decision won by the Association through its President, Mr. Moorfield Storey, did stamp it out, was the work of years. To test the right of the state to segregate passengers in interstate travel will be a matter, perhaps, of many more years. To reduce southern representation by enforcing the Fourteenth Amend- ment will be a gigantic task to enter upon. But every day there is the unceasing battle, in smaller matters, against the tendency in the United States, North and South, to treat the Negro as one less worthy of regard than the white. The only way to progress is to take up each case as it comes and work to win it. . . . It may be rescuing a woman from being convicted as a vagrant under the "work or fight" law in Georgia; it may be securing the right to sit in the orchestra of a the- atre in a northern city; but each time it is a bit gained in the great movement for the destruction of racial discrimination in a democracy that has preached to the world freedom and justice to all. . . .

Increasingly, in this world, we are learning that there is no half-way status—a man must be a man or a slave. When he ceases to be a slave, he can never be a safe element in the population until he becomes a man. America might as well face this. Europe is facing it among the many nationalities that have, of a sudden, sprung into prominence demanding their full manhood rights. We in the western hemisphere had hardly heard of these recalcitrant groups but their rulers had heard of them for centuries and with all their despotism had never been able to stifle the spirit that kept them a restless, menacing factor in the community life. They were the stumbling blocks to reform; to keep them "in their place" the empires that ruled them lost in finer forms of civilization. Now these peoples are coming into their own. And in the United States the oppressed Negro race, rich in genius, kindly, hard-working, is also coming into its own. The way may be long, but a good start has been made along the road.

THE MESSENGER

Migration and Political Power

July 1918

A. Philip Randolph and a new generation of black activists—who sometimes referred to themselves as the "New Crowd" (as opposed to the "Old Crowd" of earlier black leaders)—emerged in the late 1910s and the 1920s. What distinguished them from their predecessors, they believed, was their rejection of a politics of racial conciliation, their refusal to appeal to whites' goodwill, and their willingness to confront aggressively blacks' second-class citizenship in the North. The Messenger, published by Randolph and Chandler Owen, was a radical black monthly that espoused socialism and racial equality.

The Negroes have come from the South in large numbers and they are still coming. Before the movement is stopped it is not improbable that from three to four million Negroes may come into the North, East and West.

Let them come!

As they leave the chief "land of the lynching bee and the home of the slave" they secure better industrial opportunities, education for their children and political power. From states in which they were disfranchised they go into states where they have a man's right to vote — the right to be freedmen in fact.

With better industrial opportunity the Negroes secure wealth. They have something to fight about.

With better educational opportunity the Negroes secure information. They then have light to see how to fight — a lamp for guidance.

With the possession of the ballot the Negroes have political power — ammunition. They then have something to fight with.

Men don't fight very strongly unless they have something to fight about, and they don't fight very effectively unless they have something to fight with. As the Negro migrates North and West he secures political power to help himself in his new abode and at the same time to strike a blow for his less favored brothers in wicked "old Dixie."

MARCUS GARVEY

What We Believe

January 1, 1924

and

The Principles of the Universal Negro Improvement Association

November 25, 1922

From the war years to the mid-1920s, Marcus Garvey and his Universal Negro Improvement Association (UNIA) advanced a program of racial pride, black economic development, and the return of African Americans to Africa. Membership figures for Garvey's UNIA are incomplete and unreliable, but contemporaries acknowledged widespread black interest in the nationalist organization. Garvey's program and style quickly attracted

"What We Believe" and "The Principles of the Universal Negro Improvement Association." Speech delivered [by Marcus Garvey] at Liberty Hall, 2 Nov. 1922 in Amy Jacques-Garvey, *Philosophy and Opinions of Marcus Garvey*, vols. 1 and 2 (1923; 1925; reprint, New York: Atheneum, 1973).

strong criticism from leading civil rights activists and radicals, including W. E. B. Du Bois and A. Philip Randolph, whom Garvey himself attacked in turn. Garvey's arrest and conviction on federal charges of mail fraud further weakened an already faltering organization. Although his insistence on racial pride continued to resonate strongly among urban African Americans, the rest of his program found few adherents after the mid-1920s.

What We Believe

The Universal Negro Improvement Association advocates the uniting and blending of all negroes into one strong, healthy race. It is against miscegenation and race suicide.

It believes that the Negro race is as good as any other, and therefore should be as proud of itself as others are.

It believes in the purity of the Negro race and the purity of the white race.

It is against rich blacks marrying poor whites.

It is against rich or poor whites taking advantage of Negro women.

It believes in the spiritual Fatherhood of God and the Brotherhood of Man.

It believes in the social and political physical separation of all peoples to the extent that they promote their own ideals and civilization, with the privilege of trading and doing business with each other. It believes in the promotion of a strong and powerful Negro nation in Africa.

It believes in the rights of all men.

The Principles of the Universal Negro Improvement Association

Over five years ago the Universal Negro Improvement Association placed itself before the world as the movement through which the new and rising Negro would give expression of his feelings. This Association adopts an attitude not of hostility to other races and peoples of the world, but an attitude of self-respect, of manhood rights on behalf of 400,000,000 Negroes of the world.

We represent peace, harmony, love, human sympathy, human rights and human justice, and that is why we fight so much. Wheresoever human rights are denied to any group, wheresoever justice is denied to any group, there the U. N. I. A. finds a cause. And at this time among all the peoples of the world, the group that suffers most from injustice, the group that is denied most of those rights that belong to all humanity, is the black group of 400,000,000. Because of that injustice, because of that denial of our rights, we go forth under the leadership of the One who is always on the side of right to fight the common cause of humanity; to fight as we fought in the Revolutionary War, as we fought in the Civil War, as we fought in the Spanish-American War, and as we fought in the war between 1914–18 on the battle plains of France and Flanders. As we fought up the heights of Mesopotamia; even so under the leadership of the U.N.I.A., we are marshaling the 400,000,000 Negroes of the world to fight for the emancipation of the race and of the redemption of the country of our fathers.

We represent a new line of thought among Negroes. Whether you call it advanced thought or reactionary thought, I do not care. If it is reactionary for people to seek independence in government, then we are reactionary. If it is advanced thought for people to seek liberty and freedom, then we represent the advanced school of thought among the Negroes of this country. We of the U.N.I.A. believe that what is good for the other fellow is good for us. If government is something that is worth while; if government is something that is appreciable and helpful and protective to others, then we also want to experiment in government. We do not mean a government that will make us citizens without rights or subjects without consideration. We mean the kind of government that will place our race in control, even as other races are in control of their own governments. . . .

We are not engaged in domestic politics, in church building or in social uplift work, but we are engaged in nation building. . . .

We of the Universal Negro Improvement Association are determined to unite the 400,000,000 Negroes of the world to give expression to their own feeling; we are determined to unite the 400,000,000 Negroes of the world for the purpose of building a civilization of their own. And in that effort we desire to bring together the 15,000,000 of the United States, the 180,000,000 in Asia, the West Indies and Central and South America, and the 200,000,000 in Africa. We are looking toward political freedom on the continent of Africa, the land of our fathers.

Not Seeking a Government within a Government

The Universal Negro Improvement Association is not seeking to build up another government within the bounds or borders of the United States of America. The Universal Negro Improvement Association is not seeking to disrupt any organized system of government, but the

Association is determined to bring Negroes together for the building up of a nation of their own. And why? Because we have been forced to it. We have been forced to it throughout the world; not only in America, not only in Europe, not only in the British Empire, but wheresoever the black man happens to find himself, he has been forced to do for himself.

To talk about Government is a little more than some of our people can appreciate just at this time. The average man does not think that way, just because he finds himself a citizen or a subject of some country. He seems to say, "Why should there be need for any other government?" We are French, English or American. But we of the U.N.I.A. have studied seriously this question of nationality among Negroes—this American nationality, this British nationality, this French, Italian or Spanish nationality, and have discovered that it counts for nought when that nationality comes in conflict with the racial idealism of the group that rules. When our interests clash with those of the ruling faction, then we find that we have absolutely no rights. In times of peace, when everything is all right, Negroes have a hard time, wherever we go, wheresoever we find ourselves, getting those rights that belong to us, in common with others whom we claim as fellow citizens; getting that consideration that should be ours by right of the constitution, by right of the law; but in the time of trouble they make us all partners in the cause, as happened in the last war, when we were partners, whether British, French or American Negroes. And we were told that we must forget everything in an effort to save the nation.

We have saved many nations in this manner, and we have lost our lives doing that before. Hundreds of thousands—nay, millions of black men, lie buried under the ground due to that old-time camouflage of saving the nation. We saved the British empire; we saved the French empire; we saved this glorious country more than once; and all that we have received for our sacrifices, all that we have received for what we have done, even in giving up our lives, is just what you are receiving now, just what I am receiving now.

You and I fare no better in America, in the British empire, or in any other part of the white world; we fare no better than any black man wheresoever he shows his head. And why? Because we have been satisfied to allow ourselves to be led, educated, to be directed by the other fellow, who has always sought to lead in the world in that direction that would satisfy him and strengthen his position. We have allowed ourselves for the last 500 years to be a race of followers, following every race that has led in the direction that would make them more secure.

The U.N.I.A. is reversing the old-time order of things. We refuse to be followers any more. We are leading ourselves. That means, if any saving is to be done, later on, whether it is saving this one nation or that one government, we are going to seek a method of saving Africa first. Why? And why Africa? Because Africa has become the grand prize of the nations. Africa has become the big game of the nation hunters. To-day Africa looms as the greatest commercial, industrial and political prize in the world.

The Difference between the U.N.I.A. and Other Organizations

The difference between the Universal Negro Improvement Association and the other movements of this country, and probably the world, is that the Universal Negro Improvement Association seeks independence of government, while the other organizations seek to make the Negro a secondary part of existing governments. We differ from the organizations in America because they seek to subordinate the Negro as a secondary consideration in a great civilization, knowing that in America the Negro will never reach his highest ambition, knowing that the Negro in America will never get his constitutional rights. All those organizations which are fostering the improvement of Negroes in the British Empire know that the Negro in the British empire will never reach the height of his constitutional rights. What do I mean by constitutional rights in America? If the black man is to reach the height of his ambition in this country—if the black man is to get all of his constitutional rights in America—then the black man should have the same chance in the nation as any other man to become president of the nation, or a street cleaner in New York. If the black man in the British Empire is to have all his constitutional rights it means that the Negro in the British Empire should have at least the same right to become premier of Great Britain as he has to become street cleaner in the city of London. Are they prepared to give us such political equality? You and I can live in the United States of America for 100 more years, and our generations may live for 200 years or for 5,000 more years, and so long as there is a black and white population, when the majority is on the side of the white race, you and I will never get political justice or get political equality in this country. Then why should a black man with rising ambition, after preparing himself in every possible way to give expression to that highest ambition, allow himself to be kept down by racial prejudice within a country? If I am as educated as the next man, if I am as prepared as the next man, if I have passed through the best schools and colleges and universities as the other fellow, why should I not have a fair chance to compete with the other fellow for the biggest position in the nation? I have feelings, I have blood, I have senses like the other fellow; I have ambition, I have hope. Why should he, because of some racial prejudice, keep me down and why should I concede to him the right to rise above me, and to establish himself as my permanent master? That is where the U.N.I.A. differs from other organizations. I refuse to stultify my ambition, and every true Negro refuses to stultify his ambition to suit any one, and therefore the U.N.I.A. decides if America is not big enough for two presidents, if England is not big enough for two kings, then we are not going to quarrel over the matter; we will leave one president in America, we will leave one king in England, we will leave one president in France and we will have one president in Africa. Hence, the Universal Negro Improvement Association does not seek to interfere with the social and political systems of France, but by the arrangement of things to-day the U.N.I.A. refuses to recognize any political or social system in Africa except that which we are about to establish for ourselves. . . .

Negroes Ever Ready to Assist Humanity's Cause

The question often asked is what does it require to redeem a race and free a country? If it takes man power, if it takes scientific intelligence, if it takes education of any kind, or if it takes blood, then the 400,000,000 Negroes of the world have it.

It took the combined man power of the Allies to put down the mad determination of the Kaiser to impose German will upon the world and upon humanity. Among those who suppressed his mad ambition were two million Negroes who have not yet forgotten how to drive men across the firing line. Surely those of us who faced German shot and shell at the Marne, at Verdun, have not forgotten the order of our Commander-in-Chief. The cry that caused us to leave America in such mad haste, when white fellow citizens of America refused to fight and said, "We do not believe in war and therefore, even though we are American citizens, and even though the nation is in danger, we will not go to war." When many of them cried out and said, "We are German-Americans and we can not fight," when so many white men refused to answer the call and dodged behind all kinds of excuses, 400,000 black men were ready without a question. It was because we were told it was a war of democracy; it was a war for the liberation of the weaker peoples of the world. We heard the cry of Woodrow Wilson, not because we liked him so, but because the things he said were of such a nature that they appealed to us as men. Wheresoever the cause of humanity stands in need of assistance, there you will find the Negro ever ready to serve. . . .

We shall march out, yes, as black American citizens, as black British subjects, as black French citizens, as black Italians or as black Spaniards, but we shall march out with a greater loyalty, the loyalty of race. We shall march out in answer to the cry of our fathers, who cry out to us for the redemption of our own country, our motherland, Africa.

We shall march out, not forgetting the blessings of America. We shall march out, not forgetting the blessings of civilization. We shall march out with a history of peace before and behind us, and surely that history shall be our breastplate, for how can man fight better than knowing that the cause for which he fights is righteous? How can man fight more gloriously than by knowing that behind him is a history of slavery, a history of bloody carnage and massacre inflicted upon a race because of its inability to protect itself and fight? Shall we not fight for the glorious opportunity of protecting and forever more establishing ourselves as a mighty race and nation, never more to be disrespected by men. Glorious shall be the battle when the time comes to fight for our people and our race.

We should say to the millions who are in Africa to hold the fort, for we are coming 400,000,000 strong.

THE MESSENGER
New Leadership for the Negro
May–June 1919

The black socialist monthly journal the Messenger, *edited by A. Philip Randolph and Chandler Owen, called on southern blacks to flee the South—that "hell hole"—to struggle for equal rights in the North. During and after the war, the journal explicitly denounced Du Bois for his*

The Messenger, 2, no. 7 (May–June 1919): 9–10.

"Close Ranks" editorial in the Crisis, *criticized most black leaders for their ostensible conservatism, and called for a new, more aggressive leadership. Although the* Messenger *was not the first to proclaim the emergence of a New Negro, it enthusiastically and repeatedly approved of what it saw as a new spirit of resistance among African Americans.*

The Negro needs new leadership. The old leadership has failed miserably. . . .

With one or two exceptions the whole group lacks information and courage. They demanded nothing during the war, and now that it has closed, they can goad nobody for having failed to keep his promises.

In the midst of the war when black men were giving their lives by the minute, Du Bois wrote his infamous "Close Ranks" editorial in the *Crisis* which will rank in shame and reeking disgrace with the "Atlanta Compromise" speech of Booker Washington. Kelly Miller's contribution to the reconstruction discussion so far has been that "just as we have been 100 per cent. Americans during the war, we want to be 100 per cent. Americans after the war"—whatever that means! William Picken's contribution was a "good nigger" exhortation with this argument: "If your mother doesn't treat you right, she's your mother just the same." This was handed out to persuade Negroes that they should not complain about lynching, disfranchisement, Jimcrowism and segregation because their mother country did it. What trash! . . .

The Negro soldier is not asking for rhetoric and praise. He wants justice and fair play—a chance to work with a decent wage, freedom from discrimination on railroads and street cars, theatres and hotels, protection of his life from lynching and his property from mob violence, the right to vote and education for his children. Leaders who have not the courage to demand these things are worthless. Our present leaders are not demanding them. We need a new leadership—a leadership of intelligence and manly courage.

If We Must Die

September 1919

The radical black monthly the Messenger *celebrated African Americans' new spirit and their physical resistance to white violence during the race riots in the summer of 1919. In this article, the* Messenger *includes Jamaican poet Claude McKay's poem as a credo for the New Negro.*

America won the war that was alleged to be fought for the purpose of making the world safe for democracy, but in the light of recent happenings in Washington, the Capital city, and Chicago, it would seem as though the United States is not a part of the world. In order to win the war President Wilson employed "force, unstinted force," and those who expect to bring any similar desirable termination to a just cause can do no less than follow the splendid example set them by the reputed spokesman of humanity. That the lesson did not take long to penetrate the minds of Negroes is demonstrated by the change that has taken place in their demeanor and tactics. No longer are Negroes willing to be shot down or hunted from place to place like wild beasts; no longer will they flee from their homes and leave their property to the tender mercies of the howling and cowardly mob. They have changed, and now they intend to give men's account of themselves. If death is to be their portion, New Negroes are determined to make their dying a costly investment for all concerned. If they must die they are determined that they shall not travel through the valley of the shadow of death alone, but that some of their oppressors shall be their companions.

This new spirit is but a reflex of the great war, and it is largely due to the insistent and vigorous agitation carried on by younger men of the race. The demand is uncompromisingly made for either liberty or death, and since death is likely to be a two-edged sword it will be to the advantage of those in a position to do so to give the race its long-denied liberty.

"If We Must Die," *The Messenger,* 2, no. 9 (September 1919): 4.

The new spirit animating Negroes is not confined to the United States, where it is most acutely manifested, but is simmering beneath the surface in every country where the race is oppressed. The Washington and Chicago outbreaks should be regarded as symptoms of a great pandemic, and the Negroes as courageous surgeons who performed the necessary though painful operation. That the remedy is efficacious is beyond question. It has brought results, for as a consequence the eyes of the entire world are focused upon the racial situation in the United States. The world knows now that the New Negroes are determined to observe the primal law of self-preservation whenever civil laws break down; to assist the authorities to preserve order and prevent themselves and families from being murdered in cold blood. Surely, no one can sincerely object to this new and laudable determination. Justification for this course is not lacking, for it is the white man's own Bible that says "Those who live by the sword shall perish by the sword," and since white men believe in force, Negroes who have mimicked them for nearly three centuries must copy them in that respect. Since fire must be fought with hell fire, and diamond alone can cut diamond, Negroes realize that force alone is an effective medium to counteract force. Counter irritants are useful in curing diseases, and Negroes are being driven by their white fellow citizens to investigate the curative values inherent in mass action, revolvers and other lethal devices when applied to social diseases.

The New Negro has arrived with stiffened back bone, dauntless manhood, defiant eye, steady hand and a will of iron. His creed is admirably summed up in the poem of Claude McKay, the black Jamaican poet, who is carving out for himself a niche in the Hall of Fame:

IF WE MUST DIE

If we must die, let it not be like hogs
    Hunted and penned in an inglorious spot,
While round us bark the mad and hungry dogs,
    Making their mock at our accursed lot.
If we must die, oh, let us nobly die,
    So that our precious blood may not be shed
In vain; then even the monsters we defy
    Shall be constrained to honor us, though dead!

Oh, kinsmen! We must meet the common foe;
    Though far outnumbered, let us still be brave.
And for their thousand blows deal one death-blow!
    What though before us lies the open grave?
Like men we'll face the murderous, cowardly pack,
    Pressed to the wall, dying, but—fighting back!

GEROID ROBINSON

The New Negro

June 2, 1920

The emergence of the New Negro by no means implied a consensus among African Americans as to the best strategy to undermine racial inequality and achieve full citizenship rights for blacks. Indeed, black leaders proposed a variety of often conflicting approaches toward the advancement of the race, reflecting attitudes not only toward strategy but toward issues of class and the prospects for change in American society as well. The following article by a white author offers an overview of the changes in sensibility among black Americans during and after the war.

Before the war, the Negroes of the United States suffered more than a full measure of all the wrongs that have led to the double revolt of small nations and suppressed classes in Europe. Individually the Negro workers, who form a very large portion of the coloured population, have borne all the hardships of their economic class, and collectively the race has been subjected to special disabilities, political, economic and social, such as the limitation of the right to vote and to hold office, the denial of justice, the practices of lynching and peonage, the discrimination of white labour unions, segregation in trains and in residential districts, and the limitation of educational opportunities. Now it is perfectly obvious that every sort of discrimination against Negroes, as such, tends to unite them as a racial group, and it is equally obvious that the appearance of economic differences among the Negroes themselves has exactly the opposite effect. During recent years, the development of economic differentiations has been very marked, but there is some evidence that racial animosity is likewise on the increase; and it is precisely this complication of class and race alinements [*sic*] that makes the Negro problem the most uncertain factor in the future of the country.

The people who are attempting to deal with this situation fall naturally into three groups, as determined by the attitude they take toward the questions of race and class. Certain politicians and an increasing

The Freeman, 1, no. 12 (2 June 1920): 278–80.

number of welfare-workers and educators hold an essentially liberal position, in that they disregard racial and economic divisions and attempt to appeal to black men and white as individual citizens. The second group champions Socialism and industrial unionism, and attempts to unite all workers, irrespective of race and colour, upon the basis of common economic interest. The third group considers white Socialists almost as hateful as white Democrats; and against them all it preaches the doctrine of racial unity, Negro nationalism, and the final overthrow of Caucasian supremacy.

In so far as it may be classed as an attempt at solution, the whole "Black Republican" movement belongs to the category of non-racial, non-economic answers to the Negro problem. Tradition and sentiment have bound the coloured people so completely to the Grand Old Party, that Republican candidates have generally secured the black vote without giving either promise or performance in return. It would be hard to find better proof of this proposition than is contained in the report on a questionnaire sent by the National Association for the Advancement of Coloured People to seventeen Presidential candidates now before the country. In the questionnaire the candidates were asked to state, among other things, whether they would favour the enactment of Federal laws against lynching, and the enforcement of the Fourteenth Amendment by the reduction of the representation of States which disfranchise some of their citizens. In reply, Senator Harding stated that it was the business of the National Conventions to frame platforms and policies, and Senator Poindexter declared himself "in favour of maintaining the legal rights and opportunities of all citizens, regardless of colour or condition." As for the rest, Citizens Hoover and Johnson were as silent as Generals Wood and Pershing. The point is this: in the northern States, where the coloured vote counts, the Negroes will vote Republican whatever happens; whereas some of the northern white men might be frightened into Democracy by too much pro-Africanism on the part of the Republican candidate. On the other hand, the coloured vote in the south isn't worth a buffalo nickel to anybody under present conditions, and can hardly be made so, at an early date, by any means short of another Civil War. . . .

If the Republicans disregard racial and economic lines, the educational-welfare groups go even farther toward universal brotherhood by dropping even political partisanship. Somewhat typical of this attitude are the rejoicings of Robert R. Moton, President of Tuskegee Institute, over the fact that "Although there are 15,000,000 Negroes in this country, not one of them was ever captured in the Federal dragnets which recently gathered in bolsheviks, anarchists and other 'reds.'" President Monton's conclusion is that "the loyalty of the Negro race can never be questioned."

The National Association for the Advancement of Coloured People fairly represents the co-operation of white and coloured citizens in the liberal "appeal to the conscience of America" on behalf of the civil and political rights of the Negro. The Board of Directors of the Association is half white and half coloured, and its membership of 91,000 is about ninety per cent coloured. The *Crisis,* a magazine published by this organization, has a circulation of about 100,000 copies per month, some of which go to Africa. The Association has no economic or political programme, and its appeal is quite specifically an appeal to the righteous; nevertheless, its work in general, and its agitation against lynching in particular, have unquestionably been of very considerable value.

The civil-rights programme of the NAACP is supplemented, on the side of industrial welfare, by the work of the National Urban League. It is the aim of this organization to open up new industrial opportunities to Negro workers, and to give attention to conditions of work and recreation in communities where Negroes are employed in considerable numbers. During 1919 the various locals of the League persuaded the managers of 135 industrial plants to employ Negroes for the first time; and during the same period twenty-two welfare workers were placed in plants where Negroes were engaged. The organization has also declared its sympathy with efforts to unionize Negro labour.

At the last National Convention of the American Federation of Labour, it became evident that trade unionism was prepared to give considerable attention to the organization of Negro workers. Forty-six or more of the hundred and thirteen Internationals included in the Federation already admit Negro members, and the Convention for 1919 voted to bring pressure to bear upon the other Internationals by organizing independent locals directly under the Federation wherever the existing unions will not accept coloured applicants. According to a statement made by President Gompers, the A. F. of L. now has two paid organizers and thirteen volunteers at work among the Negroes.

But respectable trade-unionism—like Republican politics, and the liberal appeal to the American conscience—is by no means satisfactory to the leaders of the second major school of thought on the Negro problem. Here, in place of a liberal disregard of class and race lines, we have the preaching of a class-war in which "the workers of the world," irrespective of race and colour, are urged to unite against their oppressors.

In politics this group is Socialist; in the field of labour-organization, it inclines to favour the I.W.W. rather than the unions of the A. F. of L. The Socialist party, on its part, has recognized the potential value of the Negro vote, and has included in its national platform a declaration in favour of full political and economic rights for Negroes; this party has also made special provision for the spread of propaganda among the Negroes, and has employed three organizers for this purpose. No statistics are available as to the number of Negro Socialists in this country; but, according to the statement of an I.W.W. organizer, ten per cent of the members of the latter organization are coloured; in other words, the membership of the IWW corresponds pretty closely with the population of the United States in the matter of colour-composition.

The chief organ of the Negro Socialist-syndicalists — a magazine with a circulation of some 20,000 copies a month — is characterized in the following terms by Attorney-General Palmer:

> The *Messenger* [he says] . . . is by long odds the most able and the most dangerous of all the Negro publications. It is representative of the most educated thought among the Negroes.

Referring to the Socialist party, and to the National Labour party, which has also adopted a demand in favour of Negro rights, this interesting publication says:

> We have constantly maintained that the solution of the Negro problem rests with the alliance of Negroes with radical organizations. . . .
> Here are two organizations largely composed of white people, who have adopted fundamental methods for the solution of the problems affecting the white and Negro races in the United States. This is not because there is any special love for the Negro on the part of the groups which compose these conventions, but because it is impossible for them to attain the ends and objects at which they are aiming unless these fundamental rights of the Negro are granted to him.

. . . It would appear then that the *Messenger* group is convinced that the solution of the Negro problem is to be found in the solidarity of all workers, white and black. And yet it is very evident that, from time to time, lynchings and race-riots put a rude strain upon the inter-racial creed of these Socialist-syndicalists. Take, for example, this quotation, also from the *Messenger*:

> We are . . . urging Negroes and other oppressed groups confronted with lynching or mob violence to act upon the recognized and accepted law of self-defence. . . . The black man has no rights which

will be respected unless the black man enforces that respect. It is his business to decide that just as he went 3000 miles away to fight for alleged democracy in Europe and for others, he can lay down his life, honourably and peacefully, for himself in the United States. . . . New Negroes are determined to make their dying a costly investment for all concerned. . . . This new spirit is but a reflex of the Great War.

And it is this spirit that, in time of pressure—in the time of such riots as those of Washington and Chicago—must unite the Negro radicals with the supporters of the third and most startling answer to the race problem—"African nationalism." Perhaps this expression will always remain strange to American ears—and then again it may become quite familiar within a few years. For, after all, a rebellious hatred of the white race as a whole is the Negro's easiest reaction to wrongs, most of which certainly seem to fall upon him rather as a black man than as a workingman; this rebellious spirit needs only a common racial objective to give it unity, and that it seems now in a measure to have gotten. The "Negro-First" propaganda is largely the work of the Universal Negro Improvement Association and African Communities League of the World—an organization which claims a million adherents in the United States, the West Indies, South America and South Africa, and announces as its final object the establishment of a black empire in Africa. The following quotation from the *Negro World* will give an idea of the nature of this remarkable movement:

Mobs of white men all over the world will continue to lynch and burn Negroes as long as we remain divided among ourselves. The very moment all the Negroes of this and other countries start to stand together, that very time will see the white man standing in fear of the Negro race even as he stands in fear of the yellow race of Japan today. The Negro must now organize all over the world, 400,000,000 strong, to administer to our oppressors their Waterloo. . . . Let every Negro all over the world prepare for the new emancipation. The Fatherland, Africa, has been kept by God Almighty for the Negro to redeem, and we, young men and women of the race, have pledged ourselves to plant there the flag of freedom and of empire.

Connected with the U.N.I.A. are the Black Star Steamship Line, capitalized at $10,000,000, and the Negro Factories Corporation, capitalized at $1,000,000. Just what these astonishing figures represent in actual cash we have no means of knowing, but this much is certain: the Black Star Line has already in operation one of the multitude of steamers which—say the prophets of the movement—will some day ply between the Negro lands of the world. To cap the climax, the U.N.I.A. will hold in New York during the month of August an "International Convention of Deputies" who will elect "His Supreme Highness, the Potentate; His Highness, the Supreme Deputy, and other high officials who will preside over the destiny of the Negro peoples of the world until the African Empire is founded."

However laughable this language may be, there is no doubt that something is happening in the Negro world—something that can not be laughed down, any more than the Germans could laugh down the Senegalese. If any further proof of this is needed, it can be found in the pages of a magazine called the *Crusader.* On the cover of this magazine is the figure of a black man bearing a spear and a shield, and inside one finds this sort of thing:

> Let us notice a combat between black boys and white boys, and we will see that the blacks exchange two or three cuffs for one. And no single white man will attack a Negro until he is first sure that he has some other help than himself, for the Negro would endeavour to greet him with such blows as only one who knows that there is no other god but God can. . . . Do not fail to teach your children the truth, for Africa is our heritage, the hope of our salvation.

And in another number, this:

> What the Negro needs to know is that in many qualities he is the superior of the white man. He needs to know these qualities and to believe in them and insist on them.

To complete the familiar paraphernalia of nationalism with historical illusion, the coloured people are urged by the *Negro World* to "restore the ancient glories of Ethiopia."

In the face of this movement, American liberalism seeks to preserve its calm unconsciousness of race; even as it has sought to keep up the appearance of moral disinterestedness in the realm of economic interests. And just as the liberals, for all their good intentions, did not succeed in forestalling class-movements among the white workers, it is pretty certain that they can not find palliatives enough to sweep back "the rising tide of colour." The Socialist-syndicalist group, on the other hand, replaces the appeal to racial unity with a frank appeal to economic interest.

The conflict between the class-movement and the race-movement is fundamental and direct. If the expansion of American unionism leaves the Negroes for the most part unorganized, the white workers may rest assured that their coloured competitors will turn to racial organizations—black unions against white. If, on the other hand, the Negro workers can be absorbed into a general labour movement, the race problem may lose some of its difficulty, as, in the course of time, the labour-problem approaches a solution. Racial division may serve the interests of the old order for the present, but in the end it will profit no one but the munitions-makers.

Black Women, Protest, and the Suffrage

COLORED FEDERATED CLUBS OF AUGUSTA

Letter to President Woodrow Wilson

May 29, 1918

Although often denied the right to vote because of their gender and, in the South, their race, African American women engaged in social, political, and economic activism in the 1910s and 1920s in significant numbers. Through the vehicle of the black clubwomen's movement, they petitioned and lobbied for recreational and educational facilities for black children, launched health and neighborhood cleanup drives, and served as unofficial liaisons to the larger white community on matters of concern to African Americans. Increasingly, they campaigned against racial violence in general and lynching in particular. By the 1910s, tens of thousands of African American women participated in club activities nationwide. In the following document, the Colored Federated Clubs of Augusta, Georgia, direct a petition against lynching to President Woodrow Wilson.

Augusta, Ga., May 29, 1918
The President of the United States

Mr. President:
Whereas, the Negro Womanhood of Ga. has been shocked by the lynching of Mary Turner at Valdosta Sunday May 19, 1918, for an alleged unwise remark in reference to the lynching of her husband;

The document is contained in the Records of the Department of Justice, RG 60, Casefile 158260, Section 1.

And whereas, we the Negro Women of the state are aroused by this unwarranted lawlessness and are discouraged and crushed by a spirit of humiliation and dread;
And whereas, we deplore the migratory movement of the Negro from the South, yet we cannot counsel them to remain in the light of these conditions under which we live.
And whereas, our labor is in these cotton and corn fields and rice swamps, and in this frightful hour of the world['s] great war, our sons and husbands are giving their lives in defense of the country we all love so dearly; And whereas, in every forward movement in our national life the Negro has come to the front and shared in the advance and crimsoned every field of strife from Boston to "No Man's Land," for principles held sacred by every true American; And whereas, we feel that our lives are unsafe as long as this iniquitous institution exists. We therefore are asking that you use all the power of your great office to prevent similar occurrances [sic] and punish the perpetrators of this foul deed and urge that sure and swift justice be meted out to them.

Colored Federated Clubs of Augusta,
Mrs. J. S. Harper, President,
#913 Ninth Street

NEW YORK AGE

Campaign for Women Nearing Its Close
November 1, 1917

The women's suffrage movement intensified its organizing efforts in the early twentieth century, expanding its ranks beyond those of middle-class reformers to include white native-born and immigrant working-class women as well. Significant numbers of African American women, in both the North and South, also took up the banner of women's suffrage before, during, and after the war, working with their white counterparts to promote the common goal of the vote for women. The National Association of Colored Women, among other black women's groups, and black leaders such as Mary Church Terrell, Mary Talbert, Ida B. Wells-

Barnett, and W. E. B. Du Bois strongly endorsed women's suffrage. If some white suffragists welcomed black support, they resisted subsequent invitations from black suffrage activists to investigate violations of the Nineteenth Amendment in the South. The referendum campaign for women's suffrage in New York, described in the black weekly newspaper the New York Age, was successful.

Mass meetings, street meetings by the hundreds, moving picture exhibits showing women's war work and illustrating the suffrage arguments, parades, Watchers' Schools, conferences, open-air rallies, hearings before clubs, the distribution of thousands of suffrage leaflets by Literature Squads operating near theatres, movie houses, synagogues, churches and clubs will wind up the suffrage campaign in the city of New York. Suffrage sermons will be preached in many churches, and next Monday every man and woman capable of presenting suffrage questions, will get out on the street corners and present the gospel of equal rights to all comers.

Colored suffragists are as busy as any. They are canvassing the voters and preparing to watch at the polls Election Day. On Thursday evening, Nov. 1, a big meeting will be held at the suffrage headquarters, 2285 7th avenue, at which Mrs. Josephine Holmes and Miss Helen Holman will make addresses.

Colored women who will act as helpers to the watchers at the polls are asked to send in their names or to call at the headquarters to register for service. Colored women are receiving congratulations on the way they turned out to march in the suffrage parade. John W. Cooper who went the entire distance on crutches, holds the record for devotion to duty in the Suffrage Party.

Street meetings will be held during the week with Miss Helen Holman as speaker. Friday evening is scheduled for the corner of 133rd street and Lenox avenue.

SAVANNAH MORNING NEWS

Negro Women Seek Permission to Vote

November 3, 1920

The Nineteenth Amendment may have granted women the right to vote, but it did not guarantee that African American women could actually vote in the South. Some white southerners—both men and women—fearing that women's suffrage had the potential to reverse the effects of disfranchisement, legally and physically resisted black women's efforts to register and vote with considerable success. Although black voter registration increased somewhat during World War II, it was only with the passage of the 1965 Voting Rights Act that black voting rights were effectively protected by the federal government.

Attempt to Cast Ballots

Movement Follows Registration of Over 1,700 in Chatham

Negro women made a concerted effort to vote yesterday but were refused admission to the polls. Their appearance there was something of a surprise to the managers as no previous announcement of their intention had been made. No white women attempted to vote....

Those who have kept in touch with the registration of women in Chatham county as well as elsewhere in the state were not altogether surprised when the negro women presented themselves at the ballot boxes. The numbers of negro women registered during the last few weeks since the passage of the Nineteenth amendment has been over 1,700. As not only the educated and well informed negro women and those who are properly owners were among those registering, but women of all classes. Many people believed that it was a Republican movement and that an effort to have them vote would follow it. This was borne out by yesterday's events.

The number of those presenting themselves at the polls was variously estimated at from fifteen to fifty. It was in any case only a very small percentage of the 1,700 odd registered. Among them were the women who are prominent in negro women's clubs and activities of this kind. The largest number was from the first political district. Accompanying some of the women was a negro lawyer.

No formal protest was taken, the registrars said. By rights this protest would have been immediately made to the board of registrars and not to the managers of the boxes, but they were at the court house during the morning and received the protest.

One explanation of the large registration of negro women voters is found in the fact that leaflets containing "Ten reasons why negro women should vote" have been widely distributed by the negro "Federation of Women's Clubs." It is understood that these leaflets have been sent home by the children attending the public schools. When inquiry was made regarding it at the office of the superintendent of schools it was learned that no permission had been given for the distribution of the leaflets through the schools. At the top of the leaflets was an admonition to register at once and "Vote Nov. 2."

4

Black Workers and the Wartime Home Front

African Americans' wartime encounters with the organized labor movement, particularly the American Federation of Labor and its constituent unions, often proved to be troubled. Numerous trade unions admitted only white members, whereas others relegated blacks to inferior and subordinate lodges. Black migrants who had worked in skilled trades in the South often found their access to comparable jobs in the North blocked by white trade unions. African American workers were caught in a bind: They were accused of being anti-union by white trade unionists who, at the same time, refused to admit blacks into their associations. White unionists continued to view blacks as potential or actual strikebreakers, willing to work at wages below union scales, regardless of black workers' actual attitudes or behavior.

Black workers responded to the issues of labor movement affiliation and exclusion in a variety of ways. Some migrants to the North were genuinely unfamiliar with unions and their goals; others were only too familiar with trade unions' racist policies in the South. In both cases, migrants kept away from unions or even became strikebreakers to secure access to jobs. Long-term black residents of the North, however, sometimes cast their lot with the white labor movement, whereas some southern black workers organized their own trade union locals, regardless of the attitude of white workers or their employers. Like white workers, blacks struggled for dignity on the job and for higher wages to counter the quickly rising cost of living. But unlike whites, black workers had to contend not only with difficult employers and hostile police but with unsympathetic or indifferent fellow workers — namely, white workers who refused to view them as equals. The tradition of black labor activism, then, overlapped with but also diverged from that of the dominant white labor movement.

CRISIS

Trades Unions
March 1918

The NAACP's journal, the Crisis, *frequently criticized the racial policies and practices of American trade unions. Although generally sympathetic to the broader goals of the labor movement, it bitterly denounced the American Federation of Labor for pursuing a course of discrimination and exclusion.*

The attitude of trades unions toward Negroes is well known to the initiated, but seldom have illustrative facts been more clearly stated than in Epstein's excellent "Negro Migrant in Pittsburgh.". . . The author says in answer to a widespread charge:

> In only one instance in our survey of the Pittsburgh Trade Unions was a complaint lodged against colored people taking the places of striking white workers. This was in a waiters' strike and was won just the same, because the patrons of the restaurants protested against the substitution of Negro waiters. In all the others there were no such occurrences. Indeed, the number of Negroes taking the places of striking whites and of skilled white workers is so small that it is hardly appreciable.
>
> They are, as we have seen, largely taking the places which were left vacant by the unskilled foreign laborers since the beginning of the war, and the new places created by the present industrial boom. No effective effort has been made to organize these unskilled laborers by the recognized American labor movement. These people, therefore, whose places are now being taken by the Negroes, worked under no American standard of labor, and the fear of these unskilled laborers breaking down labor standards which have never existed is obviously unfounded.

In only two Pittsburgh Unions are Negroes freely admitted: the Hod-Carriers' and the Hoisting Engineers'. In both these cases "the colored man has proved to be as good a unionist as his white fellows."

Crisis, 15, no. 5 (March 1918): 234–35.

As to other unions the author gives several illustrative instances:

An official of a very powerful Union which has a membership of nearly five thousand said that it had about five colored members. He admitted that there are several hundred Negroes working in the same trade in this city, but his organization does not encourage them to organize and will admit one of them only when he can prove his ability in his work—a technical excuse for exclusion. This official was a man who was born in the South; he believed in the inferiority of the Negro, deplored the absence of a Jim-Crow system, and was greatly prejudiced.

Another official of an even more powerful trade union was greatly astonished when he learned that there are white people who take an interest in the Negro question. He absolutely refused to give any information and did not think it was worth-while to answer such questions, although he admitted that his Union had no colored people and would never accept them. There are, however, several hundred Negroes working at this trade in the city. White members related numerous incidents of white unionists leaving a job when a colored man appeared. Several other unions visited had no Negroes in the Union, although there were some local colored people in their respective trades.

On January 1, 1917, a group of about thirty unorganized Negro plasterers sent the following letter to the Operative Plasterers' and Cement Finishers' International Association of the United States with offices at Middletown, Ohio:

Pittsburgh, Pa., Jan. 1, 1917.
"We, the undersigned Colored Plasterers of the City of Pittsburgh, met in a session on the above-named date, and after forming an Organization for our mutual benefit voted to petition to you our grievances on the grounds of being discriminated against because of our color. We, therefore, would like to have a Local Body of our own for our people. We also voted to ask you for the advice and consideration of such a movement, and hereby petition you that you grant us a license for a local of our own, to be operated under your jurisdiction, praying this will meet with your approval, and hoping to get an early reply. . . ."

The International then sent the following reply:

"Replying to your letter, we are writing our Pittsburgh Local today in reference to your application for charter. According to the rules and regulations of our organization, no organization can be chartered in any city where we have a Local without consulting the older Organization."

This was signed by the Secretary of the International Association.

The Pittsburgh Local then invited the Secretary of the colored organization to appear at their regular meeting. When the Secretary came, they told him he could have five minutes time in which to present his claims. Nothing resulted from the meeting and no written statement whatsoever was made by the Pittsburgh Local in spite of attempts to secure such. . . . .

Another illustration of the difficulty confronting the colored person when he desires to join a Union, is the following: Two colored migrants, J. D. and C. S., painters from Georgia, had applied to the Union for membership in November and December, 1916, respectively. Both of these persons have their families here, and claim fourteen and sixteen years' experience in the trade, stating also that they can do as good a job as any other union man. Each one of these claims to have made from $25 to $30 a week in the South by contracting. The official in the office of the Union whom they approached to ask for membership unceremoniously told them that it would take no colored men into membership. The result was that one of these men was fortunate enough to find work in his own line in a non-union shop, receiving twenty dollars per week for eight and one-half hours, as compared with $5.50 for an eight hour day, the union scale. The second man, however, was not so fortunate, and unable to find work in his own line, he is now working as a common laborer in a steel plant making $2.70 for ten hours per day. . . . .

The following case which throws light on the general situation, and illustrates the resultant effects of this injustice was related by the head clerk of the State Employment Bureau of this city:

"In the month of June, 1917, a man giving the name of P. Bobonis, a Porto [sic] Rican, came to our office and asked for work as a carpenter. Mr. Bobonis was a union carpenter, a member of the Colorado State Union. The first place he was sent they told him they were filled up, and when a call was made to determine if the company had sufficient carpenters, the foreman said that it was impossible for them to employ a colored carpenter as all of the white men would walk out, but that they were still badly in need of carpenters. It was then decided to call upon the different companies recognizing the union, to see if they all felt the same way. Much to our amazement we found it to be the general rule— the colored man could pay his initiation fee and dues in the Union, but after that was done he was left little hopes for employment. Four large companies were called for this man and he could not be placed. As a last attempt, a call on the Dravo Contracting Company was made and as they have some union and others non-union men, they employed the man.

"Mr. Bobonis was not a floater, but a good man. He is a graduate of Oberlin College and is now working to raise enough money to enable him to study medicine."

UNITED MINE WORKERS JOURNAL

From Alabama:
Colored Miners Anxious for Organization
June 1, 1916

Despite the hostility or indifference of much of organized white labor, some southern blacks—particularly on the docks, in the coal mines, and in timber fields—managed to forge alliances with whites and organize biracial unions. Blacks organized for many of the same reasons that whites did: to protest low wages and harsh working conditions, to gain higher wages and the on-the-job protections that unions could sometimes offer, to secure better working conditions, and to eliminate abusive or discriminatory treatment. In the case of the coal fields of Alabama, black miners denounced deteriorating conditions and complained of being "no more than slaves" in the pages of their union's monthly magazine, the United Mine Workers Journal, *which had a national, and largely white, readership.*

ACTON, ALA.

I want to say just a few words through the columns of our great industrial organ; that is, my heart was filled with joy when I read the article from some brother miner in the Journal of the 4th inst., under the caption, "Praying for the Dawn."

Yes, we want a real union in Alabama, and almost every negro miner in the district has sworn never to give up the struggle until we have planted the banner of unionism in every camp in the B'ham [Birmingham] district. We, the negro miners, are tired of our hard and unreasonable taskmasters, as we are no more than slaves, for it is a fact that the contractors get the cream and we are compelled to take the skimmed milk or do without; that is to say, we do the work and they get the money. The thing that makes it so bad is that instead of getting better, they grow worse every day and we have almost got to the place that we are making bricks without straw.

We have some negro preachers in the district who are nothing more than stool-pigeons for the coal operators, and instead of preaching the Gospel of the Son of God, they preach the doctrine of union hatred and prejudice, but I thank God the tide is fast changing and we are beginning to see the light for ourselves and realize the fact that they are only selling us out to the bosses for a mere mess of porrage. We are growing tired of the beautiful promises made us by the operators and we see for ourselves that they are just so much "bull," and I am putting it to you in a mild way when I say we are simply catching hell on every side.

We are today like the children of Israel. They prayed for deliverance, and we are praying for the dawning of new and brighter days, when God, our common Father, will send us a leader—one that will be loyal and faithful and true—whom we can wholly confide in, and if the United Mine Workers of America will stand in those shoes we will hail their coming with unexpressable joy. . . .

. . . But with your stupendous organization working as a unit throughout the realms of the B'ham [Birmingham] district, these unbearable conditions will be transformed into industrial peace and freedom and plenty.

Lastly, permit me to just say a word about the most damnable evil that lives and has its being in every camp in the district, that is, the white brute in human form called the "shack rouster," who rides from sunrise until the going down of the same with his billy and revolver hanging to his saddle, going from house to house beating up negro men and using their women to suit his fancy, and if any negro opens his mouth in protest of his cowardly and inhuman acts with their women they are either beaten almost to death or shot down like a dog and there is absolutely nothing said or done about it save the compliment paid him by the bosses for killing an insolent negro. But I am sure, with the union's banner floating over the different camps of old Alabama, this white brute in human form would have to hunt more congenial climes, as the camp life would be too warm a place for him to live.

Hoping to be able to speak with you again in the near future and say more about the commissionary and schools of the mining camps, I am,

Yours for the organizing of the union,
A NEGRO MINER.

RAYMOND SWING

The Birmingham Case

1918

The National War Labor Board (NWLB), a federal World War I–era agency created in 1918, was responsible for investigating cases of industrial unrest that interfered with the war effort. Opposed to strikes and lockouts for the duration of the war, the Board supported the right of workers to bargain collectively at the same time it sought to maintain "existing conditions." Board investigator Raymond Swing traveled to Birmingham in May 1918 to determine whether the Board had the authority to intervene in a labor dispute involving white and black workers in the steel industry. Although Swing recommended NWLB intervention, board members in Washington rejected his advice. The news hit union supporters, who counted on government support, hard. The Birmingham strike, and the union's efforts to organize the Alabama steel industry, ultimately collapsed.

The Birmingham steel district is economically dominated by the Tennessee Coal, Iron and Railway Company. Not only had this Company the largest number of individual plants, but most of the other companies doing steel work are in a measure dependent on the Tennessee Company for orders and supplies. Working conditions at the steel plants of the Tennessee Company do not conform with the standars [*sic*] set up by the National War Labor Board. Ten hours constitute the usual day. Labor men report that frequently the men work twelve and even fourteen hours, whereas men on night shift work a minimum of twelve hours. The company has a policy, according to its President, of not paying extra wages for overtime. Many of the smaller plants in the district work only nine hour shifts, and some of them pay time and [a] half for overtime. An exceptional few observe the eight hour basic day.

Of the skilled labor in the Birmingham district, about 70% is organized. A movement to form unions of the colored unskilled labor has resulted, up to the present, in the enrollment of about 500 members,

National War Labor Board, Record Group 2, Casefile 2, National Archives, Washington, D.C.

but the organization[s] of labor are unable to deal in most cases as organizations with their employers. . . .

The strike of metal workers was called on February 20th. The trades involved were machinists, iron molders, boiler makers, pattern makers, blacksmiths and electrical workers. The nature of the work performed by these men was not as a rule in production, but in maintaining operation. For this reason the strike did not in an acute way curtail the output of the district. . . . The employers . . . claim that they were largely able to find high grade men to replace the strikers. It is the position of the employers that the strike, save in a few exceptions, has been in all respects a failure, and that, for this reason, there is no cause for interference by the Board. . . .

There is no question that the plants have been able to operate on a basis nearly normal. There is, however, no question that they have been greatly hampered by the strike. . . .

Discussion of Facts

It must be pointed out that the situation in the Birmingham district is complicated by many issues. The long working day is not the only complaint raised by the men. There is a spirit of bitter hostility which in itself is a considerable obstacle to efficiency. The element of negro laborers is one which deserves careful consideration by the Board. It was my impression that a new spirit has reached the colored worker and that this spirit is worth encouragement. In times past the negro worker was wholly shiftless, unreliable and unsatisfactory. Attempts to improve his conditions were generally hopeless. There was a strong racial sentiment among white labor against recognizing industrial equality, and there was in consequence no possibility of effectual cooperation in winning concessions from employers. This has now begun to change. The American Federation of Labor is actively engaged in organizing the colored men and is making a little headway. Inasmuch as nearly all of the unskilled work in the district is performed by negroes, the companies view the efforts to unionize their colored help with great alarm. Most of the bitterness between labor and capital of the Birmingham district results from efforts direct or indirect by the companies to discourage the organization of colored men. The companies are supported by a strong social prejudice, but their first motive is to insure the survival of present conditions and with apparent advantages of long hours.

The case of Ulysses W. Hale, a negro organizer of the American Federation of Labor, is indicative of the difficulty put in the way of organizing the colored men. . . . and on June 7th he was carried away from Collegeville, near North Birmingham, taken to the woods, abused, tarred and feathered and warned to discontinue his work.

There was no complaint that Hale had been actually unpatriotic. There was no complaint that he had incited colored men to violence. The only objection to him was his activity in organizing negro labor. He was about to address a meeting of colored men when two automobiles carrying probably nine men, drove up to the door where he was sitting. One of the occupants of these cars went to look for the proprietor of the hall, probably to warn him not to permit labor meetings on his premises. He returned and with several of his colleagues forced Hale to get into one of the cars. A white organizer by the name of Crough was also taken. The cars drove five miles to Lewisburg and in the woods nearby, Hill and Crough were blindfolded and handcuffed together. The men who abducted them were not masked, but Crough says that he was forced to join them at the point of a revolver. They waited for nearly an hour for another automobile to come and then the two prisoners were subjected to abuse and examination. Crough was able to induce his abductors to release him. After his departure, Hale was cross examined about his work. He was told that he had been preaching the industrial equality of the negro and that this would cause labor unrest, which would be unpatriotic. He says that one of the men told him "You were warned already once; your house was blown up." Here another man spoke up—"What, is this the same man whose house we blew up?"—and the speaker struck Hale on the head with his fist. Hale was told that he was getting off easier this time than he would [next time;] the men left him with a warning that if he did not discontinue his work he would hear from them again. He has, in consequence, given up his position as organizer with the American Federation. . . .

It is an assumption of labor that this outrage was perpetrated by gunmen of some other companies. I believe in this particular instance the assumption will be difficult to prove. I have precise knowledge that a local committee of responsible citizens, calling itself the "Vigilantes," had made a practice of discouraging the organization of negro labor as being unpatriotic. I know that this committee had spies at meetings held by organizers of the Department of Justice. I know that W. Reese Murray, Special Counsel of the Department of Justice, in disloyalty cases, summoned three negro organizers to his office and read to them reports of their remarks at recent meetings. Mr. Murray told these organizers that their activities were within the law, but he warned them not to exceed their rights. He said, according to one of the organizers, that there should be no labor troubles during the war because it would curtail production and that the Vigilantes were watching them and that his office stood behind the Vigilantes. . . .

But the use of gunmen throughout the district is a problem of great gravity even if the Hale outrage and the dynamiting of Hale's house were not acts of company employees. There is no question that the companies have wrongfully used their armed guards to intimidate organized labor, to domineer unorganized labor, to spy upon their men and to break up peaceful meetings. . . .

The labor men . . . say that these men are used to interfere in any way possible with meetings where labor is being organized and they tell of many incidents, possibly exceptional in nature, where these men have resorted to violence. They say that at almost all meetings of negroes recently the companies sent gunmen in automobiles who pointed their cars at the doors of the meetings, lighting it with their searchlights, and noted down the names of all who attended. They say at some meetings, gunmen have entered and dispersed those assembled. For instance, I was given the account of how three meetings of negroes at Tuxedo, near Ensley, had been broken up and of how three meetings of negroes in Machinists' Hall at Ensley itself had been prevented by guards standing at the doors and forbidding colored men to enter. This same procedure, I was told, was also followed at Mason City nearby. At Bessemer the local authorities passed an Ordinance forbidding inter- ference with labor meetings, but the labor men averred that the Ordi- nance was not enforced. At Avondale the proprietor of a hall, a negro woman, received a letter threatening the dynamiting of her building if she permitted labor meetings to be held there. . . .

. . . The gunmen have not tried to interfere with organized white men [involved in the metal workers strike], but have been used almost exclusively to frighten the negro employees. The practice of arming guards is an old one in the district and is followed in many of the mines, as well as at the plants. . . . I believe that there can never be complete peace in this industrial district until the Companies discon- tinue the use of their guards to intimidate their men. . . .

In closing I wish to recommend, in accordance with my instruc- tions, that there is sufficient ground to warrant the Board's taking jurisdiction, and to say that beyond reasonable doubt, the adjudication of this strike will serve to increase the war production of the Birming- ham district. . . .

Negro Organizer Tarred

June 14, 1918

Southern white employers and political officials did not take black challenges to their authority lightly and frequently resorted to violence against black trade unionists. Ulysses Hale, a black organizer from Oxmoor, Alabama, who worked for the AFL's International Union of Mine, Mill and Smelter Workers, focused on the iron ore miners of Russellville, Alabama. During an organizing drive, he and a white co-organizer, Edward Crough, were kidnapped by white vigilantes; Crough was beaten and released while Hale was beaten, tarred and feathered, and threatened with death. In protest, ore miners conducted a one-day strike, but their organizing drive collapsed when the War Labor Board refused to become involved. The white daily, the New Orleans Times-Picayune, reported on the strike in a matter-of-fact tone.

Miners Walk Out in Protest against Alleged Rough Methods

WASHINGTON, JUNE 13.—Iron miners employed by the Sloss-Sheffield Steel and Iron Company at Russellville, Ala., today notified the War Labor Board that they had gone on a one-day protest strike yesterday because gunmen had been stationed at one of their meetings last Friday night. A negro organizer of the American Federation of Labor, they said, was thrown into an automobile, taken into the woods, tarred and feathered, brutally beaten and warned to leave.

The men returned to work after a one-day walkout, but notified the War Labor Board of the incident, and asked investigation and speedy adjustment of their differences. The board ordered several investigators to go to Russellville.

The workmen struck some weeks ago, but returned to work pending arbitration. They demanded more pay, shorter hours and the right to organize. The War Labor Board has since been working on the case.

Negro Strikers Return to Work

October 3, 1918

Southern black workers, some of whom were enrolled in small labor associations, engaged in countless small-scale work stoppages and protests during the war over wages, poor working conditions, and abusive treatment by management. The walkout of Louisville and Nashville freight handlers in Birmingham over the shooting of a black man by a railroad officer, described by the white paper the Birmingham Ledger, ended when officials from the U.S. Railroad Administration promised to investigate. In the end, the company took no action and the leader of the freight handlers, Will Perry, and several other participants were arrested, charged with interfering with the operation of the railroad. They were eventually released for lack of evidence.

Shooting of Negro Leads to Strike
Reese Murray Acts as Mediator

A strike of 250 negroes at the freight house of the Louisville and Nashville railroad was prevented yesterday by the efforts of J. Reese Murray, head of the department of justice. Tuesday afternoon a railroad officer shot a negro who was caught breaking into a freight car and who attempted to run. Following the incident, the negro laborers held an indignation meeting threatening to strike unless the officer was transferred to another division or discharged.

R. N. Hudson, special attorney for the railroad administration called on Mr. Murray asking for assistance and after a conference Special Agent Jim McAdory was sent to confer with the leaders. When the workmen appeared and were told the company had refused to discharge or transfer the officer they refused to go to work and a patriotic talk and appeal to the negroes was made.

They were told they were helping the Kaiser by going on strike and going against their own government as the railroads were controlled by the government. Mr. McAdory assured the men that Mr. Murray would investigate the case and straighten out their grievances. The leader, Will Perry, when he understood the men were interfering with the government advised the negroes to return to work which they did.

HOUSTON LABOR JOURNAL

Colored Women of Houston Organize

May 6, 1916

Outside of agriculture, domestic service had long been the primary occupation open to African American women in the South and North. Laboring in individual homes, black women possessed relatively little bargaining power with their white employers; their wages were low, hours were long, and working conditions were poor. Until World War I, few alternatives were open to them, but war-induced labor shortages changed the situation dramatically, at least temporarily: Many black women rapidly moved out of positions as domestic servants into newly available wartime jobs. The war also afforded some African American women employed as domestic servants and washerwomen in the South the opportunity to organize associations aimed at improving wages and working conditions. Although short-lived, these associations demonstrated the willingness—and ability—of black women workers to take collective action when conditions permitted. The Houston Labor Journal *was a local weekly newspaper published by white trade unionists affiliated with the American Federation of Labor.*

To Protect Themselves against Low Wages and in Other Ways

On Thursday night, April 27, the colored women of Houston met at the Carnegie Library and organized for the following purposes: To organize a Woman's Domestic Union, affiliated with the American Federation of Labor, for the purpose of protecting ourselves against low wages, long hours and insanitary conditions; also to help all organized crafts and to promote the union label.

Some of the best class of colored women of this city were present and manifested an earnest desire to do all in their power to perfect the organization. The following temporary officers were elected: Mrs. J. N. Dodson, president; Mrs. A. L. Feagan, secretary; Mrs. E. L. Banks, treasurer; Mrs. L. A. Pinkney of Galveston, representing Local 14,673, was instrumental in the organization and in an effective manner set forth the necessities and benefits of organization.

TAMPA MORNING TRIBUNE

Negro Washerwomen to Have Union Wage Scale

October 10, 1918

Domestic workers attempting to organize encountered numerous obstacles, including the difficulty of enforcing discipline among their members and the opposition of not just white employers but some black leaders as well. The Tampa Morning Tribune, *a white daily newspaper, reported on one such organizing effort in St. Petersburg, Florida.*

St. Petersburg, Oct. 9. — (Special.)
Negro washerwomen and others who work by the day at housework have formed a union to increase the wages paid for such labor and the organizer, a woman, has announced that any woman who works for less than $2 a day, the union scale, will be run out of town. It is suspected here that some white person has been instigating the forming of the union in an effort to bring about trouble among the blacks. The negro women held a meeting in the negro Knights of Pythias hall and agreed to work for not less than $2 a day and several white families have received notice of the increase in scale which is an advance of 50 cents to 75 cents a day. The negro preachers here have been furthering the movement for a union of the women. The superintendent of the negro school and the negro in charge of the building refused to permit the negro women to meet in the school house as they did not consider this a proper subject to be discussed at a meeting in that building.

MOBILE REGISTER

Workers Strike in Laundries to Get Higher Pay

April 23, 1918

Black female laundry workers in Mobile, Alabama, explain the reasons for their strike in the Mobile Register, *a conservative white daily.*

Those in Walkout Claim About 250 Persons Involved — Make Statement

About 250 laundry workers of Mobile are on a strike, according to figures given out last night at the Central Trades Council hall. Increased wages and shorter hours are asked. The strikers claim that the walkout today will be practically complete. Yesterday the walkout was more or less effective in the American, Imperial, Troy and White Swan laundries. The Imperial Laundry's drivers, it is said, were out yesterday. The situation at the American laundry was not announced. The strikers claim that all workers of the White Swan and Troy laundries were out.

The following statement, officially signed, was issued from the Central Trades Council hall last night:

"We the laundry workers of Mobile desire to state our reasons for cessation of work in the Mobile laundries.

Unable to Sustain Selves, They Say

"We have been unable to sustain ourselves on the small wages received for our work. The inside workers have been working 12, 14 and 16 hours at day for $2.50 and $4 per week. The drivers have been working for a small wage, insufficient to meet the high cost of living. The laundry work has been raised 40 per cent, but the worker's wages have not been raised.

"The inside workers have asked for a minimum scale of $1 per day and the drivers have only asked for a fair and just wage and better working conditions.

"The laundry employe[r]s have had ample time to consider our agreement but they have entirely ignored us. The services of the Central Trades Council were requested by the workers and the offer of the Central Trades Council to arbitrate this matter has also been ignored by the employers and proprietors of these laundries.

"We are protesting against this discourteous treatment and we intend to stay out until our communications are answered and they agree to deal with our committee. We feel sure the general public is with us in demanding a living wage and proper consideration."

MOBILE NEWS-ITEM

Negro Women Are Under Arrest in Laundry Strike

April 25, 1918

The white daily the Mobile News-Item *recounts the events that led to the collapse of the laundry workers' strike.*

Nine Taken into Custody and Fined When Charge of Attempting to Interfere with Laundry Workers Is Made

Nine negro women, armed with sticks, who attempted to prevent employes of the American Laundry from going to work Thursday morning about 6:30 o'clock were arrested by a detail of police sent to the corner of Franklin and St. Louis streets by Lieutenant H. E. Davis, and fined $10 or twenty days by Recorder D. H. Edington two hours later. Recorder Edington warned the women that if they attempted to interfere with the laundry workers in the future, that he would put them on the state docket and give them three months hard labor.

G. U. Potter, of the American Laundry, testified that the woman [*sic*] came to the place early this morning and made threats and tried to dissuade employes from going to work. The women who were arrested gave their occupations as washerwomen and it is said some of them worked in the laundry before the strike. Those who were fined were Sarah Stephens, Martha Davis, Ella Roberson, Carrie Belle Grant, Julia Lawson, Geneva Williams, Barbara Raine, Pinkey Cook and Bertha Williams.

Wednesday afternoon from 5:30 o'clock until after 6 o'clock a crowd of several hundred negro men and women, some of them said to have been carrying sticks, gathered near the American laundry and it is alleged made threats against the employes. A call to the police station for help was sent by Mr. J. H. Bancroft, manager of the laundry. A squad of police officers and the patrol went to the scene and succeeded in breaking up the assembly by arresting ten persons for not moving on, all of them negroes. The ten were tried Thursday morning before the recorder and discharged with a warning. . . .

143

Negro Women Living in Idleness
Must Go to Work or to Jail

October 17, 1918

Labor shortages and white expectations of black female subservience led southern white officials to force those black women who chose not to work for wages back into the labor market. Charged with "idleness" or "vagrancy," black women were required to accept whatever work was presented to them or pay a substantial fine or go to jail.

At a prominent meeting of the legal and military committee of the Hillsboro County Council of National Defense which will be held this afternoon, the problem of the negro woman who lives in idleness, drawing an allotment from the government on account of having a relative in the army, and who refuses to accept employment of any kind, will be considered.

It is expected that a basis of co-operating between the defense council and the police department can be arrived at so that effective action can be taken to stamp out this nuisance, as it is not the intention of the government that negro women who have always worked for a living be supported in idleness at this time. Tampans who have endeavored to employ negro women for domestic purposes have complained bitterly recently.

A prominent Tampa physician who has been kept too busy to even change his clothes during the last six days and whose family are all suffering from illness also, yesterday tried to employ a negro woman to wait on his wife during her illness and could not get anyone to accept employment, even though he offered $5 per day, he stated.

A typical case has been brought to the attention of the defense council in which a negro woman who is being supported by her husband also is receiving $10 per month from the government because her brother is in the army, she having made a false claim that she was partially dependent on the latter for support. Steps have been taken in this case by the defense council.

Negroes to Demand Work at Charleston Navy Yard

May 19, 1917

Some Southern black communities registered protests over discrimination in employment during the war. Denied access to clothing factory jobs at the Charleston navy yard in 1917, members of Charleston's African American community invoked their rights as American citizens to justify their claims to employment. The Savannah Tribune *was a weekly African American newspaper that gave extensive coverage to racial violence and civil rights protests.*

Negro Women Refused Work at Government Clothing Factory

The announcement from officials in charge of the clothing factory at the Charleston navy yard that only white women would be employed as operators, in spite of the insistent demand of colored women in the last two days that they be employed, was published in the daily papers in this city, and has met with instant protest from the Negroes of the community. The statement made last night by representatives of the Negroes, was that demands had been made on the recorder of the labor board at the navy yard for application blanks for employment, and at the post office and the office of the director of labor in the custom house, but the response has been that no Negroes would be employed at the clothing factory. The reasons given, it was said, were those advanced already by officials at the yard, that there could be no mingling of the races, and there was no provision for segregation.

On the other hand, the Negroes claim that as American citizens, in a national emergency called upon to do their patriotic duty in offering themselves for employment at a government plant, they have the same right to employment in the clothing factory as the white people. The further claim is made that the new building of the clothing factory, to be opened June 1, will need 600 operators, and they can fill the building with Negro women, thus avoiding any mingling of the races.

The officials of the clothing factory in a statement last night, say that if there is any discussion in regard to employment the Navy Department will move the clothing factory and Charleston will lose the benefit of a finely equipped, efficient plant that means a great deal to this community in many ways. They indicate that there will be no backward step in their attitude to employ only white women in the factory, as outlined in their statement published yesterday, and that the contention of the Negroes for employment will only lead to a disagreement that will mean the loss of the factory to Charleston. There the matter stands.

The Negroes state that they have made preparations for a determined fight for what they consider their rights. The matter is one, they claim, that affects their rights as citizens of the United States, and they will carry the fight to the highest court in the land to effect a settlement.

The navy yard clothing factory officials say that the matter is already closed; as far as employment of the Negroes is concerned, and they will stand back of the announcement made that there shall be only white women employed in the factory.

Yesterday an effort was made by the Negroes to obtain application blanks at the post office, at the office of the director of labor in the custom house and the office of the recorder of the labor board at the navy yard. A black Negro woman was sent to each place. She was refused. Directly following her a light colored Negress asked for an application blank, and was given one at each place. The Negro leaders, who instigated the requests, immediately asked why one was refused and the other granted blanks. The answers were identical, that in the case of the light colored Negress the impression was that she was a white woman—otherwise she would not have been given the blank. Thus, the Negroes claim it is made plain that the Negroes will be refused blanks.

The Negroes are calling for 1,000 of their race to apply today for application blanks for employment at the clothing factory. They say that one of three applicants may be thrown out by the labor board, and thus at least 600 of their race will be given the opportunity of employment in the clothing factory.

5

Opportunities and Obstacles
in the Postwar Era

Wartime labor shortages had prompted the unprecedented employment of blacks in northern industries. With the end of the war came the critical question: How would black workers fare once labor surpluses replaced labor shortages? African American commentators attempted to assess the nature of black economic gains and the success with which blacks had performed their new jobs, as well as to predict their economic prospects in the future. For their part, black workers continued to take advantage of whatever opportunities they could find to better their circumstances, avoiding traditional, disagreeable jobs (like domestic service) and organizing labor associations to protect themselves against harsh conditions or unscrupulous employers. The white attack on wartime black gains, however, was swift, decisive, and harsh. Black soldiers were attacked, race riots erupted, and southern whites struggled to restore the prewar racial status quo.

An Uncertain Future

JAMES W. JOHNSON

Views and Reviews: Now Comes the Test
November 23, 1918

In the pages of the New York Age, *a black weekly, James Weldon Johnson viewed the immediate postwar period as one of uncertainty for African Americans, requiring greater efforts by black workers to demonstrate their competence to northern employers. Johnson was an African American*

New York Age, 23 Nov. 1918.

writer, composer, poet, journalist, and civil rights activist who became executive secretary of the NAACP, succeeding John R. Shillady, a white cofounder of the NAACP who resigned after receiving a beating in Austin, Texas, at the hands of three white men, in 1919.

Now Comes the Test

For more than three years every thoughtful colored writer and speaker has been dwelling on the permanent effect the war and its outcome would have on the Negro in the United States.

Ever since the United States entered the war many high hopes have been expressed regarding the changes that "a war to make the world safe for democracy" and black men's participation in the struggle would bring about in the status of the Negro as an American citizen. But, before the United States entered the war, two years before, the economic phase of the situation was being earnestly discussed.

We all remember what a revolutionary change was wrought in the industrial condition of the Negro during the first few months of the war. Thousands and hundreds of thousands of Southern colored men and women came North and found employment such as had never before been given to Negroes. The American Negro suddenly came into his own in the industrial world; that is, in an infinitely greater degree than ever before.

We all remember the steady flow of our people from the South to the North and West which these industrial opportunities set in motion. All of the clear-thinking men and women of the race realized the tremendous advantages which would result from the movement; the only doubt in their minds arose from the question, "Can the Negro hold what he has gained when the war is over?"

As long as the war was in progress this question did not cause a great deal of worry. Opportunities opened up every day so fast and so wide that it seemed like borrowing trouble to spend time thinking about when they might be closed. But now the war is over. To-day the question, "Can the Negro hold the industrial advantage he has gained?" looms up big and demands immediate answer. It is now plain that the Negro should have borrowed some trouble by thinking more seriously about the time when the opportunities might be closed; and he should have made better preparations to meet the situation.

What new conditions will confront the Negro in the industrial world of the North in the coming months no one can tell. What new forces will be set in motion no one can foresee. Will the demobilization of the army oust colored men from many of the places which they now hold? Will the alien laborer return and force the Negro out of the steel mills and railroad construction gangs? Will a greater tide of immigration than ever before set in from Europe and drive the Negro entirely out of competition in this section of the country?

Nobody but a prophet could answer these questions, yet it is possible to make a few reasonable forecasts. It is quite probable that colored women and girls who are now doing work which was hitherto limited exclusively to white women and girls will be the first to be affected. Miss Mary E. Jackson is making a study of the colored woman in industry, and she finds them engaged in almost every sort of work. They are in garment factories, shoe factories, button factories, paper box factories, knitting mills, chemical works, packing houses; they are employed in the manufacture of underwear, embroidery, corsets, feathers, flowers, furs, dolls and toys, candy; in fact, they have made an entry into almost every industry in which it is possible for women to engage.

The position of these colored women is precarious because those whose places they filled were white women who were called to more preferable and better paid employment on account of the war. These white women have not left the country nor have they been killed in battle; and now that the war is over and thousands of the dressy jobs of war workers and clerks and stenographers will soon be abolished, it is certain that these women will again seek their former jobs. The situation for the colored women is rendered more serious by the fact that these industrial jobs will also be lessened by the close of the war.

The position of the colored men is not quite so precarious. Most of the aliens who at the outbreak of the war left their jobs to join the colors of their native countries are dead or incapacitated for work. And the question of a great, returning tide of immigration from Europe to the United States is very problematical. It may be that the rehabilitation of Europe will require all of the industrial workers and laborers available; and, perhaps, the European countries will not only discourage emigration but in some measure prohibit it. On the other hand, the economic conditions in the countries of Europe may be so hard on account of the exhaustion caused by the war that as many people as possible will leave and seek easier livelihoods in the United States.

At any rate, this much is certain: the close of the war will reduce the demand for workers in many of the lines in which colored men are now engaged, and the demobilization of the army and some immigration will put a large number of white men in keen competition for the work which these colored men have been doing for the past two to three years. This competition has not yet been felt; colored men have been getting well paid employment for the mere asking, in many cases they did not even have to ask; now in the face of competition it remains to be seen if they can keep the new foothold which they have gained.

The weakness for the race in the whole situation lies in the fact that colored men were given these jobs for the sole reason that white men could not be found to take them. Since this is true, the danger is always present that as soon as white men can be found to take them the colored men will be thrown out. Those of us who have been studying this question have also been hoping that during the progress of the war there would be worked out some sort of inclusive relationship between Negro labor and the recognized labor unions which would enable the colored industrial to entrench himself and be protected; or that the Negro workers would develop a united strength of their own. Neither of these hopes have been fully realized.

A great deal may be expected from the action of the Government in giving consideration to Negro labor as a whole by according it representation in the Labor Department at Washington, and in appointing so able a man as Dr. George E. Haynes for that purpose. Dr. Haynes has a tremendously important task before him, one that will call for skill, far-sightedness and dogged determination, and in which he cannot succeed without the cooperation of all whose interests are involved.

But the main task for the moment is up to the Negro industrial himself. Heretofore, Negro workers in general have not placed a high enough value on a job. I have known colored men to quit their jobs to go on an excursion or to "turn out" with their lodge. This may be excused in part by the fact that they did not have jobs that were worth very much, and that they lived where it was an easy matter to get another one just as good. But that is not the situation to-day and in the North. Northern manufacturers and employers of labor expect steady workmen; and not only steady workmen, but workmen who will do their job as well as it can be done.

Colored workers have got to learn to stick to their job—that is, until they get a better one—and to do it just as well as anybody else, and even a little better. It is only by strictly adopting such a policy that the Negro can strengthen his hold on what he now has; a thing which he needs to do immediately.

These new industrial opportunities and the migration from the South which they brought about have given the Negro many undreamed of advantages. Advantages which have been gained in the South as well as in the North. If he fails to hold on to these opportunities and has to return to the South and ask "Marse" John for the job so contemptuously thrown aside a year or two ago, may God help him.

Then let him clench his teeth and make up his mind that he is going to fight to hold what he has gained. And it is a fight that is as important and will require as much courage and stamina as any he has put upon the fields of France.

FORRESTER B. WASHINGTON

Reconstruction and the Colored Woman

January 1919

The prospects for postwar employment, black social worker Forrester B. Washington concluded, were not good, especially for African American women. Life and Labor was the monthly journal of the Women's Trade Union League, an organization that brought together elite and middle-class white women reformers and female trade unionists to promote women's union organizing in the American Federation of Labor.

Chicago's famous loop district was a riot of color and a bedlam of noise. By the Red, White and Blue, held high above all else, the throngs proclaimed that the Allies were at last victorious. Joy, wild-mad, unrestrained joy was the prevailing emotion.

"What's the matter, Sally? Ain't you glad the war is over?" shrieked one bus girl to another in the dairy lunch, trying to make herself heard above the ceaseless din outside, as they picked up the soiled dishes from the arms of the chairs where the customers had left them.

"I don't know," replied Sally, as she mechanically wiped off another varnished chair-arm with her towel. "I suppose now us colored girls will all lose our jobs."

Life and Labor, 9, no. 1 (Jan. 1919): 3–7.

Shocking, isn't it, that even one individual should be so unpatriotic at such a time? Unfortunately, however, subsequent developments have proved that Sally was correct in her deduction as to what the termination of the "war for democracy" would mean to her and her race. Sally was reasoning from bitter experience. Isn't it somewhat tragic also that what meant happiness to so many should mean to one racial group a plunge back into hopelessness?

They pulled a bedraggled mass of cloth and mud out of a creek of the Toledo River recently. "Why, it's a colored girl," the policeman said. "I didn't know they committed suicide." Her landlady, when interviewed, said that on account of the end of the war they were discharging colored girls from the "decent" jobs which they had secured during the labor scarcity. The suicide, who was a graduate of a Southern college, had declared, she added, that she would kill herself before she would go back to work in a kitchen. "There's no chance for us colored girls, even if we have an education," the unfortunate girl had told her friends. "In the South they try to make us immoral, and in the North they won't let us keep a decent job."

Everyone is aware that almost as soon as the armistice was signed, the cancellation of war orders began, and factories engaged in production dependent upon the continuation of hostilities commenced to release their women employe[e]s. But it is not generally known that in the majority of plants in Chicago the first persons to be released were colored women. If only those were discharged who had taken soldiers' positions, it is doubtful if any serious distress would be caused the colored people; but the fact is that many colored people who had obtained their positions as a result of the labor vacuum caused by the cessation of immigration a year or two before we entered the war are now being discharged as well as those hired more recently. The history of the experiences of colored women in the present war should make fair-minded Americans blush with shame. They have been universally the last to be employed. They were the marginal workers of industry all through the war. They have been given, with few exceptions, the most undesirable and lowest paid work, and now that the war is over they are the first to be released.

It is especially significant that Chicago, which now has the third largest negro population in the country, should be the most inconsiderate in its treatment of the colored woman worker. As a matter of fact, the country as a whole has not treated the colored working woman according to the spirit of democracy. The essential difference between Chicago and elsewhere is that in the other cities the colored woman made some little progress into the skilled and so-called semi-skilled industries. In Chicago, while she did get into many occupations into which she had never gained entrance before, they were only the marginal occupations. She became the bus girl in the dairy lunches, the elevator girl, the ironer in the laundry, etc. Now she is being discharged rapidly from even these menial and low-paid positions. . . .

In Philadelphia the Hog Island shipyards are adjusting their working force to present conditions by letting the colored women go and retaining the white women employe[e]s. Would it not be fairer to retain those of each race who have made good? . . .

The packing houses constitute the only Chicago industry employing many colored women which is not releasing them. This fact has not much significance, because so far as the packing industry is concerned the war is not over. The packers have to supply just as much food to the soldiers now as when they were fighting, and the greatly increased number of civilians and released prisoners who must be fed are keeping this industry running to 100 per cent production. Just now the packing houses cannot afford to make any changes in help.

Detroit, perhaps, stands foremost among the cities of the country in the industrial opportunities offered colored women during the war. Here they were found working on machines in many of the big auto plants. They were engaged in making Liberty motors. It is in Detroit that the Banner Garment Company has been conducting a factory for two years with a working force of colored women from machine operators to clerical employes. Colored women in Detroit earned as high as 60 and 70 cents an hour in some plants. . . .

Colored women were also employed in Detroit as assemblers, inspectors and shippers in auto plants, as core makers and chippers in foundries, as shell makers in munition factories, as plate makers in dental laboratories, as garment makers and as armature winders in insulated wire factories.

There was practically no difference in pay for colored girls and white girls in the same occupation or process. In some cases the colored girls were entirely segregated from the white girls. In the majority of cases, however, white and colored girls were found working amicably together.

Next to Detroit in the advance of colored women in industry during the war comes Newark, New Jersey. While colored women in Newark did not get as far up the industrial scale as colored women in Detroit, they made more progress than those of any other city. We find here a group of 250 loading shells at the munition factory of the American

Can Company, working on a night shift. Colored women are also employed at cigar making, fur dyeing, awning making, shirt making, handkerchief making, as helpers on knitted sweaters, at making celluloid novelties, as helpers on aprons and towels, at pasting and lining trunks, packing suitcase handles, garment making, busheling and thread cutting on soldiers' garments, as helpers in laundries, at top and doll, button and feather making; fur cutting, candy making, picking fowls and pasting labels in packing houses. As an example of the hard work that is offered colored women in some places, the colored women track workers employed in Newark by the Pennsylvania Railway and the Public Service Railway Companies may be cited. . . .

The American employer in his treatment of colored women wage-earners should square himself with that democratic ideal of which he made so much during the war. During those perilous times white and black women looked alike in the factory when they were striving to keep the industry of the country up to 100 per cent production, just as white and black soldiers looked alike going over the top to preserve the honor of the country. Moreover, organized labor cannot afford to sink below the high standard to which it rose during the war.

If either the American employer or the American laborer continues to deny the colored woman an opportunity to make a decent living, the Bolshevik cannot be blamed for proclaiming their affirmation of democratic principles a sham.

GEORGE E. HAYNES, WILLIAM B. WILSON, AND SIDNEY J. CATTS

Letters from the U.S. Department of Labor Case Files

1919

During and after the war, white planters, industrialists, and politicians in the South resented the intrusion of the federal government into labor matters in their region. In particular, they objected to the U.S. Department of Labor's Division of Negro Economics, under the direction of George Edmund Haynes, a Fisk University professor of economics and

Chief of Clerk's Files, U.S. Department of Labor, Record Group 174.

sociology and a member of the National Urban League. Contrary to charges by southern whites, neither Haynes nor the division was in any way radical. The division's mission was to keep an eye on race relations, to discourage racial conflicts in the workplace, and to increase job opportunities for blacks. Nonetheless, southern whites accused the division's black personnel of fomenting discord and encouraging unionization and radicalization among otherwise contented black workers.

GEORGE HAYNES, DIRECTOR OF NEGRO ECONOMICS
MARCH 22, 1919
REPORT
FROM: THE DIRECTOR OF NEGRO ECONOMICS
TO: THE SECRETARY [OF LABOR]
SUBJECT: *NEGRO ECONOMICS IN FLORIDA*

1. On February 19 I was called into conference by the Solicitor and Acting Secretary and the Assistant Secretary with a Mr. Ward, Auditor of the Georgia-Florida Sawmill Association, headquarters Jacksonville, Fla., about alleged unfavorable activity of the Supervisor of Negro Economics for Florida, W. A. Armwood, among the Negro workmen in Florida. Mr. Ward had telegrams and a letter about secret and dangerous actions of Negroes in certain sawmill camps of his state, which actions had been erroneously confused with the work of Negro economics.

2. It happened that Mr. Armwood, Supervisor of Negro Economics for Florida and President N. B. Young of the Negro State College, . . . were in the city and I asked them to come into conference with Mr. Ward, which they did. We explained fully to Mr. Ward the organization of the work, emphasizing that it was cooperative and that in connection with all our committees there were white citizens of each locality, either serving on the committees directly, or acting as cooperating members, and that the work had been started by a call of the Governor. . . . Mr. Armwood had been at all times under the supervision of the Federal Director and had submitted to his office all plans, reports, etc., for approval.

.   .   .

4. About February 28, 1919, in conference with Mr. Densmore, Director General of the U.S. Employment Service, he said that complaints were being made that Negro economics was attempting to unionize Negroes. . . .

5. I had known, favorably, Congressman Drane who helped us in our campaign in Florida last fall, so I went to him.... Congressman Drane explained that the general opinion in Florida about the Department of Labor's work was that it was mainly a union labor proposition and that any complaints which had come from that quarter on Negro economics was probably not due to any specific action of this Service but because of the general atmosphere and attitude toward the Department of Labor....

Also ... Mr. Armwood (Supervisor of Negro Economics for Florida) made inquiries of the Georgia-Florida Sawmill Association in Jacksonville and reported that they had asked him to advise Negroes not to join unions. To this he replied that as a public official he could not do this. In a conference with Mr. M. J. Scanlon, President of one of the sawmill firms operating in Florida, I mentioned this matter to him and afterwards wrote him on that point ... to the effect that officials of this Department could not advise Negroes either to join the unions or not to join them, it being our business to leave private citizens to follow their own judgment and choice....

MARCH 27, 1919
MEMORANDUM FOR THE DIRECTOR, INVESTIGATION AND INSPECTION SERVICE

Information has come to me that extremely radical racial literature is being circulated amongst the negroes of Florida and that secret organizations are being formed amongst the negro population for the purpose of putting these radical racial ideas into effect. It is further intimated that our negro representatives in Florida have been giving encouragement to the organization of these societies.

The Department of Labor does not look upon it as being a governmental function to promote the organization of associations or societies amongst the people of the United States, and if our representatives have been using their official status to promote such organizations it is in violation of the policy of the Department.

I therefore desire that the Investigation and Inspection Service send a white man and a colored man to Florida to quietly investigate the alleged activities of our representatives in this connections.

W. B. Wilson [Secretary of Labor]

APRIL 7, 1919
GOVERNOR SIDNEY J. CATTS, TO WILLIAM B. WILSON, SECRETARY OF LABOR

Dear Mr. Wilson:
. . . I looked hurriedly into the matter of the Bureau of Home Economics for negroes in this State, and found that since this bureau had been established there were conditions which made it hurtful for it to continue; I, therefore, wired you to discontinue same for the present. . . . I am frank to admit that, unless the denunciatory editorials being published by several negro papers in the West and extreme North, against the white people of the South, inflaming the minds of the negroes against the white people of Florida, is not stopped, and the Bureau of Home Economics for negroes discontinued, it will cause more trouble right now than ever, because the white people of the South had a great deal of trouble in the old Reconstruction days with the scallawag negro officers and white carpet bagger officers, who came down to rule over them. . . .
. . . That on account of the inflamed condition of the minds of the negroes who are making a great many demands on the white people of the State, which demands will not be granted, it is best for you to discontinue the Bureau of Home Economics for negroes for some time to come. . . .
I recommend that it would be best for the Labor Department, if possible, to have all of the inflamed editorials, coming out in negro papers from the North and West, curtailed and stopped as far as possible, for some white newspaper in the State may publish these editorials, and the Governor of Florida could hardly call out troops enough to suppress the riots which would take place. In fact the War conditions have so changed the negroes in the South that everything had best ease up in Florida and go as slow as possible.
I am doing all in my power to keep the white people in a good frame of mind until this condition can prevail universally. Of course it may be that I am looking upon this question from the standpoint of a white man, and being a Southern born man I could look upon it from no other viewpoint than that of the white race, for this race will always dominate and control the South. . . .

WILLIAM B. WILSON TO GOVERNOR SIDNEY J. CATTS
APRIL 16, 1919

My dear Governor:
Thank you for your letter of April 7....
In describing the Negro work of this Department as the "Bureau of Home Economics for Negroes", you are under a misapprehension. There is no such bureau, the Director of Negro Economics being simply a special adviser to the Secretary of Labor. The Department is charged by law with fostering the welfare of all wage workers. So far as those of the white race are concerned it of course needs no special adviser. But following the "exodus" of Negro labor from the South during the war, and the importance of avoiding reduced production many citizens urged and the Advisory Council of this Department recommended to me that a Negro adviser be appointed. This was done and a field service provided to make his advice intelligent and trustworthy—a necessity which has not ended with the armistice. This work is for convenience of reference called "the Division of Negro Economics." It is not a separate Negro bureau but always has been associated with and subordinate to our Employment Service....
With reference to your recommendation that the Department of Labor "have all the inflamed editorials coming out in Negro papers from the North and West curtailed and stopped as far as possible," I am officially helpless as you will see upon reconsideration. It is indeed regrettable that inflammatory matter should be published by either race or any industrial interest at a time when friendly relations between workers and employers of both races are so important; but although we endeavor to discourage it, we have no legal authority to prevent it....

SIDNEY J. CATTS TO WILSON
APRIL 22, 1919

Dear Sir:
... Regardless of what the work [of the Bureau of Home Economics for Negroes] is called, it will be deeply resented by the white people of the State if a negro is employed and sent through Florida doing this work ... if men like Dr. Haines [*sic*] and Armwood are to be sent over the State to organize the negroes, it will foment and stir up trouble in this Country.
The trouble about the situation is that your Department is being mislead [*sic*] by Dr. Haines [*sic*] in doing things that are not the best for the section involved and the Democratic party has enough to answer for without also answering for the carpet bag negro Federal

Officers going over this State engendering strife between the white and black race, which the white race will not submit to. I, therefore, hope you will take what I have written, in the spirit intended, for if a negro organizer is put back in Florida, I fear that before two years is out we will have trouble and possibly have to call Federal troops to Florida to put down the uprising. . . .

MARY WHITE OVINGTON

Bogalusa

January 1920

The year 1919 was a year of tremendous labor upheavals across the United States. Many of the white unions affiliated with the American Federation of Labor offered little assistance to black workers and excluded them not only from union membership but from key jobs, too. In Bogalusa, Louisiana, however, established white trade unionists offered genuine aid to black lumber workers. In this article, white NAACP leader Mary White Ovington reports on racial violence directed against black and white labor activists in the lumber town of Bogalusa.

On Saturday morning, November 22, in the town of Bogalusa, in the state of Louisiana, three men marched down the street. One was black; the other two, armed, walking on either side, were white. A negro criminal, one says at once, guarded by two officers of the law. No, there was no look of criminal or of policeman on any one of the three faces. Those men, marching abreast, one black, the others white, were brothers, comrades-in-arms in the interminable battle of the worker for the product of his toil. The black man had dared to organize in a district where organization meant at the least exile, at the most, a death by lynching. On either side of him two white union men, carpenters by trade, risked by their espousal of the black man's cause, not only their lives, but, if they were permitted to live, their reputations. They knew every vile taunt the cheap type of southerner, whom Dixon has made familiar to the world, would cast upon them. Yet together the three men marched down the broad highway of the Southern lumber town.

Unionism is far from popular in Bogalusa. The town is controlled by the Great Southern Lumber Company which this autumn ordered 2500 union men to destroy their union cards. Those refusing were thrown out of work. The Lumber Company has at its command the Loyalty League, a state organization formed during the war, not of soldiers but of men at home, part of whose business it was to see that every able-bodied man (Negro understood) should work at any task, at any wage, and for any hours that the employer might desire. They had back of them the State "work or fight law," and might put to work men temporarily unemployed, save that the provision of the act did not apply to "persons temporarily unemployed by reasons of differences with their employers such as strikes or lockouts." Under this legislation it was small wonder that unionism was forbidden by the Lumber Company; or that, though the war was ended, the Loyalty League continued its work. Returning soldiers joined it, and the night before the three men marched down the city street five hundred armed Leaguers held up a train half-a-mile from the railroad station and searched it for undesirables. Failing to get any one on the train, they turned back into town and proceeded to chase undesirables there. A number of union negroes were beaten up, but their chief quarry, Saul Dechus, president of the local timberman's union, they could not find. They wanted the "nigger" to be handed to them to be lynched, and failing to get him, they went discontented to their homes.

The next morning, members of the Loyalty League saw Saul Dechus, Negro union labor leader, protected by Daniel O'Rourke and J. P. Bouchillon, white union carpenters, parading their city street. Astonishment gave place to action; the three men were permitted to reach their destination, a garage owned by L. E. Williams, district president of the A. F. of L., but after they had entered, the Loyalty League demanded that they be immediately given up. This Williams refused to do, and as he raised his gun he was shot dead. The Loyalty Leaguers then rushed into the garage and killed two other men, Thomas Gaines a carpenter, and Bouchillon. O'Rourke, the second man to stand with the negro, was severely wounded. Dechus himself escaped. Two members of the Loyalty League were reported seriously wounded.

To understand the story of November 22, one needs to know the determined and successful efforts of the southern lumber men in these recent extraordinary years of prosperity, to keep unionism out of their camps and mills.

Fred W. Vincent, writing in an interesting article on the lumber industry in *Sunset,* August, 1918, says: "On the Pacific Coast all logging camps and everyone of the big lumber mills operate on the eight-hour schedule. Of the 70,000 West Coast timber workers, virtually every man holds union membership. The government practically guarantees them high wages, sanitary camps, plentiful food, and the eight-hour day. In Dixie there isn't a single organization among the 237,000 workers. They toil ten and eleven hours. Their wages are from one-half to two-thirds what is paid in the Douglas fir region. Forty percent of the Southern timber workers' wages range between $1.50 and $2.25 a day. Organization is prohibited. Once the I. W. W. tried it seriously. When the gun fire ceased in that small Louisiana mill town, 14 radicals and their sympathizers were dead. Southern labor is unprotected. The majority of unskilled laborers are black. They are not allowed to vote. The whites, excepting the skilled men, are poor, ignorant, and are denied the power of the ballot box because they are unable to pay the poll tax. The South is a land of only one political faith controlled by the business element wholly. The workers are at its mercy."

The timber workers of Bogalusa, white and black, were in this helpless state. Not even the Federal Government was protecting them, all the war-time recommendation and commands of the labor department, which were accepted by the West, being quietly passed over by the southern employer. One Federal mediator, awarding an eight-hour day in the oil fields of Houston, was told to leave and mind his own business. "Organized labor is not recognized in the South," was the statement of the superintendent of the United States Shipping Board, Gulf District.

But since Mr. Vincent wrote his article, organized labor has been at work; and even in the town of Bogalusa—though it is owned by the Lumber Company, and has its Loyalty League armed to show the poor whites and the poorer blacks the virtue of a government of the employer, for the employer and by the employer—white and colored men have joined together to secure better conditions for themselves and their families. They have striven for some of the advantages of the Pacific timber workers, who indeed need an advance in wage less than their southern brothers, for the western timber worker is usually single while the southern supports a wife and children. And they have done this at the risk of their lives.

My first knowledge of labor disturbances at Bogalusa was in June, 1919, at the annual conference of the National Association for the Advancement of Colored People, when the president of the New Orleans Branch of that body reported on the work of his section. Among other matters he made the following statement:

"At Bogalusa, Louisiana, men who had violated no law, but who refused to advise colored people not to join the unions—among them a doctor owning about $50,000 worth of property—were visited by a committee of the district and told to leave town. They were given so many minutes to get out of the city, some twenty minutes, some an hour, some six hours, depending upon their condition. When they asked why this was done, they were given no reason. They carried the matter to the head of the town and he refused to hear them. The police refused to hear them. No local authority would give them any answer except—'what we ask is that you go.' Finding that they could get no protection these citizens came to New Orleans. We took their statements and the Branch strove to assist them. The colored people are fast leaving Bogalusa, and as a result the employers of the town are going throughout the country to get men for their work.

"We have tried in every way possible to get into the white papers something in respect to this particular matter, but not one will say a word about it."

The next word that came to our office concerning Bogalusa was news of a particularly atrocious lynching. The negro's body was riddled with bullets, dragged through the streets to be burned outside the house of the woman who had accused the murdered man of assaulting her. No arrests, of course, were made.

The night before the attack on Dechus, when the Loyalty League were hunting the town for undesirables, more than one negro was beaten up. One of them, George Williams, age 65, escaped to New Orleans and gave his story to a courageous little colored paper, the *Vindicator*, of that city. Among other things he said:

"I moved to Bogalusa in 1907. I worked off and on for the Great Southern Lumber Company up to the time the labor troubles began. In November I met a member of the so-called strong-armed squad and he said to me: 'Why don't you go back to work?' I said that the Company demanded that I tear up my union card and that was the only condition under which we would be allowed to go back to work— renounce our union membership and get back into the old rut where we had always been until just a short while ago when we joined the union. He replied to me: 'Well, you had better get out of this town.' I thought little of the remark at first because I have always tried to live peaceable with everybody; and secondly I could not think that any civilized man in this day and time could think of killing a man because he tried, in a legal way, to get all that he could for his labor. This man proved to be one of the gang that came to my house Friday night and dragged me out and beat me. I know him well and he knows me. I know a lot of others, too, and before this matter is over, there is going to be more dirt uncovered in Bogalusa than the average man would think possible.

"About eleven o'clock Saturday night, as I sat in my home—I was tired, having worked rather late that night—I was aroused by some one at the door. I was nodding and did not know what was happening until the gang had hold of me, dragging me outside. They cursed and swore declaring they were going to kill me that night. They beat me with clubs and sticks until, almost lifeless, I dropped to the ground. I reckon I did not drop sooner because they were holding me up so that they could hit me better. When I fell, helpless, a man weighing in the neighborhood of three hundred pounds jumped upon me and stamped me. I could do nothing but take it.

"I have something like sixteen hundred dollars worth of household goods, and a very large house. I hope some way can be arranged that my things can be taken care of."

This is the story of one man, beaten so that his hands were broken as he tried to ward off the blows. "And just like I know these things," he says, "a lot of other men know them, and it is hardly likely we will all be killed before the cover is pulled back. In fact, if anyone is killed it will make all the rest that much more anxious and willing to tell."

After all, with all its tragedy, there is much of this story of Bogalusa that is commonplace, and nothing about it is more a commonplace than the way in which it is hushed up in the press. William L. Donnels, General Secretary of the United Brotherhood of Carpenters and Joiners, telegraphing to the Attorney General and Samuel Gompers and the Secretary of War, concerning the murder of the three men, said: "We have asked repeatedly that an investigation be made of conditions in Bogalusa without avail. If something is not done at once we are going to take the law into our own hands."

But it is very doubtful if there will be any investigation. Special protection has been accorded the southern lumber companies and it is not likely to be withheld now. And in this the present government is like many another government that this republic has known.

Bogalusa is a commonplace story of the attack upon organized labor by force, but there is one thing unusual in it. Not since the days of Populism, has the South seen so dramatic an espousal by the white man of the black man's cause.

The three white men who died in protecting a negro in that lumber town, marked, let us dare to hope, the turning point in the history of southern labor. For centuries the white and the colored laborers of the South have been taught to despise one another. The slave despised the poor white trash, and the poor white despised the bondsman; and both grew up in ignorance and dirt and heart-rending poverty. Freedom brought little change in the status of labor. By an appeal to race pride, by clever playing up of old animosities, the master class has prevented the white and the black from uniting to secure decent labor conditions. Something of the same sort has been done in the North in pitting American-born against foreigner, but it has been less successful than the southern pitting of race against race.

If they wished, the influential people of the South could stop lynching to-morrow. They have only to recognize the Negro as a citizen, to mete out justice to those who commit crimes against him, to stop the orgies whose records defile our daily press. They make entertaining excuses for refusing the black man his citizenship, but the excuses are camouflage. Far back in their minds is the undefined realization that if white and black laborers come together, if they pool their interests, profits will grow less. And so, we find the Florida legislature, with a fine gesture of contempt, tearing up a Negro petition for better schools, throwing it unread into the waste-paper basket. This is a bow to the poor white, part of the policy of impressing him with his immense superiority over the black. It is a policy which leads to many a lynching, but it also prevents many a strike.

Lawlessness and cruelty will continue in the South so long as this carefully stimulated race hatred keeps the working class apart. We know then how to judge the splendid courage, the spiritual dignity, of the two carpenters who walked down the street of Bogalusa guarding their colored brother.

CHICAGO WHIP

Colored Labor Delegation Demands Rights in Alabama
February 28, 1920

Despite white hostility and repression, many southern blacks continued to press for their rights. The Chicago Whip, *a militant black weekly newspaper, applauded the actions of black Birmingham laborers, finding in their actions evidence of the spirit of the New Negro.*

BIRMINGHAM, ALA., FEB. 16TH —

Commissioner Henry Page Burress received a set back today when he was confronted by a delegation of colored laborers, who in a militant mood, presented their grievance. Mr. Burress was so surprised in what he termed the "impudence" of the Negroes that for once he was speechless.

The men, who were street cleaners, have been somewhat irksome under the typically Southern Policy of docking them for two days work when they missed one. The delegation presented their grievance without the least show of that "bow and scrape" attitude which the commissioner expected.

Mr. Burress declared he does not know what the world is coming to. You don't know Mr. Burress, but you will soon find out where the "NEW NEGRO" is going.

GEORGE SCHUYLER

Negroes in the Unions

August 1925

To northern employers, one of the advantages of southern black labor was black workers' reputation for avoiding trade unions and their reluctance to participate in labor strife. Although undoubtedly true to some extent, numerous black workers during and after the war did experiment with labor organizing and enrolled in unions affiliated with the American Federation of Labor. George Schuyler was an African American journalist who regularly contributed to the Messenger.

. . . It is generally thought by both Negroes and whites that Negroes are the chief strikebreakers in the United States. This is far from the truth. The Negro workers' part in strikes has been dramatized by virtue of the striking contrast of race which invariably provoked race riots. But the fact is that there are many more scabs among the white than black workers, partially because there are numerous industries in which Negroes are not permitted to work, which, too, are by no

George Schuyler, "These 'Colored' United States. New York: Utopia Deferred," *The Me senger,* 7, no. 8 (Aug. 1925): 303.

means 100% organized. Out of 30 or more millions of workers in the United States, less than five million are organized. Note the potential scabs! The great majority of strikes in this country are broken by white scabs. This is due to the fact that the great majority of strikes in America have been in industries where not a sufficient number of Negro workers could be mobilized to break them. Besides there are many more Negroes in the organized labor movement than is usually imagined. In New York there are thousands of Negroes in the teamsters'[,] longshoremen's, foundation workers', needle trades' and building trades', unions. Of course, not as many as there should be, but many more than the race is given credit for. What is true of the number of Negro workers in the unions in New York is true of the Negro in every big city in the country. Contrary to the general opinion of the Southern Negro being more backward, he is the more forward in organizing his labor power. In some cities of the South, one of which is Jacksonville, Florida, they control the district council of the building trades. The task of the future, however, is to carry forward with greater efficiency and determination the work of bringing the Negroes into the trade union movement.

1919 Riots

WASHINGTON BEE

The Rights of the Black Man
August 2, 1919

The "red summer" of 1919 witnessed the outbreak of bloody racial violence in dozens of communities across the United States. Whatever the immediate cause of this "racial counterrevolution"—white disdain for returning black soldiers, labor market competition, white fears of black "crime," or white resentment of black migrants' very existence—riots against African Americans broke out in numerous cities. In many cases, local police did little to combat the violence. In contrast to some past encounters with white rioters, contemporaries observed, African Americans fought back, forcefully defending their communities against attack. Two of the most dramatic instances of racial violence in the summer of 1919 occurred in Washington, D.C., and Chicago. The Washington Bee was an African American weekly newspaper.

The rights of the people have been violated by a class of irresponsible people. The recent riot was started by certain soldiers and marines. When the colored men in the Southwest [section] were attacked, they defended themselves. When they exercised their constitutional rights, they were called "crapshooters and bootleggers." The attack upon colored citizens of every description, standing and occupation began Sunday, July 19. The colored citizens were taken by surprise. Colored women were taken from street cars and assaulted; colored men were also taken from street cars and assaulted, and the only persons arrested were colored citizens. Those who had arms to protect themselves were arrested and charged with carrying concealed weapons. They were carried to the Police Court, and no matter what their defense was, they were convicted. White men who were assaulting colored citizens were not arrested. Soldiers, marines and policemen sided with the white mob. The killing of young Neal was one of the most cowardly murders that was ever perpetrated upon a young man who had been to France to fight for world democracy. At the time young Neal was killed he had committed no offense. Colored citizens were told to disarm, while the white mob killed them. It is said that it was cavalry that kept the mob from invading South Washington and the Northwest colored section. It was the well-organized citizens who were prepared to meet all invaders; it was the determination of the black man to protect his home, his wife and his children; it was the determination of the law-abiding citizens to protect themselves, because the police authorities were powerless to protect them. As an evidence of that, Sergeant Detective Jackson was shot in the presence of his brave partner, while hundreds of the mob looked on. The time has come in the history of the colored Americans to protect themselves against the cowardly attacks of a mob, no matter what its nationality may be. The mob did not select those upon whom it committed assaults. No respectable colored person—woman or man—was respected.

If colored citizens had been appointed on the police force, conditions would have been different. It is so strange that white women are qualified to serve as policewomen, regardless of their age, but colored men who saved the day upon French soil are not qualified to be appointed on the police force. No; no black man with flat feet was disqualified to serve in the recent war. No black man was too short to be drafted into the army, but when it comes to appointing them on the police force, they are weighed in the balance and found too light, or measured with a tape measure and found too short, or they have flat feet. No doubt many a colored soldier who kept the Germans from invading France had flat feet, but the French generals found them to be the bravest and the most courageous soldiers.

The black man is loyal to his country and its flag, and when his country fails to protect him, he means to protect himself.

JACKSON (MISSISSIPPI) DAILY NEWS

Race Riots in Chicago

July 28, 1919

In July 1919, Chicago exploded in a fury of racial violence, the most intense in the nation, lasting five days. The Jackson (Mississippi) Daily News, *a white conservative daily, contrasted race relations in the South favorably with race relations in the North; it also misidentified the NAACP as the "American Association for the Advancement of Colored People" in this article.*

The only surprising feature about the race riot in Chicago yesterday is that it did not assume larger proportions.

Trouble has been brewing in that city for several months, and nothing short of exceptionally good work by the police department can prevent further clashes.

The native white population of Chicago bitterly resents the influx of negro labor, and especially the housing of blacks in white neighborhoods.

On numerous occasions since the first of the year bombs have been exploded in houses occupied by negroes, but very little was said about these affairs in the press, chiefly for the reason, perhaps, that they didn't take place in the South.

And, now that the trouble is apparently about to reach a crisis in Chicago, it is to be hoped that it will receive proper attention from the American Association for the Advancement of Colored People, and other negrophiles of the nation; that they will vent some of the spleen that has been directed at the South on the people of the Windy City.

In the meantime, the decent, hard-working, law-abiding Mississippi negroes who were lured to Chicago by the bait of higher wages, only to lose their jobs, or forced to accept lower pay after the labor shortage became less acute, are hereby notified that they will be welcomed back home and find their old positions awaiting them.

Mississippi may lynch a negro occasionally when he commits the most heinous of all crimes, but we do not blow up the innocent with bombs, or explode sticks of dynamite on their doorsteps.

GRAHAM TAYLOR

Chicago in the Nation's Race Strife

August 9, 1919

Graham Taylor was a prominent minister, educator, social worker, and urban reformer who was involved in the Chicago Commons, a settlement house for immigrants; he became a member of the Chicago Commission on Race Relations investigating the 1919 riot. The Survey *was the most important white journal of political reform and social work of the era.*

The lightning that set Chicago's race antagonisms aflame did not strike out of a clear sky. Only those who did not care or want to see could have failed to be aware that the storm clouds had been gathering a long while, and that the very air was charged with electricity. . . .

. . . Thus somewhat thrown off their guard, the Negro workers continued steadily at work, and great crowds of them resorted to the bathing beaches where sections of the shore were informally set apart for their use, although without any warrant for segregation either by ordinance or statute. Across this watery line a Negro boy on a raft drifted Sunday afternoon, July 27, when the beach was thronged both by whites and blacks immediately adjacent to each other. A white man threw a stone at the lad which knocked him into the water. Some of the Negroes demanded the arrest of the assailant and, when a white patrolman refused, he was beaten, and later suspended by the chief of police. The fugitive was captured by other Negroes, placed under arrest by other officers, and held under $50,000 bail, to be tried for

Survey, 42, no. 19 (9 Aug. 1919): 695–97.

murder. Meanwhile those seeking to save the boy from drowning were prevented by the whites from rescuing him. Then and there came the first clash which led to the week of rioting. The first man killed was a Negro shot by a Negro officer for firing at a white policeman. Great credit is given the police by Negro citizens, with very few exceptions, for standing up to their duty, especially when and where contending with very insufficient force against overwhelming odds in the midst of mobs of infuriated blacks and whites numbering as many as three thousand. This is the more creditable since many of them are Irishmen and had to contend with the most aggressive element from an Irish district bordering the Negro quarter.

The fury spread like wild-fire, first back in the "black belt" where safeguards disappeared as rapidly as the perils to life and property increased. Workers in the stockyards, 10,000 or more of whom are Negroes, were at first guarded as they entered and left, but few of them could get to their work when rioting made passage through the streets unsafe and the street-cars were completely stopped by the carmen's strike. Groups and crowds gathered, grew and loitered. Gangs of white and black hoodlums appeared and ran amuck. Armed men of either color dashed through the district in automobiles and beyond, firing as they flew. Two white men, wounded while shooting up the district, were found to carry official badges, one being thus identified as in the United States civil service and the other as a Chicago policeman. White men firing a machine gun from a truck were killed. White and Negro policemen were in turn attacked and badly beaten by mobs of the opposite color. The torch followed attacks upon Negro stores and dwellings, scores of which were set on fire.

Fighting the Fire

At last the mayor, recognizing the inadequacy of the police force to cope with the situation, called upon the governor for the assistance of the state troops, seven regiments of which are at this writing in Chicago under arms, five of them on patrol duty in the most disturbed district. While a suspension of organized hostilities has thus been secured, sniping continues. Like a prairie fire the flames of hatred leap over all such barricades to other parts of the city, not only where Negroes live and work, but in some instances where they are passing through the thoroughfares, more thronged than ever by pedestrians and vehicles while all street-cars were strike-bound. A colored soldier wearing a wound stripe on his sleeve was beaten to death while limping along one of the main streets. He was heard to exclaim, "This is a fine reception to give a man just home from the war." One cannot but wonder what might have happened if any of these outrages had occurred a day or two before when a Negro regiment of Chicago men, 1,800 strong, carrying their rifles, marched through these same streets on their way direct from France to the demobilization camp.

The situation within the military lines has been temporarily relieved at many points. Negro stockyard employes received wage payments at their homes. Their return to work has been postponed till the responsibility for incendiary fires in the Lithuanian district has been fixed. Deliveries of food and fuel which had been suspended for several days were restored, the wholesale grocers uniting to relieve many families who could not get supplies. The district office of the United Charities kept open, but its visitors were not permitted to expose themselves to the violence on the streets in making their rounds. The playgrounds were also closed. The vacation session of the public school was forced to suspend, being at the very center of the disturbance. The Provident Hospital, served by Negro physicians and nurses, ministered to wounded blacks and whites alike, which exposed them to the threats and even raids of blacks seeking vengeance upon wounded white[s]. The buildings of the Y. M. C. A. and the League on Urban Conditions among Negroes, managed respectively by two very courageous and capable colored men, A. F. Jackson and T. Arnold Hill, have throughout the crisis been the centers within the district for communication and cooperation for philanthropic and civic effort and have promoted understanding, interpretation and mediation among many influential groups in the city at large.

Causes and Remedies

... In justice to Chicago, its citizens and those of other cities should recognize this humiliating experience to be a local symptom of a national disturbance which can be effectively remedied only by the broadest interchange of views and the most active cooperation in effort and by eliciting and applying locally all the social and economic, legislative and administrative, educational and religious resources of the whole nation.

NEWPORT NEWS TIMES-HERALD

Slowly Restore Order Today in Riot Districts

October 3, 1919

In the South, white violence was also directed against black sharecroppers who insisted upon a "fair settlement" with white landholders. Claiming that blacks were planning a violent "insurrection," white Arkansas planters, politicians, and police violently suppressed an organization of black share-croppers seeking fairer conditions in early October 1919. The treatment in the Newport News, Virginia, Times-Herald, a white daily, is typical of the white southern press, which gave the "uprising" ample coverage.

Two More Colored Men Killed Today
When They Refused to Obey Command

HELENA, ARK. OCT. 3—With military control established at Elaine, eighteen miles south of this city, center of the negro disorders, which for 48 hours have thrown Helena and Phillips county in tourmoil, [sic] and other villages where the negro population predominates, the task of restoring order was declared well under way today.

Two negros who failed to obey a command of a military patrol early today, were fired on by the soldiers near Elaine and killed and another was wounded. A fourth member of the party was arrested. Otherwise, with the exception of the firing of several shots, comparative quiet prevailed in the county districts. The white casualties as a result of the clashes, which occurred at intervals since the first outbreak Tuesday night, stood today at five dead and five wounded. With the exception of Ira Proctor, a deputy sheriff, who was seriously wounded, all of the inpured [sic] were reported recovering.

So far more than 200 negroes have been taken into custody by the military and held under guard at Elaine. About sixty arrests have been made by the civil authorities.

The known [number of] negro dead today was fourteen with other bodies reported in the canbrakes [sic] and underbrush about Elaine, where most of the fighting occurred.

A large amount of literature tending to show that the outbreak was due to propaganda circulated among negro tenant farmers, making roseate promises if the negroes would band together. The agitators, the literature indicated, represented themselves as agents of the Federal government, and gave promise of fifty cents a pound to be paid for cotton direct to the small farmer to replace the method of settlement now in force between the landowner and tenant.

Federal troops from Camp Pike and local possemen [*sic*] and State officers [are] on riot duty at Elaine, a small town near here, where race disturbances have occurred intermitiently [*sic*] since Thursday. . . .

The race trouble, late reports indicated, was fomented by agitators, who had aroused the negroes to participate in an organized uprising and the authorities were determined to prevent further trouble by obtaining possession of all firearms in the hands of negroes.

To accomplish their purpose they sent parties of men through the negro quarter searching houses and the outbuildings, where gun caches were suspected. . . .

Wholesale arrests of negroes have been made, according to officials, who announced today that 285 prisoners had been taken to date. Of that number 225 were under guard by Federal troops at Elaine, and 60 had been brought here.

The known white dead in connection with the fighting remained at five, including one soldier, Corporal Luther Earles. Five white men have been wounded. Eleven negroes are known to have been kiild [*sic*] and officials said that number probably would be increased when outlying spots where skirmishes took place have been searched.

The feeling prevailed among officials here today that the worst of the trouble was over.

WALTER F. WHITE

The Race Conflict in Arkansas

December 13, 1919

At the time he visited Arkansas to investigate the Elaine massacre, Walter White was a twenty-six-year-old assistant secretary of the NAACP. A graduate of Atlanta University, White was an extremely light-skinned, blue-eyed black man who "passed" for white. His fair complexion allowed him to interview officials and mob participants in Arkansas until the

Survey, 43, no. 7 (13 Dec. 1919): 233–34.

discovery of his racial "identity" forced him to flee the region to avoid being lynched. The Survey *was an important white journal of social work and political reform that provided frequent coverage of race relations in the United States.*

Associated Press dispatches of early October informed the country in detail of a plot, by a fortuitous circumstance checked, of Negro assassins conspiring to stage a massacre and to murder, without reason or warrant, twenty-one white citizens of Phillips county, Arkansas. Following closely upon the widespread publicity given this account, an investigation was made by the National Association for the Advancement of Colored People who sent me as their representative into the county. The facts thus secured are totally at variance with the published accounts sent out from the community.

The trouble began on October 1, when W. D. Adkins, special agent for the Missouri Pacific Railway, Charles Pratt, deputy sheriff, and a Negro trusty were driving past a Negro church at Hoopspur in Phillips county, Arkansas, where a meeting of a branch of the Progressive Farmers and Household Union of America was being held. According to Pratt's story, Negroes without cause fired at the party from the church, killing Adkins and wounding Pratt. Negroes in the church at the time, however, declare that Pratt and Adkins fired into the church apparently to frighten the Negroes gathered there, and that the Negroes returned the fire. This started the conflict which spread to all parts of Phillips county.

About the same time that the meeting was being held at Hoopspur, sixty-eight Negro farmers at Ratio, another small town in the county, had met for conference with the son of a white lawyer of Little Rock, to pay retainers' fees for the prosecution, in court, of their landlord who they alleged had seized their cotton and was about to ship it away. During 1918 these same share-croppers charged that their cotton had been taken from them and a settlement had not been made until July, 1919. Fearing that this action would be repeated with this year's crop, the Negroes were taking legal means to prevent it. The lawyer's son and all of the Negroes in the conference were arrested. The white man was kept in jail thirty-one days without a hearing, charged with "barratry"—fomenting legal action. He was finally released on his own recognizance.

When the news of the killing of Adkins spread—vague rumors of the farmers' organization having meanwhile come to the ears of the whites—the entire community was at once thrown into a state of antagonism. White men poured into Helena, the county seat of Phillips county, from all parts of Arkansas, Mississippi, and Tennessee; Negroes were disarmed and arrested; their arms were given to the whites who rapidly thronged the little town of Helena. Those Negroes who escaped arrest took refuge in the canebrakes near the town where they were hunted down like animals. According to the final death list, five whites and twenty-five Negroes were killed. Several white men in Helena told me that more than one hundred Negroes were killed, and that in his opinion the total death list would never be known. The Negroes arrested were herded together in a stockade and were refused communication with relatives, friends, or attorneys. Though a Negro might have been able to prove his innocence, he was released only when a white man vouched for him; a thing which was not done until the Negro agreed to work for the white man for a period of time and for wages determined upon by the employer.

Five times as many Negroes as white persons were killed, according to statements given out in the community, and many more times as many according to unofficial statements. According to the census of 1910, there were 7,176 white people and 26,354 Negroes in the county.

When the alleged conspirators were brought up for trial they were assigned counsel by the court; witnesses for the defense were not allowed to testify; no change of venue was asked, although the trials were held in Phillips county one month after the alleged massacre took place while the feeling was still intense. The first six defendants were jointly indicted, tried and found guilty in exactly seven minutes by a jury from which Negroes were excluded. The six were sentenced to electrocution on December 27, for murder in the first degree. In all, twelve Negroes have been sentenced to death and eighty have been sentenced to terms ranging from one to twenty years—all of these convictions taking place within five days.

These Arkansas Negroes like others in certain parts of the South, have been living under a state of subjection for more than fifty years. The system, known as "share-cropping" or "tenant farming," had become so abusive that these farmers felt its continuance meant nothing except peonage.

The basis of the system in theory is this: Land together with implements, seed, and supplies, is furnished by a landlord; labor is furnished by the share-croppers; and at the end of the year the crop is divided share and share alike. The system, however, rarely works out in actua practice according to this theory. When the season is ended the cotton is taken by the owners, ginned at the plantation gin, and sold. The Negro share-cropper is not allowed to know the weight of the cotton which he raised nor the price at which it is sold. Instead of an itemized statement of the goods received during the year from the plantation commissary (where in most cases he is compelled to purchase his supplies), the Negro is given a lump statement generally marked "to balance due." By always having the charge for goods received larger than the value of the Negro's share of the crop the owner can keep him perpetually in debt. There is an unwritten law which is rigidly observed in this Arkansas district that no Negro can leave a plantation while he is in debt. Thus the owner not only takes the Negro's crop out but is assured of his workers for the following year.

Attempts had been made by individuals to protect against their failure to secure from landlords itemized statements of their accounts and equitable settlements; these resulted not only in failure but in many cases in further persecution of the worker. The organization of the Progressive Farmers and Household Union of America was the Negro's answer—a legitimate alliance of colored farmers in Phillips county to end a vicious system of economic exploitation.

A few of the actual cases taken from court records and from personal interviews with share-croppers, owners, and their agents, will show how the system has worked there and the condition which the farmers' union attempted to remedy.

A Negro raised during the season of 1918, 40 bales of cotton. An average bale of cotton weighs 500 pounds, and at the time that this crop was sold cotton was selling at $.28 a pound. To every bale of cotton there is approximately one-half ton of seed which sells at $70 a ton. The total value of the Negro's crop was, therefore, $7,000, and when this Negro asked for a settlement he was told that he had not only "taken up" goods worth over $7,000 but that his "balance due" amounted to over $1,000.

During the same year in Keo, Lonoke county, Arkansas, a Negro by the name of George Conway, raised 20 bales of cotton, the value of which was $3,500. His landlord refused to furnish him shoes or clothing, so that he was forced to work his crop bare-footed and often hungry. The worker's family consisted of himself, a wife, and two children. Although the value of goods he "took up" did not amount to more than $300, when he asked for an itemized statement at the end of the year he was told that his purchases amounted to $40 more than the value of his crop. When he demanded a settlement and an itemized statement his landlord beat him severely and threatened to kill him if he persisted in his demand. For the $40, balance due, the landlord seized the Negro's household goods and drove him off the plantation, penniless.

A Negro who lived at Watson, Arkansas, produced, during the year 1919, a crop of which his share was 14 bales. The price of cotton when his crop was sold was $.43 a pound, so that the value of the 14 bales with the seed was $3,500. The man "took up" during the year goods valued at $23.50, yet in the statement he received the value of the goods received exactly equaled the value of his crop. This man, though paralyzed in his right leg, walked 122 miles to Little Rock, hoping to secure a lawyer to bring suit against the landlord. But being without funds he was unable to secure one.

Phillips county, in October, is relatively unimportant as an isolated case. As an example of the underlying corruption and injustice that will lead to further and more disastrous conflicts, it is of grave import. Unless there is immediate interference on the part of federal or state officials—and there is little hope of the latter—twelve Negroes will be legally lynched and eighty will continue to serve prison sentences in Arkansas, victims of America's negligence and denial of common justice to men.

PITTSBURGH COURIER

How the Arkansas Peons Were Freed

July 28, 1923

The NAACP defended the black sharecroppers who had been convicted in connection with the Arkansas "uprising," pursuing the case to the U.S. Supreme Court. In its landmark 1923 decision, Moore v. Dempsey, *the Court overturned the lower court's convictions on the historic grounds that the "due process clause" of the U.S. Constitution had been violated and that those convicted had not received a fair trial. Although the brutal suppression of the Arkansas sharecroppers' association was somewhat unique in its scope and ferocity, sporadic white violence against southern blacks continued into the postwar years. Like numerous other weekly African American newspapers, the* Pittsburgh Courier *covered the case closely.*

N.A.A.C.P. Issues History of Famous Elaine Riot Case, Which Just Recently Entered Its Closing Chapters with the Release of Six of the Men, Thrice Convicted and Sentenced to Death

NEW YORK, JULY 26—In response to nation-wide interest in the freeing of the colored farmers of Arkansas, sentenced to death in connection with the Arkansas riots in 1919, the National Association for the Advancement of Colored People, 69 Fifth Avenue, New York City, issued the following history of the case.

In October, 1919, the country woke to the existence of slavery in the form of peonage on the farms of Arkansas. Several white men and 250 colored men, women and children were killed in the canebreaks of that state. While the disorders were still going on, a representative of the National Association for the Advancement of Colored People, Walter F. White, assistant secretary, hastened to the scene from New York. Armed with a letter appointing him special correspondent of the Chicago Daily News, Mr. White interviewed the Governor of Arkansas and was permitted to travel into the center of the disturbance. He escaped just in time from the Arkansas mob of white men who had discovered that a "yaller nigger" was investigating their reign of terror.

Mr. White returned to New York and reported that colored people had been held in peonage or perpetual debt slavery on the farms. Contrary to [the] report sent out by white news services the Negroes had no [sic] organized to "massacre whites," but in order to employ a lawyer to obtain settlements from their landlords. Following the riots, colored people were arrested by hundreds, penned in stockades in Little Rock, and after being tortured to make them give false evidence in court, 67 of them were railroaded to long prison terms and 12 colored men were sentenced to death.

Acting upon information obtained by Mr. White, the National Association for the Advancement of Colored People stepped in to defend the 12 men sentenced to death. U. S. Bratton, the white lawyer to whom the peons had originally appealed, was enlisted in the cause. Mr. Bratton, owing to threats against his life, had to leave Arkansas. So the brunt of the work fell upon Scipio A. Jones, a colored lawyer of Little Rock, who carried six of the cases to the United States Supreme Court, where their sentences were reversed on February 19 of this year, and took the other six cases to the Supreme Court of Arkansas, which freed the men on June 25th of this year.

The entire power of the N.A.A.C.P. was invoked to win these cases, [said] Moorfield Storey, former president of the American Bar Association and now president of the N.A.A.C.P., travelling from his home in Boston to argue the cases before the U.S. Supreme Court in Washington. About $14,000 has been spent on these cases and the victories have brought commendation from the most distinguished lawyers, including Louis Marshall, of New York, counsel for Leo Frank, and Charles Nagel, of St. Louis, former secretary of the interior in President Taft's cabinet.

The victories in the Arkansas cases constitute one of the most damaging blows ever struck against peonage in America. Scipio Jones, for the N.A.A.C.P., will file as soon as possible in the federal court, a petition for a writ of dismissal in behalf of those of the 67 colored people still serving prison terms in connection with the riots.

6

Postwar Migration

The migration of the World War I years brought roughly half a million southern blacks to the North. The scale of the migration was unprecedented, as were the often violent racial conflicts over jobs, housing, and other resources that accompanied it. The wartime migration rapidly became the subject of considerable discussion in the press, as black and white contemporaries struggled to comprehend the causes, character, and consequences of this dramatic movement of people. The end of the war, however, signaled neither a cessation of migration nor commentary on it. Following a brief postwar economic depression, even greater numbers of southern blacks—perhaps as many as seven hundred thousand—settled in northern communities. The conditions in the South that prompted blacks to leave, including poor wages, lynching and other forms of violence, inadequate education, and enduring poverty and powerlessness, persisted. So too did the demand for labor in the North. Although racial inequality in the North hardly diminished, black migrants established new roots in their adoptive communities and supported a growing number of black newspapers, political organizations and movements, businesses, and cultural institutions.

JACKSON (MISSISSIPPI) DAILY NEWS

"Chi" Negroes Ask to Return to Mississippi

August 1, 1919

Some white southerners, concerned over the dwindling availability of cheap black labor, continually sought to stem the migration or even reverse its flow through efforts to persuade migrants to "return home." Advancing the proposition that life in the North was inhospitable to southern blacks and that life in the South was vastly preferable, white daily newspapers like the conservative Jackson Daily News *of Mississippi contrasted what they viewed as black prosperity in the postwar South with the brutal race riots and rising black unemployment in northern cities in 1919.*

Newspaper in Telegram to Gov. Bilbo on Behalf of Leaders Solicits Number the State Can "Absorb"

News of the first "home coming" of southern negroes from Chicago, the week's riot center of the north, reached Jackson this morning in the form of a telegram to Governor Theodore G. Bilbo from the Chicago Herald-Examiner, requesting information in behalf of negro leaders of the industrious element as to the number Mississippi could absorb.

Said the telegram:

"Many negroes who came here for war work are anxious to return south if the south needs them. Their spokesman asks us to inquire how many your state can absorb. They are of the most industrious type, distinct from the bad element responsible for the recent difficulties here."

Governor Bilbo will be reached by long distance phone, and his reply is expected to be in the affirmative as to needing negroes. Labor authorities, including the U. S. Employment Service, will probably be consulted as to the number Mississippi can "absorb."

A few individual cases of returning negroes have been reported, but this is the first general movement southwa[r]d.

Negroes Who Come to South Are Better Off

August 24, 1919

and

Find the Southern Negro Prosperous

October 5, 1919

The Tampa Morning Tribune, *a white Florida daily paper, joined the campaign to portray the South as more hospitable to blacks than the North.*

Negroes Who Come to South Are Better Off

Improved Conditions of Life for Race

Planters Anxious to Get Southern Raised Negroes — Better Wages and More Work

MEMPHIS, TENN., AUG. 23.—Plenty of farm and mill work, better wages than ever before paid and improved living conditions await southern negroes who have gone to the North and who now are said to be clamoring to return to the South, according to employers here.

Southern farmers and plantation owners want the southern negroes back. If there were some method of getting in touch with them it is declared the expense of their return to Dixie would be willingly borne. This will hold especially true for the next few weeks, because there is need of negroes who know how to take care of the cotton crop.

But these employers say they do not want northern-born and reared negroes. They would prefer to bring in foreign labor, they assert.

"We would not hesitate to pay the expense of a hundred or more negroes from Chicago or other northern cities to our place if we can get southern negroes, particularly negroes who have gone from Mississippi, Arkansas and Tennessee," said A. C. Langer, vice-president and general manager of the Chicago Mill and Lumber Company, which owns more than 70,000 acres of timber and agricultural lands in northeastern Arkansas. "I think it is safe to say that every southern negro in the north would be brought back without expense to him if southern farmers and plantation owners knew where and how to get in touch with the southern born. We don't want and will not have northern negroes."

The question of how to get in touch with negroes who have gone north was discussed at the Memphis meeting of the Southern Alluvial Land Association several days ago, and the subject will be a special order of business at the next meeting. The association is an organization of bankers, land owners, chambers of commerce, planters and lumbermen of the lower Mississippi Valley formed to serve, in a measure, the same purposes for the delta country as the chamber of commerce serves the town or city. At the last meeting it was said that there is great need for more labor in the lower Mississippi Valley and especially for negro labor acquainted with southern agricultural methods and with cotton-growing and handling.

Find the Southern Negro Prosperous

CHICAGO, OCT. 4.—Exceptional happiness, contentment and prosperity among the negroes of Mississippi is reported by a committee of Chicago white and negro men after an investigation of conditions in that state. The committee was delegated to visit Mississippi by the Chicago association of commerce, the federal bureau of labor and by organized labor to which had been referred a question of aiding the return of southern-born negroes to the South.

A written statement prepared by the committee said:

"The happiness, contentment and prosperity among the colored race in Mississippi is much greater than the committee expected to find. We know no place where greater happiness and prosperity prevail among them."

School facilities were found to be good, churches adequate, housing conditions being improved rapidly and race relations good, according to the report, while the industrious negro is afforded excellent opportunities to become a landowner. No police oppression, imposition or "lawlessness" was found. Negro workers in the sawmill districts were reported happy and contented. . . .

T. ARNOLD HILL

Why Southern Negroes Don't Go South

November 29, 1919

However inaccurate the claims of appealing conditions in the South, the 1919 race riots demonstrated that the North was far from a "promised land" where equality for African Americans prevailed. In the pages of the influential white weekly journal of reform, the Survey, *T. Arnold Hill, the Chicago Urban League's secretary, responded to those white southerners who sought to convince migrants living in the North to return to the South. For good reason, Hill argued, few blacks were persuaded by southern whites' invitations to resettle permanently in the South.*

An anticipated result has followed the wholesale migration of Negroes from the South. Negro labor is seriously in demand, and the South is trying to get it back. Thousands of acres of rice and sugar cane are going to waste because of lack of labor. The turpentine industry is threatened. The milling interests of Tennessee are hard pressed for laborers to man their plants. Cotton growing, especially in the rich and fertile Delta region of Mississippi, and the cotton industry throughout the South are profoundly affected through lack of husky black hands to carry it on. The situation is a critical one and resolves itself into a fundamental economic problem for the South. Realization of this has prompted organized efforts to develop a replacement scheme and, through the use of persuasion, suggestion, and subtle diplomacy, to stimulate a tide of return. . . .

The press throughout the country has been made use of to spread broadcast the South's needs, its kind treatment of Negroes, its opportunities and its growing change of heart on the embarrassing question of race relations. The efforts are manifest in newspaper articles from sections of both North and South. The Chicago Tribune prints:

LOUISIANA WANTS NEGROES TO RETURN.

The Washington Post:

SOUTH NEEDS NEGROES.

Try to Get Labor for Their Cotton Fields.

Tell of Kind Treatment.

Survey, 43, no. 6 (29 Nov. 1919): 183–85.

The New York Sun:
To Aid Negro Return.
The Philadelphia Press:
South Is Urging Negroes to Return.
Many Districts Willing to Pay Fare of Those Who Come Back.
The Memphis Commercial Appeal:
South Is Best for Negro, Say Mississippians.
Colored People Found Prosperous and Happy.

Though these reports have been circulated over the entire North, the actual efforts of the commissions from the South have centered around Chicago. This is due in large part to the fact that the southern states most acutely in need were, during the migration, tributaries to the state of Illinois. . . .

Immediately following the riots in Chicago and Washington, rumors gained astounding currency that scores of refugees were leaving for sections of the South. So strong was the belief in the authenticity of these that one Chicago newspaper sent telegrams to the governors of southern states inquiring the number of Negroes they needed. Southern agents representing the Association of Commerce and the Department of Immigration of Louisiana and officers of the Mississippi Welfare League and of the Southern Alluvial Land Association came north with a view to providing means for handling this anticipated supply of labor. Free transportation was offered, together with promises of increased wages and better living conditions.

Nonetheless, the various commissions were most unexpectedly disappointed.

The Chicago Urban League, in an effort to gauge the actual movement of the Negro population, conducted a brief but direct inquiry into the numbers leaving and arriving in the city. The period selected covered the week following the riot and concurrent with the strongest efforts of southern interests. During this period 261 Negroes arrived in the city and 219 left. Of these last, 83 gave some southern state as their destination. For the most part, they were persons returning from vacations, visiting the South, or going on business. Some of them were joining their families. Fourteen were leaving because of the riot. None, however, stated or gave any evidence of going South to work.

. . . Personal interviews with Negroes now living in the North, however, revealed to the delegation the fact that there exists among the migrants a pronounced indisposition to return to those conditions, in revolt against which they left two years ago. . . .

Accordingly an effort was made by the Chicago Urban League to ascertain the precise state of affairs as viewed by the people most concerned. This was done through questioning hundreds of Negroes living in the South as to their opinions regarding improved relationships. Replies to this query are of this nature:

I fail to see any improvement.

There has been no change for the better.

Why, conditions are worse than ever.

Anyone who says conditions now are better than before the war is crazy.

Some deceitful, lying Negroes may say times are better, but he would at the same time know that he was not telling the truth.

Haven't you been hearing more reports of lynching of Negroes than you ever did in your life since the war?

Ain't all the judges, all the police and constables, all the juries white men as ever? Does the word of a Negro count for more now than it did before the war? Don't white men insult our wives and daughters and sisters and get off at it, unless when we take the law into our own hand and punish them for it ourselves, and get lynched for protecting our own just as often as ever?

How much more schooling from public funds do our children get now than they got before the war? How much more do we have to say now than we had to say before the war, about the way the taxes we pay shall be spent for schools, or for salaries, or for anything connected with administration and government? Why even the colored man in Caddo parish who subscribed for $100,000 in Liberty bonds and bought lots of War Saving stamps, and others who bought less, but in the hundreds and thousands of the bonds and War Saving stamps, have no more to say about affairs now than they ever had. Where then, is the improvement?

There has been no change. The Lincoln League organized in this city has been denounced by the white newspapers as a movement that will cause trouble, and the National Association for the Advancement of Colored People, and the Urban league of various cities have been called "strife breeders["] and meddlers in southern affairs, Jim Crow accommodations are just the same as ever. If there is any change for the better, I can't see it.

In only one thing do I see greater efforts being made to better conditions for Negroes here, and that is along public educational lines. The state and parish school authorities are giving more attention to the needs of colored people for primary schools. A number of parishes have planned for additional primary schools and for better pay for colored teachers. The average pay has been $20 per month for an average of four months' term. It is proposed in about twenty of the sixty-four parishes of the state to extend the term to six months and to increase the average pay of colored teachers to $30 per month. Some of these twenty parishes are proposing to pay colored primary teachers as much as $40 per month and to run the colored schools of that character as long as eight months. In the cities like New Orleans, Shreveport, Alexandria, Monroe, Baton Rouge, Lake Charles, Natchitoches, and one or two others, the pay of colored teachers and the terms of the school have always been better than in the rest of the state, and offered better facilities in the matter of equipment for the work. As you know, however, even in these places conditions have not been half as good for colored as for white people, by comparison either in buildings used, in equipment, in pay of teachers, or in the number of schools or grades.

Colored laborers are getting better pay on the plantations and farms, but no shorter hours, than before the war, and plantation and farm hands have as usual no rent to pay for the cabins occupied and the garden spots given them on which to grow vegetables. They can get credit for provisions, etc., at the plantation store, but contract is understood or written to bind the laborer to work, and not to leave. Share-workers and tenants raising cane or cotton or rice are advanced tools, implements, mules, etc., to work the land when needed, but they are not allowed weighters at the scales or representatives to check the weighing of their produce.

It is ridiculous, not to say absurd, for any Negro to say he finds conditions better here. Don't you remember that Negroes answering an invitation to meet the welfare committee of white men not long ago were told as soon as they got into the meeting place that the committee was ready to hear what Negroes wanted, but that the question of the Negro's right to exercise the right of voting would not be allowed to be discussed at all, and that that must be agreed to before any discussion whatever would be entertained, and that the Negroes left the meeting place without a chance to demand the one main thing that they wished to enjoy?

Though here and there throughout the South improvement is reported, southern Negroes living in the North are not returning South. On the contrary, there is still a small but steady stream to the industrial centers of the North. A letter strikingly setting forth the

present attitude among Negroes will explain what many of those solic-
iting labor assert that they cannot understand:

Editor of the Chicago Defender:

I notice that the town is flooded with representatives from various
parts of the South trying to persuade our people to return. They are
offering good housing conditions and high salaries as an incentive.
For twenty years, I taught school in the state of Mississippi and with
all things equal, would return there never again to leave, but my
twenty years of experience taught me that even those who are supposed to enforce the law in that state had no conception of its func-
tions and were themselves its greatest violators.

After twenty years of seeing my people lynched for any offense
from spitting on the sidewalk to stealing a mule, I made up my mind
that I would turn the prow of my ship towards the part of the country where the people at least made a pretense at being civilized. You
may say for me through your paper, that when a man's home is
sacred; when he can protect the virtue of his wife and daughter
against the brutal lust of his alleged superiors; when he can sleep at
night without the fear of being visited by the Ku Klux Klan because
of refusal to take off his hat while passing an overseer, then I will be
willing to return to Mississippi.

(Signed) "A SUBSCRIBER."

The failure of this section to attract Negroes is not surprising. The
promises of fairer treatment and unrestricted economic development
are powerless because they are barren. Negroes know they are barren. The good intentioned white persons of the South in serious
moments confess their own impotence to deal with community problems. They are, unfortunately, as helpless as Negroes themselves in
changing conditions. It is possible that with the present restraints on
immigration and the persistent determination of southern Negroes to
remain away from home, some of these recalcitrant sections will be
shocked into a change of heart by the force of economic necessity.

BUFFALO AMERICAN

Mighty Exodus Continues; Cause Not Economic

July 22, 1920

The New York African American weekly the Buffalo American *joined the debate on the causes of the continuing migration, downplaying economic conditions and emphasizing racial violence.*

CHICAGO, JULY 21.—There is another mighty exodus of the Negro on from the South. The chief cause this time is not economic, although practically all who come are able to get work, but the movement is due to an epidemic of intimidation and lynching. Since the first of July there has been an astounding epidemic of murder and lynching in several sections of the South.

The Associated Negro Press is carefully investigating the conditions from every angle. According to the Memphis Times, Colored people are leaving the South at the rate of more than 100 a day. This is frankly very conservative. A leading professional man from Mississippi, who has just reached Chicago, stated that the people are leaving at the rate of more than 1,500 a day.

The newspapers of the country, daily and otherwise, had not ceased commenting editorially on the semi-annual report of Dr. Robert R. Morton [Moton] of Tuskegee Institute, as gathered by Prof. Monroe N. Work of the research department, on lynchings for 1920— where an appreciable decrease is shown—when the trouble started.

James Spencer, a postal clerk, Meridian, Miss., who had an altercation with a white traveling postal clerk, was taken from the officers, and "quietly" lynched. He leaves a wife and two children. Says the Meridian Star of July 6th: "The killing of the Negro was the quietest and most orderly lynching that ever took place in this section. Not an inkling of any intention to deal out summary vengeance having been allowed to become known and the identity of the man who did the work is a profound mystery which probably will never be solved." While the whites are remaining "mystified," thousands of people, many of them with large property holdings, the accumulation of a lifetime, are leaving Mississippi.

A white policeman shot and killed two Negro firemen in Elberton, Ga., July 1st; Ed. Rosch was "shot to death by a posse of farmers nea

Roxboro, Va.," July 6th; Irving and Herman Arthur were mobbed and burned at the stake in Paris, Tex., July 6th, and thus goes the great American pastime of human slaughter.

Scattered newspapers, here and there, speak out against lynching, but it goes merrily on, and the people do not know what the next day will bring. "There is never any justification of lynching," says the Raleigh Observer, and "Where the law is respected, and it should be respected everywhere, there is no reason for mob," says the Anniston, Ala., Star. The big fact is: The Law is Not Respected. The Albany (N. Y.) Press declares: "Primarily the weakness and incapacity of local officers of the law are to blame for lynching. Thirty seconds' use of a machine gun might cost some lives, but it would enforce respect for law and for civilization, and it ought to be applied."

BUILDING A NEW LIFE IN THE NORTH

CHARLES S. JOHNSON

These "Colored" United States
December 1923

Black sociologist and Urban League editor Charles S. Johnson was intimately familiar with Chicago, having studied and written about the city while working for the Chicago Commission on Race Relations following the 1919 race riot. His contribution to the Messenger's *"These 'Colored' United States" series—which examined black life in many states—balances the positive gains migrants made with warnings about the persistent "race question" reflected in racial tensions and economic competition.*

... Chicago is in more than one sense the colored capital and in every sense the top of the world for the bruised, crushed, and thwarted manhood of the south. In ten years its colored population jumped from 44,000 to 109,000, an increase of 148 per cent. Here they are in open country and on their metal. In a slice of the city between nineteen blocks live 92,000 of them, nauseated by the stench of the stockyards on the west and revived again by the refreshing breezes of Lake

"Illinois: Mecca of the Migrant Mob," *The Messenger,* 5, no. 12 (Dec. 1923): 928, 933.

Michigan on the east. Forward and effective in politics, they boast of three aldermen at various times, one the floor leader for the administration, a half-dozen state representatives, assistant state's attorneys, a traction attorney for the city drawing a salary of $25,000 a year and a standing army of smaller political appointees. Their combined strength elected one mayor and now threatens to send a representative to Congress. It is indeed nearer to that body than any other section having achieved, through their enforced concentration, one congressional district in which they out-number their white neighbors four to one. Although Republicans by birth they have shown, as in a recent election, that they could break ranks when their interests were threatened.

Here also is the home of the world's greatest weekly with a circulation of more than a hundred thousand and a plant valued at as many dollars; the Liberty Life Insurance Company with $3,500,000 worth of insurance in force after two years' work, the only such institution in the north; two banks; two hospitals; 200 churches ranging from the air-tight store fronts of illiterate cults, dissenters and transplanted southern churches to the imposing structure of the Olivet Baptist Church with a membership of ten thousand; and 1,800 business establishments, varying in size and characteristics from nondescript fly-traps called restaurants to the dignified Overton Building.

These are its boasts. Besides, it points with pride to the physician who made the first successful operation on the human heart, indeed, to Jean De Baptiste, Pointe de Saible, San Domingo—a Negro, the very first settled in Chicago, to the largest number of successful young Negroes of any city in the country. Other things make it the capital. It is the headquarters of the peripatetic Knights of the Whiskbroom—the generic George; of the largest independent Negro labor union in the country; and of the fighting Eighth Illinois Regiment with a colonel who went further into service than the gentlemen in Washington intended.

The story of the rise of Negroes in Chicago has its high lights and deep shadows. Fifteen years ago over 60 per cent of all those working were engaged in domestic and personal service. There was nothing else to do. Then the fashion changed in servants as Irish and Swedish and German tides came on. An unfortunate experience with the unions lost for them the best positions in their traditional strongholds as waiters and poisoned their minds against organized labor. Racial exclusiveness, tradition and inexperience, kept them out of industry. Then a strike at the stockyards and the employers miraculously and suddenly discovered their untried genius, while the unions elected to regard them as deliberate miscreants lowering wage standards by design and taking white men's jobs. Smoldering resentment!

When the war brought another shortage they came in again, this time in a torrent. The migration to Chicago has continued to this day, and industry has absorbed fully 80 per cent of the working members. They have overrun the confines of the old area and spread south in spite of the organized opposition of Hyde Park and Kenwood, where objection was registered with sixty bombs in a period of two years. They have bought homes and put money in the bank. Three banks alone have $3,150,000 of Negro money on deposit. One bank has 4,000 depositors. One can make money in Chicago. This is its most respectable attraction.

The second ward is both a political unit and an expression used to characterize an exclusive residential area. It is an institution in itself. On one corner once lived the wealthy first residents, now departed for the north shore; at another, the city's protected red light district, dispersed by a wave of reform and driven into the neighborhoods of the Negroes to be enumerated by the reform papers and purity leagues in their convincing statistics on the "frightful immorality of the Black Belt."

No one escapes Chicago without an impression of State Street, in the second ward. Tawdry stretches of brick and frame decrepitude, leaning in rather discordant obliquity, here and there snapped into order by the rigidly erect lines of a new building. Crowds—almost static crowds—a rich but impossible mixture. Each strain of this enforced homogeneity must set up its own antitoxin of indifference, for "the stroll" appeals in motley indiscriminateness to the Negro in Chicago. . . .

The race question is a big issue in Chicago as well as the state. That is because relations are not fixed, and they are not fixed because Chicago is the open ground for myriad transplanted traditions. Sentiment shifts with majorities and recently the migration of whites from the south has almost equalled that of the Negroes.

These authorities on the character and methods of handling of the Negro race are most advantageously distributed from the point of view of peaceful penetration. One stronghold is the press. The Chicago *Tribune* is a scourge, though perhaps no worse than some of the others who with the brave hundred percenters and the Nordics by fiat and the propaganda of protective associations are quite capable of lashing the low-browed graduates of the stockyards, the moron population, job-scared aliens, the innumerable gangs organized as athletic clubs and the city's massive criminal fringe to a state of murder lust, and lulling the respectable into blind complacency.

Economic competition is severe. It is severe because the groups in contact are so nearly equal. Combine with this the tricks of employers to get the cheapest labor, the tricks of labor to keep Negroes out of white men's jobs, talk mysteriously about sex and black and tan cabarets, and the deed is done. . . .

GEORGE E. HAYNES

Negro Migration: Its Effect on Family and Community Life in the North

October 1924

The postwar North continued to offer African Americans economic, political, social, and educational opportunities that the postwar South denied them. Few observers, however, could miss the discriminatory treatment blacks in the North faced in the job market, in labor unions, in schools, and in other aspects of urban life. Despite the conditions they found themselves in, southern migrants built homes, churches, theaters, businesses, fraternal lodges, and even unions in their new communities. White and black journalists, scholars, and activists attempted to analyze the position of migrants in the North, with an eye not only toward understanding the migration and the migrants but also to helping the migrants adjust to urban life or inspiring them to challenge racial inequality there. Writing in the pages of Opportunity, *the monthly journal of the National Urban League, George Edmund Haynes, formerly with the U.S. Labor Department's Division of Negro Economics, offered this assessment of the characteristics of different types of migrants, northern black institutions, and the migration's impact on northern white communities.*

Opportunity, 2, no. 22 (Oct. 1924): 303–6.

Types of Migrants

The types of Negro migrants are interesting. In 1916 and 1917, the earlier years of the present migration, the majority of the newcomers were men—particularly detached men—either men without families or men who would not venture to bring their families with them into an unknown country. Included among them were a great many younger men, with the "floaters" and ne'er do wells, who had been easily attracted away from southern towns and cities by the stories of easy work at high wages and by free transportation offered promiscuously by labor agents and railroad companies. A second class was made up of a large number of single women, detached from their families, who came because of the large opportunities for remunerative work, particularly in domestic service.

These gradually were accompanied and followed by the third type, the substantial laboring man of unskilled or semi-skilled abilities. For the most part these men either brought their families, soon married, or sent for their families as soon as they could find remunerative employment. Fourth, with parts of such families as fathers and sons had left behind came a great many broken families—widows with children, attracted by the opportunities for an education for the children in public schools and wages in domestic service. There came also the aged relatives of the wage earning men and women of families. As those in the larger southern cities and towns moved on to the North, others moved in from the hamlets and rural districts to fill their places and to swell the proportions. Thus much of the movement was by successive stages.

Beginning about 1919 those who had come in the two or three years preceding had gained a substantial economic footing and knowledge of being able to stand the climate and other living conditions. Consequently a general assurance spread throughout cities, towns and rural districts of the South. Frequently whole families or neighborhoods, sometimes with previous arrangements for employment in some of the industrial communities, migrated in a group. A few cases have been recorded of whole church congregations bringing their pastors with them.

As the types described above settled, they furnished a field for the small tradesmen and the professional class who either came along with the crowd or followed closely after. In many cases, of course, the more enterprising wage earners, finding themselves in the midst of a large Negro population with considerable wages to spend, ventured into business. Along with this host of mixed humanity, there came a vicious and criminal element. It is the testimony, however, of social workers, railroad officials, law officers and other observers, that to an unusual degree these people are law-abiding, unoffending folk who are seeking larger opportunities in a new environment. . . .

Some of the outstanding effects of migration on the average Negro family are better standards of food and clothing due to higher wages. The children have better school buildings with teaching equipment and higher paid, better trained teachers. . . .

Negroes believe that the Negro community in the North, although considerably segregated, has advantages over their former homes in the South, such as theatres, public libraries, parks, playgrounds, museums and non-"Jim Crow" railroad and street cars. Negroes are taking part more and more in the civic and political affairs of the community. Newspapers and magazines, especially Negro newspapers and magazines, are being read as never before. Negro newspapers and magazines with the largest circulation are published in Chicago and New York. The headquarters of nearly every one of the Negro betterment organizations are now in northern cities and many of the general officers of the Negro churches have moved North. Small Negro business enterprises are increasing rapidly. A study of "The Negro at Work in New York," in 1910, before the present migration, listed about 475 enterprises in Manhattan; in 1921, a similar survey showed at least 584 such business enterprises in the Harlem district alone — a larger number than in the three Negro neighborhoods of Manhattan in 1910. General observations in Philadelphia, Chicago, Detroit and Cleveland give a similar impression of increase.

EFFECTS ON NEGRO CHURCH

What has been the effect of migration on the Negro church, which we saw was the most influential institution in Negro life in the South? In the northern cities it has increased greatly in membership, although many small mushroom store-front churches have sprung up and often become a hindrance to progress. There have developed some strong organizations in every one of these cities. Their great need is better trained leadership. In a few cities Negro congregations have bought or built institutional plants and are employing trained social workers. Abyssinia Baptist Church, St. Philip's P. E. Church, Williams Institutional C. M. E. Church, and Mother Zion A. M. E. Church in New

York City; St. John's Congregational Church in Springfield, Mass.; Mount Zion Congregational Church and St. John's A. M. E. Church in Cleveland; Olivet Baptist Church and two community churches in Chicago; and Sharpe Street M. E. Church in Baltimore, are prophecies of great community service and show the possibilities. . . .

EFFECTS ON NORTHERN WHITE COMMUNITY

This leads us logically to the effect of Negro migration on the white community in northern cities. In such communities the reaction of public opinion seems to have become one of our foremost problems. For instance, anyone would have been considered an alarmist twenty years ago had he predicted that public opinion would allow 58 Negro homes in Chicago to be bombed with impunity as increasing numbers forced Negro residents to spread beyond the areas where they had formerly lived. Race riots and outrages in East St. Louis, Omaha, Chicago and Washington paralyzed these cities for days and shocked the Nation. In public schools in more than a dozen northern cities Negro children are being directly or indirectly segregated. In one small city recently a company of leading white citizens spent a whole evening deliberating how they might control the adjustment of Negroes in the community with some fairness and yet not make it favorable enough to attract additional numbers. In some cities the former Negro residents have felt an unfriendly reaction toward their former free participation in community life.

This reaction of white public opinion has shown itself decidedly in the housing situation. These newcomers meet tremendous racial friction which grows out of their efforts to improve their housing conditions. It is very important that northern public opinion should not regard Negroes as things, nor as serfs, nor as half-men and half-women. Many of them are handicapped by ignorance, previous conditions and poverty, yet they possess all the rights and needs of whole men and women and are seeking the opportunities of free citizens.

The newspapers, the pulpits and other community channels of information may influence public opinion toward friendly racial attitudes. The Inter-racial Committee of Youngstown, Ohio, recently had an educational campaign which included a pageant produced by five hundred of the Negro people of the community on two nights at the leading the-in the city. It received the praise of the leading newspapers and ːr two thousand white citizens who packed the theatre. The music ₋d dramatic ability were a revelation to the performers as well as to ₋ie community. During the Sunday that preceded the performance, the ministers of the leading churches gave strong addresses or sermons on the problems of inter-racial adjustment and on two days following in the elementary and high schools through songs and addresses information was given to the pupils about the achievements of Negroes along lines of art, literature, science, and invention. The newspapers gave liberal space to reports of these events.

The effect upon political life in northern communities when large numbers of Negro voters come in is too extensive a subject to be considered here.

The dramatic and musical contributions of Negroes have greatly changed the comedy, the song and the dance of the North where opportunity the past fifteen years has brought ragtime, jazz, comic acting and art songs of high quality which have influenced the whole community.

The effects of increasing thousands of Negro workers in northern industries is of great importance, for in this field the masses meet face to face. In the past Negroes often got chances to work when white workers went on strike. They were then taunted as scabs by white workmen who had previously objected to their being on the job and had excluded them from their unions. Gradually, however, Negro workers are winning their way into the ranks of labor. The Negro worker is not militant-minded. He is drawn more to persons than to property. He often considers the interest of the other group as a part of his own. Is not this spirit of conciliation the ethical value that must more and more control both white capitalist and white worker before we shall have democracy in industry or industrial peace? The Negro worker needs help that his preference for persons above property may not make him a tool in the hands of employers who may wish to use him to fight the unions. As the Negro worker gets into labor ranks he may bring a spirit of cooperation that the new day in industry requires.

There is a special call to social workers for types of service in addition to the usual case work for dependents, defectives, and delinquents. What is needed by the large majority of the Negro migrants is friendly integration fully into the economic, educational, civic, and religious life of the community. These people by their brain and brawn are seeking to pay their way by their labor in the expanding industries of northern communities. They are not a group of economic dependents or social delinquents. Many are ignorant and unused to the complex life about them, but they are very teachable and most adaptable. They need help, for instance, against the exploitation of real estate sharks, white and Negro, who exploit them for the houses and shacks they buy or rent; from the shameless profiteers who sell them goods on the installment plan; from commercialized vice which flourishes unmolested by public authorities in their tenements and neighborhoods. They need the liberal interest of white citizens such as prompted the Americanization efforts for the foreign-born. The Negro, however, only needs help in securing the opportunity to embrace American advantages. . . .

THE NEW NEGRO AND THE HARLEM RENAISSANCE

ALAIN LOCKE

The New Negro

1925

Born in 1886 in Philadelphia, Alain Locke studied at Harvard University, Oxford, and the University of Berlin and was the first African American to win a Rhodes scholarship. For much of his professional life, he was a professor of philosophy at Howard University, a black institution in Washington, D.C. In 1925, his edited collection, The New Negro, *was published, bringing to a wide readership the voices of the "Harlem Renaissance," a cultural and literary movement of African American artists, writers, and intellectuals that emerged in the 1920s.*

In the late decade something beyond the watch and guard of statistics has happened in the life of the American Negro and the three norms who have traditionally presided over the Negro problem have a changeling in their laps. The Sociologist, the Philanthropist, the Race-leader are not unaware of the New Negro, but they are at a loss to account for him. He simply cannot be swathed in their formulae. For the younger generation is vibrant with a new psychology; the new spirit is awake in the masses, and under the very eyes of the professional observers is transforming what has been a perennial problem into the progressive phases of contemporary Negro life.

Alain Locke, *The New Negro* (New York: Albert & Charles Boni, Inc., 1925), 3–16 (excerpt).

Could such a metamorphosis have taken place as suddenly as it has appeared to? The answer is no; not because the New Negro is not here, but because the Old Negro had long become more of a myth than a man. The Old Negro, we must remember, was a creature of moral debate and historical controversy. His has been a stock figure perpetuated as an historical fiction partly in innocent sentimentalism, partly in deliberate reactionism. The Negro himself has contributed his share to this through a sort of protective social mimicry forced upon him by the adverse circumstances of dependence. So for generations in the mind of America, the Negro has been more of a formula than a human being—a something to be argued about, condemned or defended, to be "kept down," or "in his place," or "helped up," to be worried with or worried over, harassed or patronized, a social bogey or a social burden. . . .

With . . . renewed self-respect and self-dependence, the life of the Negro community is bound to enter a new dynamic phase, the buoyancy from within compensating for whatever pressure there may be of conditions from without. The migrant masses, shifting from countryside to city, hurdle several generations of experience at a leap, but more important, the same thing happens spiritually in the life-attitudes and self-expression of the Young Negro, in his poetry, his art, his education and his new outlook, with the additional advantage, of course, of the poise and greater certainty of knowing what it is all about. From this comes the promise and warrant of a new leadership. As one of them has discerningly put it:

> We have tomorrow
> Bright before us
> Like a flame.
>
> Yesterday, a night-gone thing
> A sun-down name.
>
> And dawn today
> Broad arch above the road we came.
> We march!

This is what, even more than any "most creditable record of fifty years of freedom," requires that the Negro of to-day be seen through other than the dusty spectacles of past controversy. The day of "aunties," "uncles" and "mammies" is equally gone. Uncle Tom and Sambo have passed on, and even the "Colonel" and "George" play barnstorm rôles from which they escape with relief when the public spotlight is off. The popular melodrama has about played itself out, and it is time to scrap the fictions, garret the bogeys and settle down to a realistic facing of facts.

First we must observe some of the changes which since the traditional lines of opinion were drawn have rendered these quite obsolete. A main change has been, of course, that shifting of the Negro population which has made the Negro problem no longer exclusively or even predominantly Southern. Why should our minds remain sectionalized, when the problem itself no longer is? Then the trend of migration has not only been toward the North and Central Midwest, but city-ward and to the great centers of industry—the problems of adjustment are new, practical, local and not peculiarly racial. Rather they are an integral part of the large industrial and social problems of our present-day democracy. And finally, with the Negro rapidly in process of class differentiation, if it ever was warrantable to regard and treat the Negro *en masse* it is becoming with every day less possible, more unjust and more ridiculous.

In the very process of being transplanted, the Negro is becoming transformed.

The tide of Negro migration, northward and city-ward, is not to be fully explained as a blind flood started by the demands of war industry coupled with the shutting off of foreign migration, or by the pressure of poor crops coupled with increased social terrorism in certain sections of the South and Southwest. Neither labor demand, the boll-weevil nor the Ku Klux Klan is a basic factor, however contributory any or all of them may have been. The wash and rush of this human tide on the beach line of the northern city centers is to be explained primarily in terms of a new vision of opportunity, of social and economic freedom, of a spirit to seize, even in the face of an extortionate and heavy toll, a chance for the improvement of conditions. With each successive wave of it, the movement of the Negro becomes more and more a mass movement toward the larger and the more democratic chance—in the Negro's case a deliberate flight not only from countryside to city, but from medieval America to modern.

Take Harlem as an instance of this. Here in Manhattan is not merely the largest Negro community in the world, but the first concentration in history of so many diverse elements of Negro life. It has attracted the African, the West Indian, the Negro American; has brought together the Negro of the North and the Negro of the South; the man from the city and the man from the town and village; the peasant, the student, the business man, the professional man, artist, poet, musician, adventurer and worker, preacher and criminal, exploiter and social outcast. Each group has come with its own separate motives and for its own special ends, but their greatest experience has been the finding of one another. Proscription and prejudice have thrown these dissimilar elements into a common area of contact and interaction. Within this area, race sympathy and unity have determined a further fusing of sentiment and experience. So what began in terms of segregation becomes more and more, as its elements mix and react, the laboratory of a great race-welding. . . . In Harlem, Negro life is seizing upon its first chances for group expression and self-determination. It is—or promises at least to be—a race capital. That is why our comparison is taken with those nascent centers of folk-expression and self-determination which are playing a creative part in the world to-day. Without pretense to their political significance, Harlem has the same rôle to play for the New Negro as Dublin has had for the New Ireland or Prague for the New Czechoslovakia.

Harlem, I grant you, isn't typical—but it is significant, it is prophetic. . . . The challenge of the new intellectuals is clear enough—the "race radicals" and realists who have broken with the old epoch of philanthropic guidance, sentimental appeal and protest. But are we after all only reading into the stirrings of a sleeping giant the dreams of an agitator? The answer is in the migrating peasant. It is the "man farthest down" who is most active in getting up. One of the most characteristic symptoms of this is the professional man, himself migrating to recapture his constituency after a vain effort to maintain in some Southern corner what for years back seemed an established living and clientele. The clergyman following his errant flock, the physician or lawyer trailing his clients, supply the true clues. In a real sense it is the rank and file who are leading, and the leaders who are following. A transformed and transforming psychology permeates the masses.

When the racial leaders of twenty years ago spoke of developing race-pride and stimulating race-consciousness, and of the desirability of race solidarity, they could not in any accurate degree have anticipated the abrupt feeling that has surged up and now pervades the awakened centers. Some of the recognized Negro leaders and a powerful section of white opinion identified with "race work" of the older order have indeed attempted to discount this feeling as a "passing phase," an attack of "race nerves" so to speak, an "aftermath of the war," and the like. It has not abated, however, if we are to gauge by the present tone and temper of the Negro press, or by the shift in popular support from the officially recognized and orthodox spokesmen to those of the independent, popular, and often radical type who are unmistakable symptoms of a new order. It is a social disservice to blunt the fact that the Negro of the Northern centers has reached a stage where tutelage, even of the most interested and well-intentioned sort, must give place to new relationships, where positive self-direction must be reckoned with in ever increasing measure. The American mind must reckon with a fundamentally changed Negro. . . .

The Negro mind reaches out as yet to nothing but American wants, American ideas. But this forced attempt to build his Americanism on race values is a unique social experiment, and its ultimate success is impossible except through the fullest sharing of American culture and institutions. There should be no delusion about this. American nerves in sections unstrung with race hysteria are often fed the opiate that the trend of Negro advance is wholly separatist, and that the effect of its operation will be to encyst the Negro as a benign foreign body in the body politic. This cannot be—even if it were desirable. The racialism of the Negro is no limitation or reservation with respect to American life; it is only a constructive effort to build the obstructions in the stream of his progress into an efficient dam of social energy and power. Democracy itself is obstructed and stagnated to the extent that any of its channels are closed. Indeed they cannot be selectively closed. So the choice is not between one way for the Negro and another way for the rest, but between American institutions frustrated on the one hand and American ideals progressively fulfilled and realized on the other.

There is, of course, a warrantably comfortable feeling in being on the right side of the country's professed ideals. We realize that we cannot be undone without America's undoing. It is within the gamut of this attitude that the thinking Negro faces America, but with variations of mood that are if anything more significant than the attitude itself. Sometimes we have it taken with the defiant ironic challenge of McKay:

> Mine is the future grinding down to-day
> Like a great landslip moving to the sea,
> Bearing its freight of débris far away
> Where the green hungry waters restlessly
> Heave mammoth pyramids, and break and roar
> Their eerie challenge to the crumbling shore.

Sometimes, perhaps more frequently as yet, it is taken in the fervent and almost filial appeal and counsel of Weldon Johnson's:

O Southland, dear Southland!
Then why do you still cling
To an idle age and a musty page,
To a dead and useless thing?

But between defiance and appeal, midway almost between cynicism and hope, the prevailing mind stands in the mood of the same author's *To America,* an attitude of sober query and stoical challenge:

How would you have us, as we are?
Or sinking 'neath the load we bear,
Our eyes fixed forward on a star,
Or gazing empty at despair?

Rising or falling? Men or things?
With dragging pace or footsteps fleet?
Strong, willing sinews in your wings,
Or tightening chains about your feet?

More and more, however, an intelligent realization of the great discrepancy between the American social creed and the American social practice forces upon the Negro the taking of the moral advantage that is his. . . .

Chronology of Events
Related to the Great Migration
(1865–1925)

1865 The Civil War ends with a northern victory; Reconstruction begins; the Thirteenth Amendment formally ends slavery.

1867 Military Reconstruction begins, launching a period of black political influence in the South.

1877 Reconstruction ends.

1879–1880 Exodusters migrate from Louisiana to Kansas.

1896 The Supreme Court upholds the constitutionality of a Louisiana state law requiring "separate but equal" railway cars in *Plessy v. Ferguson,* in effect constitutionally sanctioning racial segregation.

1898 Race riot in Wilmington, North Carolina.

1900 The "Robert Charles" race riot in New Orleans.

1906 Race riot in Atlanta, Georgia.

1908 Race riot in Springfield, Illinois.

1909 The National Association for the Advancement of Colored People (NAACP) is formed.

1914 Fighting breaks out in Europe, inaugurating World War I.

1914–1915 With a significant falling off of European immigration to the United States because of the war, industries in the northern, industrial states experience labor shortages. Black migration from the South to the North slowly increases to meet the demand for labor; by 1919, perhaps a half million southern blacks have migrated to the North. A new Ku Klux Klan (KKK) is founded by whites.

1916 President Woodrow Wilson is reelected, promising to keep the United States out of the European war. Black migration to the North intensifies. Marcus Garvey founds his Universal Negro Improvement Association (UNIA). The *Chicago Defender* calls on southern blacks to migrate to the North.

1917 *April:* The United States enters World War I.

July: Race riot in East St. Louis.

August: Members of the black Twenty-fourth Infantry, stationed in Houston, Texas, battle white soldiers, resulting in swift military court-martials, imprisonment, and in some cases executions of black soldiers.

1918 *June:* Emmett J. Scott convenes a conference of African American newspaper reporters and editors to increase black support for the war.

July: W. E. B. Du Bois publishes his "Close Ranks" editorial in the *Crisis.*

November: The signing of the armistice ends World War I with an Allied victory.

1919 National wave of labor strikes affects the packinghouse, steel, coal, and longshore industries, among many others. Nineteenth Amendment to the U.S. Constitution grants women the right to vote. Racial violence breaks out in the "red summer." *July:* Race riots in Longview, Texas, Washington, D.C., Chicago, Illinois, and other cities.

October: Elaine, Arkansas, massacre destroys the Progressive Farmers and Household Union.

November: Violence against black and white trade unionists in Bogalusa, Louisiana.

1920s A second wave of the Great Migration brings roughly seven hundred thousand more southern blacks to the North.

1921 *June:* Race riot in Tulsa, Oklahoma.

1923 Supreme Court issues its decision in the landmark case of *Moore v. Dempsey,* overturning the convictions of Elaine, Arkansas, black sharecroppers and establishing the right to a fair trial. Marcus Garvey is convicted of mail fraud in federal court.

1925 Alain Locke publishes *The New Negro.* Brotherhood of Sleeping Car Porters is formed and selects A. Philip Randolph as its president.

Questions for Consideration

1. What was the social, economic, political, and legal status of southern African Americans on the eve of World War I? To what extent did the wartime experience affect southern blacks' status in the postwar era?
2. How did southern elites analyze the origins and impact of the migration? What arguments did they advance to convince southern blacks to remain in the South?
3. Was the Great Migration the result of organized efforts? How did the migration process actually work?
4. How did white southerners respond to the wartime migration?
5. Not all black southerners endorsed migration as a solution to African Americans' problems. On what grounds did those who opposed the wartime exodus base their stand?
6. What conditions, negative and positive, did southern migrants encounter in the North during and after the war? Why did some migrants view the North as a "promised land"? In what ways did the North live up to, and fall short of, this reputation?
7. In what ways did African Americans respond to the United States's entry into, and participation in, World War I? Did black participation in the war produce lasting gains for them?
8. How did the political perspectives of African Americans change during and after World War I?
9. Who was the "New Negro"?
10. What was the attitude of the organized labor movement toward African Americans during and after the war?
11. How did African American men and women respond to trade unionism and labor activism during and after the war?
12. To what extent did black men and black women experience the opportunities and challenges of the war years in the same way? In different ways?
13. At the end of the war, what concrete advances had black migrants made? How did the end of the war affect those advances?
14. What was the "racial counterrevolution" of 1919? How did it affect African Americans? How did they respond to it?
15. How, precisely, did those writers who were sympathetic to the migrants portray those who migrated from the South?
16. Was the Great Migration a strike or a "great American protest," as some sympathetic contemporaries claimed? How would you interpret the meaning of the migration?

Selected Bibliography

EMANCIPATION, SHARECROPPING, AND JIM CROW IN THE PRE–WORLD
WAR I SOUTH

Ayers, Edward. *The Promise of the New South: Life after Reconstruction.* New
York: Oxford University Press, 1992.

Brundage, W. Fitzhugh. *Lynching in the New South: Georgia and Virginia,
1880–1930.* Urbana: University of Illinois Press, 1993.

Daniel, Pete. *The Shadow of Slavery: Peonage in the South, 1901–1969.* New
York: Oxford University Press, 1972.

Dray, Philip. *At the Hands of Persons Unknown: The Lynching of Black America.* New York: Random House, 2002.

Fite, Gilbert. *Cotton Fields No More: Southern Agriculture, 1965–1980.* Lexington: University Press of Kentucky, 1984.

Foner, Eric. *Reconstruction: America's Unfinished Revolution, 1863–1877.* New
York: Harper & Row, 1988.

Gilmore, Glenda Elizabeth. *Gender and Jim Crow: Women and the Politics of
White Supremacy in North Carolina, 1896–1920.* Chapel Hill: University of
North Carolina Press, 1996.

Jaynes, Gerald David. *Branches without Roots: Genesis of the Black Working
Class in the American South, 1862–1882.* New York: Oxford University
Press, 1986.

Lichtenstein, Alex. *Twice the Work of Free Labor: The Political Economy of Convict Labor in the New South.* New York: Verso, 1996.

Litwack, Leon F. *Been in the Storm So Long: The Aftermath of Slavery.* New
York: Random House, 1974.

———. *Trouble in Mind: Black Southerners in the Age of Jim Crow.* New York:
Alfred A. Knopf, 1998.

McKiven, Jr., Henry M. *Iron and Steel: Class, Race, and Community in Birmingham, Alabama, 1875–1920.* Chapel Hill: University of North Carolina
Press, 1995.

McMillen, Neil R. *Dark Journey: Black Mississippians in the Age of Jim Crow.*
Urbana: University of Illinois Press, 1989.

Mandle, Jay. *Not Slave, Not Free: The African American Economic Experience
since the Civil War.* Durham: Duke University Press, 1992.

Rabinowitz, Howard N. *Race Relations in the Urban South, 1865–1890.* New
York: Oxford University Press, 1978.

Royster, Jacqueline Jones, ed. *Southern Horrors and Other Writings: The Anti-Lynching Campaign of Ida B. Wells, 1892–1900.* Boston: Bedford Books, 1997.

Schwalm, Leslie A. *A Hard Fight for We: Women's Transition from Slavery to Freedom in South Carolina.* Urbana: University of Illinois Press, 1997.

Tindall, George B. *The Emergence of the New South, 1913–1945.* Baton Rouge: Louisiana State University Press, 1967.

Trotter, Jr., Joe William. *Coal, Class, and Color: Blacks in Southern West Virginia, 1915–32.* Urbana: University of Illinois Press, 1990.

Woodward, C. Vann. *Origins of the New South, 1877–1913.* 1951. Reprint, Baton Rouge: Louisiana State University Press, 1971.

PRE–WORLD WAR I BLACK MIGRATION

Armstead, Myra B. Young. *"Lord, Please Don't Take Me in August": African Americans in Newport and Saratoga Springs, 1870–1930.* Urbana: University of Illinois Press, 1999.

Clark-Lewis, Elizabeth. *Living In, Living Out: African-American Domestics in Washington, D.C., 1910–1940.* New York: Kodansha International, 1994.

Cohen, William. *At Freedom's Edge: Black Mobility and the Southern White Quest for Racial Control, 1861–1915.* Baton Rouge: Louisiana State University Press, 1991.

Hahamovitch, Cindy. *The Fruits of Their Labor: Atlantic Coast Farmworkers and the Making of Migrant Poverty, 1870–1945.* Chapel Hill: University of North Carolina Press, 1997.

Jones, Jacqueline. *The Dispossessed: America's Underclasses from the Civil War to the Present.* New York: Basic Books, 1992.

Painter, Nell Irvin. *Exodusters: Black Migration to Kansas after Reconstruction.* 1976. Reprint, New York: W. W. Norton & Company, 1986.

AFRICAN AMERICAN URBAN HISTORY

Anderson, Jervis. *This Was Harlem: A Cultural Portrait, 1900–1950.* New York: Farrar, Straus & Giroux, 1981.

Bigham, Darrel E. *We Ask Only a Fair Trial: A History of the Black Community of Evansville, Indiana.* Bloomington: Indiana University Press, 1987.

Blassingame, John W. *Black New Orleans, 1860–1880.* Chicago: University of Chicago Press, 1973.

Drake, St. Clair, and Horace R. Cayton. *Black Metropolis: A Study of Negro Life in a Northern City.* Vol. 1. 1945. Revised and enlarged edition. New York: Harcourt, Brace and World, 1970.

Gerber, David. *Black Ohio and the Color Line, 1860–1915.* Urbana: University of Illinois Press, 1976.

Johnson, James Weldon. *Black Manhattan.* 1930. Reprint, New York: Atheneum, 1968.

Katzman, David. *Before the Ghetto: Black Detroit in the Nineteenth Century.* Urbana: University of Illinois Press, 1973.

Kusmer, Kenneth L. *A Ghetto Takes Shape: Black Cleveland, 1870–1930.* Urbana: University of Illinois Press, 1976.

Lewis, Earl. *In Their Own Interests: Race, Class, and Power in Twentieth-Century Norfolk, Virginia.* Berkeley: University of California Press, 1991.

Mohl, Raymond A., and Neil Betten. *Steel City: Urban and Ethnic Patterns in Gary, Indiana, 1906–1950.* New York: Holmes and Meier, 1986.

Osofsky, Gilbert. *Harlem: The Making of a Ghetto.* New York: Harper Torchbooks, 1966.

Philpott, Thomas Lee. *The Slum and the Ghetto: Immigrants, Blacks, and Reformers in Chicago, 1880–1930.* 1978. Reprint, Belmont, Calif.: Wadsworth Publishing, 1991.

Rudwick, Elliot, and August Meier. *Black Detroit and the Rise of the UAW.* New York: Oxford University Press, 1979.

Spear, Allan H. *Black Chicago: The Making of a Negro Ghetto, 1890–1920.* Chicago: University of Chicago Press, 1967.

Trotter, Jr., Joe William. *Black Milwaukee: The Making of an Industrial Proletariat, 1915–45.* Urbana: University of Illinois Press, 1985.

Wolcott, Victoria W. *Remaking Respectability: African American Women in Interwar Detroit.* Chapel Hill: University of North Carolina Press, 2001.

Wright, George C. *Life Behind a Veil: Blacks in Louisville, Kentucky, 1865–1930.* Baton Rouge: Louisiana State University Press, 1985.

TRADITIONS OF BLACK PROTEST AND RESISTANCE

Arnesen, Eric. *Brotherhoods of Color: Black Railroad Workers and the Struggle for Equality.* Cambridge: Harvard University Press, 2001.

———. "Following the Color Line of Labor: Black Workers and the Labor Movement before 1930." *Radical History Review,* no. 55 (Winter 1993): 43–87.

———. *Waterfront Workers of New Orleans: Race, Class, and Politics, 1863–1923.* 1991. Reprint, Urbana: University of Illinois Press, 1994.

Bates, Beth Tompkins. *Pullman Porters and the Rise of Protest Politics in Black America, 1925–1945.* Chapel Hill: University of North Carolina Press, 2001.

Fox, Stephen R. *The Guardian of Boston: William Monroe Trotter.* 1970. Reprint, New York: Atheneum, 1971.

Gutman, Herbert. "The Negro and the United Mine Workers of America: The Career and Letters of Richard L. Davis and Something of Their Meaning: 1890–1900." In *The Negro and the American Labor Movement,* ed. Julius Jacobson. New York: Anchor Books/Doubleday & Company, 1968.

Hunter, Tera W. *To 'Joy My Freedom': Southern Black Women's Lives and Labors after the Civil War.* Cambridge: Harvard University Press, 1997.

James, Winston. *Holding Aloft the Banner of Ethiopia: Caribbean Radicalism in Early Twentieth-Century America.* New York: Verso, 1998.

Jordan, William. "'The Damnable Dilemma': African-American Accommodation and Protest during World War I." *Journal of American History* (March 1995): 1562–83.

Kelley, Robin D. G. "'We Are Not What We Seem': Rethinking Black Working-Class Opposition in the Jim Crow South." *The Journal of American History,* 80, no. 1 (June 1993): 75–112.

Kelly, Brian. *Race, Class, and Power in the Alabama Coalfields, 1908–21.* Urbana: University of Illinois Press, 2001.

Letwin, Daniel L. *The Challenge of Interracial Unionism: Alabama Coal Miners, 1878–1921.* Chapel Hill: University of North Carolina Press, 1997.

Levine, Lawrence W. "Marcus Garvey and the Politics of Revitalization." In *Black Leaders of the Twentieth Century*, ed. John Hope Franklin and August Meier. Urbana: University of Illinois Press, 1982.

Lewis, David Levering. *W. E. B. Du Bois: Biography of a Race, 1868–1919.* New York: Henry Holt and Company, 1993.

———. *W. E. B. Du Bois: The Fight for Equality and the American Century, 1919–1963.* New York: Henry Holt and Company, 2000.

Rachleff, Peter. *Black Labor in Richmond, 1865–1890.* 1984. Reprint, Urbana: University of Illinois Press, 1989.

Rudwick, Elliott M. *W. E. B. Du Bois: Propagandist of the Negro Protest.* 1960. Reprint, New York: Atheneum, 1969.

Walker, Clarence. "The Virtuoso Illusionist: Marcus Garvey." In *Deromanticizing Black History: Critical Essays and Reappraisals.* Knoxville: University of Tennessee Press, 1991.

THE ERA OF THE GREAT MIGRATION

Adero, Malaika. *Up South: Stories, Studies, and Letters of This Century's African-American Migrations.* New York: New Press, 1993.

Barbeau, Arthur E., and Florette Henri. *The Unknown Soldiers: African-American Troops in World War I.* 1974. Reprint, New York: Da Capo Press, 1996.

Barrett, James. *Work and Community in the Jungle: Chicago's Packinghouse Workers, 1894–1922.* Urbana: University of Illinois Press, 1987.

Bontemps, Arna, and Jack Conroy, *Anyplace But Here.* Originally published as *They Seek a City,* 1945. Reprint, New York: Hill and Wang, 1966.

Canaan, Gareth. "'Part of the Loaf': Economic Conditions of Chicago's African-American Working Class during the 1920's." *Journal of Social History* (Fall 2001): 147–74.

Chicago Commission on Race Relations. *The Negro in Chicago: A Study of Race Relations and a Race Riot.* Chicago: University of Chicago Press, 1922.

Cortner, Richard C. *A Mob Intent on Death: The NAACP and the Arkansas Riot Cases.* Middletown, Conn.: Wesleyan University Press, 1988.

Dittmer, John. *Black Georgia in the Progressive Era, 1900–1920.* Urbana: University of Illinois Press, 1977.

Ellsworth, Scott. *Death in a Promised Land: The Tulsa Race Riot of 1921.* Baton Rouge: Louisiana State University Press, 1982.

Epstein, Abraham. *The Negro Migrant in Pittsburgh.* 1918. Reprint, New York: Arno Press, 1969.

Gottlieb, Peter. *Making Their Own Way: Southern Blacks' Migration to Pittsburgh, 1916–30.* Urbana: University of Illinois Press, 1987.

Greenwald, Maurine. *Women, War, and Work: The Impact of World War I on Women Workers in the United States.* Westport, Conn.: Greenwood Press, 1980.

Grossman, James. *Land of Hope: Chicago, Black Southerners, and the Great Migration.* Chicago: University of Chicago Press, 1989.

Haiken, Elizabeth. "'The Lord Helps Those Who Help Themselves': Black Laundresses in Little Rock, Arkansas, 1917–1921." *Arkansas Historical Quarterly,* 49, no. 1 (Spring 1990): 20–50.

Halpern, Rick. *Down on the Killing Floor: Black and White Workers in Chicago's Packinghouses, 1904–54.* Urbana: University of Illinois Press, 1997.

Harrison, Alferdteen, ed. *Black Exodus: The Great Migration from the American South.* Jackson: University Press of Mississippi, 1991.

Henri, Florette. *Black Migration: Movement North, 1900–1920.* Garden City, N.Y.: Anchor Books, 1976.

Huggins, Nathan. *Harlem Renaissance.* New York: Oxford University Press, 1971.

Kirby, Jack Temple. "The Southern Exodus, 1910–1960: A Primer for Historians." *Journal of Southern History,* 49, no. 4 (November 1983): 585–600.

Kornweibel, Theodore, Jr. *"Seeing Red": Federal Campaigns against Black Militancy, 1919–1925.* Bloomington: Indiana University Press, 1998.

Lewis, David Levering. *When Harlem Was in Vogue.* New York: Vintage, 1982.

Lewis, Ronald L. "From Peasant to Proletarian: The Migration of Southern Blacks to the Central Appalachian Coalfields." *Journal of Southern History,* 55, no. 1 (February 1989): 77–102.

Locke, Alain, ed. *The New Negro.* 1925. Reprint, New York: Atheneum, 1980.

MacLean, Nancy. *Behind the Mask of Chivalry: The Making of the Second Ku Klux Klan.* New York: Oxford University Press, 1994.

McCartin, Joseph. *Labor's Great War: The Struggle for Industrial Democracy and the Origins of Modern American Labor Relations, 1912–1921.* Chapel Hill: University of North Carolina Press, 1997.

Norwood, Stephen H. "Bogalusa Burning: The War against Biracial Unionism in the Deep South, 1919." *Journal of Southern History,* 63, no. 3 (August 1997): 591–628.

Phillips, Kimberly L. *AlabamaNorth: African-American Migrants, Community, and Working-Class Activism in Cleveland, 1915–45.* Urbana: University of Illinois Press, 1999.

Reich, Steven A. "Soldiers of Democracy: Black Texans and the Fight for Citizenship, 1917–1921." *Journal of American History,* 82, no. 4 (March 1996): 1478–1504.

Rodgers, Lawrence R. *Canaan Bound: The African-American Great Migration Novel.* Urbana: University of Illinois Press, 1997.

Rudwick, Elliot, *Race Riot at East St. Louis, July 2, 1917.* 1964. Reprint, Urbana: University of Illinois Press, 1982.

Sernett, Milton C. *Bound for the Promised Land: African American Religion and the Great Migration.* Durham: Duke University Press, 1997.

Spero, Sterling D., and Abram L. Harris, *The Black Worker: The Negro and the Labor Movement.* 1931. Reprint, New York: Atheneum, 1969.

Stein, Judith. *The World of Marcus Garvey: Race and Class in Modern Society.* Baton Rouge: Louisiana State University Press, 1986.

Trotter, Jr., Joe William, ed. *The Great Migration in Historical Perspective: New Dimensions of Race, Class, and Gender.* Bloomington: Indiana University Press, 1991.

Tuttle, Jr., William M. *Race Riot: Chicago in the Red Summer of 1919.* 1970. Reprint, New York: Atheneum, 1985.

Woodruff, Nan Elizabeth. "African-American Struggles for Citizenship in the Arkansas and Mississippi Deltas in the Age of Jim Crow." *Radical History Review,* no. 55 (Winter 1993): 33–51.

Zieger, Robert. *America's Great War: World War I and the American Experience.* Lantham, MD: Rowman & Littlefield, 2000.

AFRICAN AMERICAN WOMEN, WORK, AND ACTIVISM

Gordon, Linda. "Black and White Visions of Welfare: Women's Welfare Activism, 1890–1945." *Journal of American History,* 78, no. 2 (September 1991): 559–90.

Harley, Sharon. "For the Good of Family and Race: Gender, Work, and Domestic Roles in the Black Community, 1880–1930." *Signs,* 15 (Winter 1990): 336–49.

Higginbotham, Evelyn Brooks. *Righteous Discontent: The Women's Movement in the Black Baptist Church 1880–1920.* Cambridge: Harvard University Press, 1993.

Jones, Beverly Washington. *Quest for Equality: The Life and Writings of Mary Eliza Church Terrell, 1863–1954.* Brooklyn: Carlson Publishing, 1990.

Jones, Jacqueline. *Labor of Love, Labor of Sorrow: Black Women, Work, and the Family from Slavery to the Present.* New York: Basic Books, 1985.

Scott, Anne Firor. "Most Invisible of All: Black Women's Voluntary Associations." *Journal of Southern History,* 56, no. 1 (February 1990): 3–22.

Shaw, Stephanie J. *What a Woman Ought to Be and to Do: Black Professional Woman Workers during the Jim Crow Era.* Chicago: University of Chicago Press, 1996.

Terborg-Penn, Rosalyn. *African American Women in the Struggle for the Vote, 1850–1920.* Bloomington: Indiana University Press, 1998.

White, Deborah Gray. *Too Heavy a Load: Black Women in Defense of Themselves 1894–1994.* New York: W. W. Norton & Co., 1999.

Index

213